# THE QUIET CANADIAN

Sir William Stephenson, M.C., D.F.C.

*'In a duty of great responsibility, he worked tirelessly and effectively . . . '*

# THE QUIET CANADIAN

*The Secret Service Story of
Sir William Stephenson*
(Intrepid)

H. Montgomery Hyde

CONSTABLE · LONDON

First published in Great Britain 1962
First published in paperback 1989
by Constable and Company Limited
10 Orange Street, London WC2H 7EG
Copyright © by H. Montgomery Hyde 1962
Printed in Great Britain by
St Edmundsbury Press Limited
Bury St Edmunds, Suffolk

ISBN 0 09 468780 3

*To the memory of Mary*
*Lady Stephenson*

'There was established, by Roosevelt's order and despite State Department qualms, effectively close co-operation between J. Edgar Hoover and British Security Services under the direction of a quiet Canadian, William Stephenson. The purpose of this was the detection and frustration of espionage and sabotage activities in the Western Hemisphere. . . . It produced some remarkable results which were incalculably valuable. . . . Hoover was later decorated by the British and Stephenson by the U.S. Government for exploits which could hardly be advertised at the time.'

Robert Sherwood. *The White House Papers of Harry L. Hopkins.* Vol. 1, at page 270.

'Bill Stephenson taught us all we ever knew about foreign intelligence.'

General William J. Donovan, Director of the U.S. Office of Strategic Services.

'Bill Stephenson worked himself almost to death during the war, carrying out undercover operations and often dangerous assignments (they culminated with the Gouzenko case that put Fuchs in the bag) that can only be hinted at in the fascinating book that Mr Montgomery Hyde has, for some reason, been allowed to write—the first book, so far as I know, about the British secret agent whose publication has received official blessing.'

Ian Fleming, author of the James Bond books.

# CONTENTS

# ILLUSTRATIONS

# ACKNOWLEDGEMENTS

VARIOUS people on both sides of the Atlantic have helped me to produce this book, and my obligation to them is great.

Not only has Sir William Stephenson put his files and private papers unreservedly at my disposal, but he has shown limitless patience and good humour in answering a multitude of harassing questions which I have put to him. To Lady Stephenson, too, I am grateful for many kindnesses, not least of which has been the friendly hospitality of their New York apartment, where the book originated and took shape.

However, I must make it clear that I accept complete responsibility for its contents.

Others in New York have made useful contributions, notably Mr. Ernest Cuneo, Mr. Whitney Shephardson, Mr. John Pepper, Mr. Sydney Morrell and Mr. David Ogilvy; also Mr. Thomas Drew-Brook in Toronto. My thanks are due to them in full measure.

In London, Colonel C. H. Ellis has read the book in manuscript and has made suggestions which have improved it in many ways. His experience and knowledge of the intelligence background of the story have been invaluable. The U.S. Ambassador, the Hon. David Bruce, has done likewise. For their help in various ways I would also thank Mr. Ian Fleming, Mr. Ingram Fraser and Miss A. M. Green.

To Cassell & Co. Ltd., publishers of *The Second World War* by Sir Winston Churchill, to Michael Joseph Ltd., publishers of *War at the Top* by James Leasor, and to Hamish Hamilton Ltd., publishers of *Seven Major Decisions* by Sumner Welles, I am grateful for permission to quote from these works.

H. M. H.

# INTRODUCTION

This work, first published in 1962 as *The Quiet Canadian* in Britain and *Room 3603* in the United States of America, tells the story of one of the most remarkable men in and between the two World Wars, Sir William Stephenson. In the first war he served in the Royal Canadian Engineers on the Western Front where he was badly gassed. During his convalescence he learned to fly and was transferred to the Royal Flying Corps, when he shot down numerous enemy aircraft, was himself shot down, taken prisoner, and escaped to make his way back successfully to the allied lines, incidentally being decorated by both the British and the French for his feats.

Between the wars he became a successful inventor in the radio-telegraphic field, his patents making him a millionaire by the time he was thirty. He also became a successful industrialist, in which capacity his contacts with German companies enabled him to obtain information about Nazi armaments which he passed on to Winston Churchill, then a backbencher in the House of Commons during the years of appeasement. Stephenson contrived to send this information to the Secret Intelligence Service (MI6), as well as to Major Desmond Morton's Industrial Intelligence Centre.

At this time Stephenson learned about Enigma, which for security reasons I did not mention in the following pages. This was a cipher machine which had been invented by a German engineer and marketed commercially by its Swedish manufacturers as a 'secret writing mechanism to frustrate inquisitive competitors.' In 1937, through his contacts in the German communications industry, Stephenson discovered that a revised and portable version of Enigma was being manufactured near Berlin for use by Hitler's armed forces. This information led to a prototype of the new mechanism being obtained by MI6 with the aid of the Polish intelligence service on the eve of Poland's invasion by the Germans and Russians, thus eventually enabling the 'most secret Ultra' signals, as they were called, being deciphered in Britain throughout much of the Second World War.

During the afternoon of 10 May, 1940, the day Churchill became Prime Minister, he telephoned Stephenson at the latter's London home, 76 New Cavendish Street, telling him that he was dining that night with Lord Beaverbrook at Stornoway House, where Beaverbrook then lived when in London, and suggesting that Stephenson should propose himself and join them. Stephenson did so with the desired effect and was warmly welcomed by the newspaper magnate. The other guests included Lord Trenchard, affectionately known as 'Boom', who as Chief of the Air Staff during the years of appeasement had striven to keep a nucleus of the Royal Air Force in being.

When the port and cigars appeared, Churchill rose from his seat at the head of the table and beckoned Stephenson to follow him. They walked over to the heavily draped dining room windows. Pointing his finger at Stephenson, the Prime Minister said to him quietly: 'You know what you must do at once. We have discussed it most fully and there is a complete fusion of minds between us. *You are to be my personal representative in the United States.* I will ensure that you shall have the full support of all the resources at my command. I know that you will have success and the good Lord will guide your efforts as He will ours. This may be our last farewell. *Au revoir* and good luck!'

They returned to the dinner table and shortly afterwards the party broke up. Stephenson went home to tell his American wife Mary that they must leave London for New York as soon as possible. This they did by air and sea from Genoa, arriving in New York a fortnight or so later and having heard during the voyage the news of the French collapse and the evacuation of the British Expeditionary Force from the beaches at Dunkirk. This heightened the urgency of Stephenson's mission, which included the establishment of a security and intelligence organisation, comprising the representation in the Western Hemisphere of MI6 (SIS), MI5 and 'special operations' (SOE). The organisation was called British Security Co-ordination (B.S.C.).

In discussing Stephenson's task as his personal representative, Churchill had told him: 'You must be intrepid.' Thus *Intrepid* became Stephenson's code name as well as the label under which the records of B.S.C. were kept. It was not the Prime Minister's intention that Stephenson should supplement his secret telegraphic correspondence with President Roosevelt in any way, save in the most exceptional circumstances. His initial task as Churchill's personal representative was to increase and enlarge American material aid to Britain during the period when Europe stood alone against the Axis enemy.

Consequently Stephenson's meetings with the President were few, and always most discreetly conducted. The first took place a few days after his arrival in New York when he went to the White House accompanied in accordance with diplomatic protocol by the British Ambassador Lord Lothian, whose tragic death a few months later was a dire blow to Anglo-American relations. The principal topic of conversation was the aid which the United States could give Britain to replace the hardware which had been abandoned as the result of the Dunkirk evacuation. On the subject of security and intelligence, the President's advice was that Stephenson should work intimately and confidentially with Mr J. Edgar Hoover, the chief of the Federal Bureau of Investigation. 'There should be the closest possible marriage between the FBI and British Intelligence,' said the President. And so, as this book reveals, there was.

With regard to Stephenson's initial task the first fruits of his efforts were to secure one million rifles and thirty million rounds of ammunition for the British Home Guard, who were training with broomsticks at the time, to combat the anticipated German invasion. Other supplies of war material followed, as will be seen, notably one hundred Flying Fortresses for Coastal Command of the RAF, as well as the secret Sperry bomb-sight. Later in the summer of 1940 came the destroyers-for-bases deal in which Stephenson also played a part along with his friend General William J. Donovan on the American side. Lord Louis Mountbatten, as he then was, described it as 'absolutely vital' for the convoying of Britain's merchant shipping across the Atlantic. As Mountbatten put it, 'Big Bill Donovan and Little Bill Stephenson were primarily responsible for persuading the President' to agree to it.

A subordinate of Donovan's, the Hon. David Bruce, who was U.S. Ambassador in London in 1962, wrote at that time that Donovan 'did not exaggerate when he said that British Security

Co-ordination was built from nothing into the greatest integrated, secret intelligence and operations organisation that has ever existed anywhere. It was Stephenson's conviction, months before Pearl Harbour, that the United States should possess a similar organisation for use abroad. He hoped it would be headed by his friend. To achieve this end he brought, through subtle influences, the merits of such a proposal to the attention of President Roosevelt . . . The resultant organisation was later known as the Office of Strategic Services (OSS), and later still, it should be added, as the Central Intelligence Agency (CIA).

Stephenson took no salary for his work. On the contrary, he ploughed $9 million of his fortune into the unique organisation which he created. Apart from Donovan and Hoover and their associates, there were other American individuals who, in Stephenson's words, 'were most helpful to me in furthering my objectives during my wartime tour of duty, all with President Roosevelt's approval.' They included the late Ernest Cuneo, co-ordinator of the President's brain trust and general liaison with B.S.C.; Averell Harriman, U.S. Ambassador in Moscow during the war, John Winant who held a similar post in London; also Vincent Astor, Nelson Rockefeller, Robert Sherwood, 'and an endless list of foresighted patriots to whom we all owe a debt of gratitude.' Among them was an American, Tom Childs, the principal legal representative in the United States of the United Kingdom and Commonwealth wartime governments. Also Wendell Willkie, the Republican nominee for President in 1940, who was defeated by Roosevelt in the latter's campaign for a third term; nevertheless he undertook not to oppose the destroyers deal.

An important branch of B.S.C. was Camp X, established by Stephenson as the first secret training school in North America primarily for the purpose of training agents and guerilla fighters in the techniques of clandestine warfare. It was also used for top secret communications in cipher by B.S.C., being known as Hydra. The camp, which was located in the neighbourhood of Oshawa on the north shore of Lake Ontario, was so secret that not even the Canadian War Cabinet knew of its existence. Although not specifically mentioned in the following pages, it was also the location of Station M, whose task was to fabricate documents for use against the enemy as is described here.[1]

I have referred above to Wendell Willkie's campaign as Republican nominee for President in 1940. For my benefit Stephenson recently amplified his recollections of Willkie, which did not appear in this book as first published.

The forty-eight-year old Willkie, a lawyer and public utilities authority from Elmwood, Indiana, was initially thought to have little chance of securing the Republican nomination; but he did so on the sixth ballot at his party's national convention in June 1940. After his defeat by Roosevelt in November, Willkie decided that he would like to make an exploratory visit to the European war theatre. Stephenson, who met him at this time in New York, suggested to him that he should persuade the President to appoint him his personal investigative representative which would be bound to result in Willkie being treated with greater confidence and would learn more of the actual situations at the points of active interest.

Willkie flew to Washington and saw President Roosevelt in the White House. The President welcomed the idea, which he considered would be a great help to him, and he gave Willkie the necessary documentation certifying the purpose of his proposed visit. On Willkie's return to New York, Stephenson met him in his office at the Commodore Hotel. 'He was a great bear of a man,' Stephenson described him to me. 'He threw his arms round me and said: "Bill you were absolutely right. Imagine one of the purple pleading with an Indiana farm boy to help him! We must all alert the American people to the real danger that confronts them. Look at this letter to Churchill which the President wrote in my presence!"' When the President had finished writing, Willkie went on, he picked up the letter and read aloud the dramatic verse it contained. 'I am most grateful for your wise suggestion,' Willkie concluded what he said to Stephenson, 'and will keep you informed.' This he did.

The letter from President Roosevelt to the British Prime Minister read as follows:

[1] In August 1984, an impressive memorial on the site commemorating the camp's activities was unveiled by the Hon. John Aird, Lieutenant-Governor of Ontario Province.

THE WHITE HOUSE
WASHINGTON
January 20, 1941

Dear Churchill

Wendell Wilkie will give you this letter. He is truly helping to keep politics out over here.

I think this verse applies to your people as it does to us:

'Sail on, O ship of State!
Sail on, O Union, strong and great!
Humanity with all its fears,
With all the hopes of future years,
Is hanging breathless on thy fate.'

As ever yours,
FRANKLIN D. ROOSEVELT

'I received Willkie yesterday,' Churchill wrote to Roosevelt on January 1941, 'and was deeply moved by the verse of Longfellow's which you had quoted. I shall have it framed as a souvenir of these tremendous days, and as a mark of our friendly relations, which have been built up telegraphically and also telepathically under all the stresses.' The Prime Minister added that all his information showed that the Germans were persevering in their preparations to invade Britain, 'and we are getting ready to give them a reception worthy of the occasion.' He also expressed his gratitude 'for all you are doing to secure us timely help.'[1]

A few days later, on February 9, Churchill made a broadcast to the British nation and Empire, his first for five months. It was one of his most vivid and dramatic of its kind. After reviewing the course of the war, he quoted Longfellow's verse which he had received from Willkie and which the President wrote in his own handwriting. 'What is the answer I shall give, in your name to this great man, the thrice-chosen head of a nation of a hundred and thirty millions?' he asked his listeners. He went on: 'Here is the answer which I shall give to President Roosevelt:

---

[1] Churchill, *The Second World War* (1950), III, 23–5. The quotation was from Longfellow's poem *Building of the Ship*. Willkie was also received by King George VI, on 4 February, 1941.

Put your confidence in us. Give us your faith and your blessing, and, under Providence, all will be well . . . Give us the tools and we shall finish the job!'

Willkie was a great internationalist besides being a warm supporter of the British cause, welcoming the Lend-Lease project. He returned to Europe in 1941 whence he made a 30,000 mile world trip as presidential envoy visiting the Near East, Soviet Russia and China, meeting De Gaulle, Stalin and Chiang Kai-chek, returning to the U.S. towards the end of the year and assuring Stephenson of his conviction that the Nazis would not defeat the Soviets.[1]


In 1963 Sir William Stephenson and his wife moved from Jamaica to a new home in Bermuda. This was Camden House at the top of Camden Hill in the parish of Paget, with a superb view of the Atlantic, which Stephenson bought from the Bishop of Bermuda. However Stephenson demolished it and on the site built the present attractive house to his own specification. It was an ideal retirement home, and a happy one, the happiness lasting for fifteen years and eventually terminating in Mary Stephenson's death from cancer on 24 December, 1978. During the last three months of her life she was nursed tenderly and compassionately by an experienced and highly qualified nurse now Elizabeth Mary Margaret Stephenson. She stayed on after Mary's death to look after Sir William Stephenson, whose adopted daughter she became.

It remains to mention the honours which Stephenson received during his retirement. He was already an honorary doctor of the University College of the West Indies in Jamaica, today the sole surviving relic of the ill-fated West Indies Federation. He was one of the first to receive an honorary doctorate in 1950, the year after the university college was created at St Andrew near Kingston. Honorary doctorates were also conferred upon him, *in absentia*, by the Royal Military College, Kingston, Ontario, in 1979, and by the University of Manitoba,

---

[1] Willkie's unexpected death in October 1944 – supposedly caused by a virus in a book he read – was a great blow to his many friends, particularly Stephenson and Roosevelt.

Winnipeg, in the following year. The latter university as well as others made an exception to a longstanding rule because of the recipient's health, and the honorary doctorate of science was consequently conferred upon him in the sitting room of his Bermuda home. Described by the university president D. R. Campbell as 'an eminent native' of the province 'turned world citizen', Stephenson received the degree from the chancellor Isabel Auld. In his reply the recipient declared the ceremony was a 'very heartwarming occasion' for him, although he admitted to being saddened by the lack of progress towards world peace in spite of all talk since the Second World War. 'In the event of a nuclear war, there would be no survivors,' he added. 'All will be obliterated. It is up to us, the people, to make the moral and philosophical choice, and since the threat to humanity is the work of human beings it is up to man to save himself from himself. The world now stands on the brink of a final abyss – let us resolve to take the practical steps to ensure that through our own folly we do not go over the edge.'[1]

In 1980 Stephenson was made a Companion of the Order of Canada, being specially invested in Bermuda by the Canadian Governor General Mr Edward Schreyer. Three years later, on 22 September, 1983, he was awarded the William J. Donovan Medal by the Veterans of the Office of Strategic Services, an award founded for 'an individual who has rendered distinguished service in the interests of the democratic process and the cause of freedom'. Of the recipients who had received it hitherto, only two were British or Commonwealth citizens, Earl Mountbatten of Burma (1966) and the British Prime Minister Margaret Thatcher (1981). The impressive ceremony for the award to Stephenson took place appropriately on board the U.S. aircraft carrier *Intrepid* in New York Harbour. The award was preceded by a dinner, of which the honorary chairman was also a medal holder, William Casey, the head of the CIA and a former OSS officer who had worked with Donovan on covert operations behind the German lines in the closing days of the Second World War.

A short time before, Casey had told President Reagan about

---

[1] *Winnipeg Tribune*, 17 December, 1979.

the award, and this led the President to send Stephenson the following letter:

THE WHITE HOUSE
WASHINGTON
September 12, 1983

Dear Sir William:

I was delighted to hear through Bill Casey that you would be the recipient of the William J. Donovan Award. I can think of no person more deserving. What an extraordinary life you have led in the service of freedom. Your career through World War I, World War II, and the postwar years adds up to one of the great legends, one of the great stories of personal valor and sacrifice for the sake of country and fellow man.

All those who love freedom owe you a debt of gratitude; but we, as Americans, are particularly grateful to you for the warmth and friendship you have always shown towards our nation. We want you to know that friendship is reciprocated tenfold; and I want to assure you that as long as Americans value courage and freedom there will be a special place in our hearts, our minds, and our history books for the 'Man Called Intrepid.'

Your accomplishments need little embellishment from me; they are your monument; they remain our inspiration. On behalf of the American people, I send you our warmest congratulations, our deepest gratitude, and our sincere wishes for many more years of friendship and service together.

Sincerely,

*Ronald Reagan*

Sir William Stephenson
Post Office Box 445
Devonshire 4, Bermuda

Although Stephenson has retired completely, he still, at the age of 93, is mentally alert and takes a lively interest in current

affairs, particularly the relations between the world's two domi-
nant powers the Soviet Union and the United States of America,
on which the peace of the world depends. The Soviet Union's
global ambitions in the field of territorial expansion and influence, notably in the Third World, occupy his attention. For
one thing he is convinced that the Soviet Union wishes to
recover Alaska, called Russian America when it belonged to the
old Tsarist empire. The sale to the United States in 1867 for a
little over $7 million, otherwise about two cents an acre, was
derisory in the opinion of the present Soviet leaders, since the
territory is so rich in commodities such as gold, copper, furs, oil,
fisheries and forestry. Territorial annexation was exemplified
before World War II in the Baltic states of Latvia, Lithuania
and Estonia as well as parts of Finland and Romania, and after
the war in Germany, Czechoslovakia and Japan. This, together
with the Warsaw Pact Communist regimes in Eastern Europe
stretching from the Baltic to the Black Sea have transformed the
Red Army into an offensive arm of Soviet imperialism, as
recently seen in Afghanistan. In addition, the Soviet Union has
approximately 24,000 military advisers in thirty countries ex-
tending from North Korea to Peru, while in Latin America it has
strong relations with the Communist governments of Cuba and
Nicaragua.

In the Western Hemisphere Stephenson attaches the greatest
importance to the free trade agreement with Canada which
President Reagan concluded in January 1988 on behalf of the
United States. As the President stated at the time, 'the people of
the United States and Canada have had a long and harmonious
friendship which is the envy of the world. Now, in addition to
sharing the world's largest free trade area . . . It will strengthen
the bonds between our nations and improve the economic
performance and competitiveness of both countries. The agreement will provide an enduring legacy of which both nations can
be proud.' The initiative, it should be added, came from the
Canadian Prime Minister Brian Mulroney, who originally
made a formal request for bilateral negotiations on the subject in
1985.

Stephenson thereupon proposed a United States-Canadian
interdependency operation with the object of Canada providing
hydro-electric energy for American industry, thereby among

other relevant matters dispensing with reliance on Middle East oil with its economic turbulence and uncertain and unpredictable Arab control. He discussed the financing of such a project with the directors of a leading international investment banking group, who, in Stephenson's words, 'have confirmed their confidence that the necessary finance can be raised for any viable energy development of this kind and have expressed their interest in forming an international financing group for this purpose. It is anticipated that, in addition to North American banks, there would be very strong support from European and Japanese banks.'

As he informed the US State Department, Stephenson forecast energy sources of potential electricity from Canada available for the US of 100 Terrawat hours – roughly equivalent to 300 million barrels of oil a day – which he believed would be attainable by the year 2000. Available exports were generated from hydro-electric stations (Quebec, British Columbia and Manitoba). He anticipated that exports from Alberta through British Columbia would start in 1991. 'The security arising from interdependence,' Stephenson concludes, 'is where the value truly lies.'

In this context it may be added that the current role of the Organization of Petroleum Exporting Countries (OPEC) is extremely unsatisfactory. Of the 13 member countries two are at war with each other (Iran and Iraq), while two have broken off mutual diplomatic relations (Saudi Arabia and Iran). The conflict in the Gulf embodies these troubles and as an intergovernmental organization it has little or no value in its object of unifying and co-ordinating the petroleum of its members and protecting their interests.


I conclude with two noteworthy incidents, one in Sir William Stephenson's career between the wars and the other quite recently.

The first was after Chamberlain's meeting with Hitler and the Munich conference in 1938 when the Nazis subsequently occupied Czechoslovakia. Stephenson was one of two individuals who undertook to shoot Hitler with high-powered sporting rifles. (The other was Colonel F. N. Mason-Macfarlane, the

British Military Attaché in Berlin.) However, Halifax, who was Foreign Secretary at the time, vetoed the proposal. 'We have not reached the stage in our diplomacy,' he said, 'when we have to use assassination as a substitute for diplomacy.'[1]

According to the former MI5 officer Peter Wright, author of the notorious book *Spycatcher*, Stephenson telephoned him 'out of the blue' from Bermuda in January 1988. They had never met, although Wright naturally knew about him and his work during World War II. 'I didn't even know he was still alive,' Wright was reported as saying. Their conversation concerned Sir Roger Hollis, Wright's former chief and head of MI5, whom he was convinced was a Soviet spy. What is more, Wright claimed that he had the evidence to prove it and that the damage caused to British Intelligence by Hollis's treachery was 'almost immeasurable.' He also claimed to have converted Stephenson to this view.

Stephenson, to whom I have spoken at his home in Bermuda, flatly denies Wright's story, which first appeared in the Australian media and was later repeated in the London *Times*.[2] 'It is completely false,' he told me. 'I have *never* been in contact with Wright by telephone or otherwise.'

H. MONTGOMERY HYDE

---

[1] Anthony Cave Brown. *The Secret Servant* (1988), at p. 195.
[2] *The Times*, 15 June, 1988.

CHAPTER I

## PRELUDE

I

ONE day in the spring of 1945, when the end of the war with
Hitler was in sight, Mr. Edgar Hoover, head of the United
States Federal Bureau of Investigation, sat dictating letters to
his secretary in his office in the Department of Justice building
in Washington. For the past four years, Mr. Hoover as Director
of the F.B.I. had been charged not only with the ordinary work
of criminal investigation in the United States of America, for
which his Bureau had always been responsible, but also with
counter-espionage and other secret intelligence activities which
he and his agents carried out on behalf of the U.S. Government
against the common enemy. Now he had learned that his close
collaborator on the British side, a Canadian named William
Stephenson, had been knighted for his services by King George
VI in Buckingham Palace, and so among the letters which went
out under the Director's signature on that particular day in
March, 1945, was one to Sir William Stephenson, M.C., D.F.C.
After congratulating him on this honour which in his view was
'both well earned and well deserved', the F.B.I. chief remarked
that in the years to come Stephenson could certainly look back
with great satisfaction to the 'very worthy contribution' which
he had made not only to his own country but to those of the
Allies in this world conflict. 'When the full story can be told',
Mr. Hoover added, 'I am quite certain that your contribution
will be among the foremost in having brought victory finally to
the united nations' cause.'

Coming from a man in the unique position of Edgar Hoover,
who was familiar with the whole pattern of enemy activities in
the Americas, this was a most remarkable tribute, particularly
to the citizen of another country. At the time Hoover wrote,
the name of William Stephenson was scarcely known outside a

I

few select Government and business circles on either side of the Atlantic. The picture which did occasionally emerge into a slightly wider field was that of a mysterious millionaire, who had been highly decorated for his gallantry as a flier in the First World War and was now engaged by the British authorities on work of a 'top secret' character which went far beyond his ostensible duties of devising and executing security measures for the protection of British shipping and cargoes of war material plying between America and Britain.

Apart from the peculiar war-time conditions under which he worked and which made secrecy essential, Stephenson has always deliberately shunned publicity, and even today the total of newspaper cuttings about him and his fantastic career barely covers half a dozen pages of foolscap. Yet his was the master mind which directed a vast range of vitally important secret operations for Britain throughout the Western Hemisphere, and at the same time showed the Americans, when the time came, how to build up their own successful intelligence service and 'special operations'. This latter achievement led President Truman to award him the country's highest civilian decoration, the Medal of Merit, Stephenson being the first and so far the only non-American to have received this coveted distinction. As General William ('Wild Bill') Donovan, head of the American Office of Strategic Services (O.S.S.), put it—Donovan was if anything closer to Stephenson than was Edgar Hoover during these momentous years—'Bill Stephenson taught us all we ever knew about foreign intelligence'.

At last, after the lapse of two decades, it is possible to lift the veil and reveal something of these astonishing activities and of the Canadian business man who directed them from the thirty-sixth floor of a skyscraper office building in New York.

Towards the middle of 1940, when France was on the verge of defeat and Britain stood virtually alone against the victorious Nazis, Stephenson had arrived in New York entrusted by the Chief of the Secret Intelligence Service in London with the task of collecting information on enemy activities aimed against the continuance of Britain's war effort and planning appropriate counter-measures. He was also invited by Mr. Churchill, who had just become Prime Minister, to exert his efforts among his business and other contacts in the United States to help Britain

in her hour of desperate need with essential supplies, and likewise to do all he could to promote a climate of public opinion
favourable to American intervention on the side of Britain.
Stephenson had been quick to realize that the mere collection
of secret intelligence of enemy activities would be quite inadequate in the prevailing situation and that other secret activities
particularly of an offensive nature would have to be undertaken.
This involved the co-ordination of a number of functions falling
within the jurisdiction of different Government departments in
London such as the Ministries of Information, Economic Warfare, Supply and War Transport, and the Intelligence branches
of the armed forces, all of which Stephenson represented in his
official capacity. Hence the name British Security Co-ordination
(B.S.C.), by which his organization was officially known, a
name which incidentally was first suggested by Edgar Hoover.

On the offensive side, Stephenson and his B.S.C. were
responsible for the training of hundreds of American and
Canadian agents who made successful parachute landings in
occupied Europe. His communications experts were able to
intercept and decode the radio signals of enemy submarines,
pinpointing their positions so that they could be destroyed by
allied naval action. In the sphere of counter-espionage he was
able to furnish extremely important information through
British censorship intercepts and other sources, which resulted
in the arrest and trial of a number of key German agents in the
United States. He was similarly able, through his own agency
network, to render harmless the activities of a vast German
sabotage ring in Latin America, as well as to expose the dummy
companies operated in various parts of the world by the powerful German industrial cartel of I.G. Farben. Stephenson also
had a finger in the 'destroyers for bases' deal with the United
States which gave Britain much-needed convoy protection for
her supplies in the crucial months following the Dunkirk
evacuation and the fall of France, just as he was involved in a
subtle manoeuvre which delayed Hitler's attack on Russia by
six vital weeks. In the penetration of enemy and unfriendly
diplomatic missions in the Western Hemisphere and the discovery of their secret codes and ciphers, B.S.C. was particularly
adept, as also in the delicate operation of discrediting their staff
members through their individual indiscretions. Stephenson's

discoveries of this kind among the Vichy French representatives in the United States were passed on to President Roosevelt, who considered them 'the best bed-time story' he had read since the last war. Finally—although this concerned a different type of enemy who was in fact a military ally at the time— Stephenson personally played a most significant part in the chain of events which followed the defection of Igor Gouzenko, the cipher clerk in the Soviet Embassy in Ottawa in September, 1945, and which revealed the existence of a widespread espionage network including the first 'atom spies' under the direction of the Russians in North America.

Of course, all this necessitated the employment of a consider- able staff both at headquarters and in the field. At one time about a thousand men and women worked for Stephenson's B.S.C. in the United States and about twice that number in Canada and Latin America. All these employees were paid by the British Government. Stephenson took nothing in the way of remuneration for himself. Much was heard at the time about the 'dollar a year' men, wealthy American business executives who undertook various key jobs in the prosecution of their country's war effort. But Stephenson did not accept even a dollar a year. On the other hand, he contributed largely to the common cause out of his own pocket. When peace came, he had spent close on one million dollars of his personal fortune in this way.

He seldom left his New York headquarters except to fly to Washington to see people like Hoover and Donovan who had their headquarters there, or to cross the Atlantic to report progress to the Prime Minister and the various departments represented by B.S.C. He was probably not known, even by sight, to more than a fraction of his carefully selected head- quarters staff. But those who did know him held him in admira- tion and indeed affection, for he was a patient and understand- ing chief who gave his subordinates their heads and invariably stood by them when they got into trouble, as sometimes happened through excess of zeal or some other cause.

William Stephenson was forty-four years old when he assumed the immense task of co-ordinating and directing British security intelligence and 'special operations' in the Americas. What those who knew him at that period recall was a small, slim, erect figure with the springy walk that boxers have. (He had boxed in his youth—indeed he was a former amateur light-weight world champion—and it was his interest in the sport which later introduced him to Gene Tunney, the undefeated American champion, who in turn introduced him to Hoover.) What you noticed when you first met Stephenson was a ruddy complexion, crisp greyish hair, a pair of most penetrating eyes, a soft speaking voice with hardly a trace of accent, and, as one observer accurately noted, a mouth that slipped easily into a wry grin. Although he could argue with conviction and even eloquence, as a rule he preferred the other chap to do the talking at an interview, a characteristic which prompted the American dramatist Robert Sherwood to describe him as 'a quiet Canadian'. Not that he was in the least unsociable. His capacity for absorbing dry Martinis was astonishing, the more so as they never seemed to have the slightest effect upon him. To his intimates he was known affectionately as 'Little Bill' to distinguish him from 'Wild Bill' Donovan who was 'Big Bill'.

In recommending William Stephenson for the award of the Medal for Merit in a citation which he personally composed and sent to the White House for the President's approval, General Donovan referred to the 'timely and valuable aid' which the Director of British Security Co-ordination had given the American effort by making available to the United States the 'extensive experience of the British Government' in the fields of Intelligence and Special Operations. 'At every step in the creation of these instrumentalities', the citation continued, 'Sir William contributed assistance and counsel of great value both to the Government of the United States and to the entire allied cause. In a duty of great responsibility he worked tirelessly and effectively . . .'

2

Stephenson grew up in Winnipeg, the capital of Manitoba and the chief city of Western Canada, where his father had a lumber mill. Situated on the eastern border of the prairies in the middle of a narrow belt between Lake Winnipeg and the boundary line with the United States, the city enjoys a unique geographical position for purposes of trade, since it is the natural centre of all commercial intercourse between the eastern and western parts of the country. At this period the population of Winnipeg was rapidly increasing, thus keeping pace with the town's mounting industrial prosperity. In 1870, when it still belonged to the Hudson's Bay Company, the place had been no more than a fur trading post with a couple of hundred inhabitants; by the turn of the century, after the settlement and its surrounding territory had been taken over by the Dominion Government, there were over 40,000 living in Winnipeg; and when Stephenson went off to join the Canadian army at the outbreak of the First World War, the local population was approaching the 200,000 mark. With its big lumber and flour mills Winnipeg was thus the scene of great industrial and commercial expansion at this period and at the same time of intense business competition and individual rivalries. Surrounded as it was by lakes, woodland and prairie, Winnipeg in those days was an ideal place, with its long and severe winters, in which to cultivate the qualities of hard work, thrift and self-reliance, and young Stephenson was seldom idle.

William Samuel Stephenson was born at Point Douglas, just outside Winnipeg, on January 11, 1896. (He was called William after his father, Samuel after an old family friend.) It was here, at the junction of the Assiniboine and Red rivers, that Thomas Douglas, Earl of Selkirk, and his Scottish Highlanders had established the first British settlement in the name of the Hudson's Bay Company towards the end of the Napoleonic Wars. And it was at Point Douglas that the elder Stephenson, who was descended from one of the early Scottish settlers, had his lumber mill, and that his son spent his boyhood. Here the lad liked to tinker around with anything mechanical he could lay his hands on. Fortunately Winnipeg, through the foresight and benevolence of its leading citizens, possessed some of the best schools in the country, and it was to one of them, the Argyle High School, that Bill Stephenson was in due course sent. At this academy his education, as befitted the place and the times, was thorough rather than elegant. He showed himself a willing learner, excelling especially in mathematics and in all kinds of handicrafts. Outside the classroom his tastes ran to boxing and he was a creditable light-weight performer in the school boxing ring, although nobody took him at the time for a future amateur world champion.

Stephenson was still at the Argyle High School in Winnipeg when German troops invaded Belgium in August, 1914, and the First World War began. He went straight from school into the Royal Canadian Engineers. Before his nineteenth birthday he had received his commission as a Second Lieutenant, and a few months later he was fighting in the trenches in France. Soon he was promoted Captain. Towards the end of 1915 he was badly gassed and invalided back to England. While convalescing he determined to learn to fly and he accordingly applied for a transfer to the Royal Flying Corps. His application was granted in due course and he received his 'wings' at the R.F.C. station at South Carlton, Lincolnshire, and sometime in 1916 he reported for duty with No. 73 Squadron of the R.F.C. in France. A stockbroker from Toronto named Thomas Drew-Brook was orderly officer at the time and he has recalled that Stephenson looked extremely pale and delicate when he arrived, for he was still suffering from the after-effects of German gas. In fact, Drew-Brook doubted whether he would ever do much as a fighter pilot and he privately advised his Flight Commander that he should be posted to a reserve flight.

There were two Flight Commanders in 73 Squadron and Stephenson himself quite soon became one of them. The other was Captain A. H. Orlebar, a most skilful and daring fighter pilot, for whom Stephenson always had a particular admiration and with whom he enjoyed a friendly rivalry in operations.

For some time Stephenson did nothing spectacular. He was always where he should be, but he certainly did nothing to call attention to himself. Then one day during the March offensive in 1918 he was out on a flight in a Sopwith Camel and a couple of German fighters got on his tail, shooting up his machine so badly that he was only able to come in to land with the greatest difficulty and at the risk of his life as his machine was more or less out of control. The small pale-faced figure which emerged from the cock-pit appeared 'hopping mad' and ready to take on the entire German Air Force, as his friend Drew-Brook also recalls. He immediately got into another machine and insisted on returning to action. The next the squadron heard of him was that he had brought down two German fighter planes in flames.

From then on there was no holding him. During the next few weeks he destroyed eighteen more enemy machines and two kite balloons. Three of the planes came down in the Allied Lines, and one of them he forced to within a mile of his own aerodrome, having had a bet in the mess on the previous evening that he 'would bring a Hun back for breakfast'. His victims included Lothar Von Richtofen, brother of the famous German air 'ace' Baron Von Richtofen. It was said of Stephenson at the Battle of Chateau Thierry that he literally 'lived in the air' over the River Marne and with thousands of well-placed machine-gun bullets was largely instrumental in preventing the enemy sappers from rigging their pontoons for the river crossing. 'You can always know when Steve is over', said a Canadian 'Tommy' who experienced the horrors of the Front Line. 'He comes right down to wave "Hello" and never forgets the boys on the ground when things are hot.' These exploits gained for him the Military Cross and Distinguished Flying Cross, while the French awarded him the Legion of Honour and the Croix de Guerre with palm.

At this time his proficiency in boxing had become remarkable, and at Amiens, early in 1918, as Royal Flying Corps member of the Inter-Services Boxing Teams he won the amateur light-weight championship of the world. Because of his punching speed in the ring, he was known as 'Captain Machine Gun'.

The episode of gallantry which brought him the high military decoration from the President of France also unfortunately brought him to grief behind the German lines. On the afternoon of July 28, 1918, Stephenson, by this time a Flight Commander, decided to go up on a lone patrol, since the regular scout patrols had been cancelled owing to stormy weather. Through a gap in the clouds he suddenly saw a French reconnaisance two-seater aircraft being attacked by seven Fokker planes. Without a moment's hesitation he dived through the clouds and attacked the leader of the enemy formation, shooting down his machine in flames. Then followed a terrific 'dog fight' in which Stephenson made brilliant tactical use of the clouds and succeeded in bringing down another Fokker, while a third was sent spinning towards the ground out of control. The remainder thereupon made off. Then, so as to make sure that the observer of the French plane recognized the markings on his own machine, he flew right alongside the reconnaisance aircraft. Unfortunately the observer who saw him out of the corner of his eye mistook him for a German and fired a machine-gun burst into Stephenson's aircraft which put the engine out of action and wounded the pilot in the leg.

Stephenson managed to land just in front of the German Front Line, crawled out of the damaged machine, and in spite of his wounded leg tried to reach the British lines. This time an enemy machine-gunner hit him again in the same leg, and this completely incapacitated him. He was immediately surrounded by the enemy and taken prisoner. In due course he was sent to the prisoner-of-war camp at Holzminden on the River Weser near Brunswick. Here he was joined by his friend Tommy Drew-Brook, who had been captured about the same time.

Only those who have experienced living behind barbed wire can realize how extremely boring the life of a prisoner-of-war can be. The unfortunate inmates of Holzminden were no exception and they found little with which to occupy themselves besides playing games and concocting plans to escape. One of the games at Holzminden, which is really self-explanatory, was known as 'Beat the Hun'; it consisted of getting the better of the camp guards, usually by the acquisition of some German property. 'If you were smart enough to get away with anything, even if it were only a potato', Drew-Brook later recalled, 'this could provide a topic of conversation and a feeling of achievement for at least a day!'

The camp commandant was a certain Hauptman Niemeyer, who bore a remarkable physical resemblance to the Kaiser. When Stephenson eventually succeeded in escaping from Holzminden, which he did in October, 1918, a few weeks before the Armistice, and in making his way back to his squadron in France, he deliberately purloined a photograph of the commandant from the latter's office, under the noses of the camp guards, and took it with him on his escape journey. It was, he said, a last gesture of contempt for his captors. He still has that photograph.

At the time of his demobilization William Stephenson, then

in his early twenties, foresaw the coming of commercial wireless and even television on a nation-wide scale, and that he determined to apply his inventive talents in this lucrative field. For a time he returned to Winnipeg, where his family still lived, but neither in Canada nor across the border in the United States could he find the opportunities he sought in his chosen field of radio, despite the current boom in broadcasting. The United States were, of course, the pioneers in large-scale broadcasting and it was there that the new medium first received its name. Soon large numbers of stations of varying power were 'on the air', while a multiplicity of radio firms sprang up and placed on the market both complete receiving apparatus to meet the differing requirements of the various stations and the components necessary for assembling the sets in the listeners' homes. One result of the haphazard erection of transmitters was to produce considerable interference between locally over-crowded stations, while large tracts of the country were either badly served or not at all. Canada, on the other hand, while following the example of the United States, did so on a much smaller scale and with a greater regard for interference difficulties that might arise. In particular, the operation of the station at Winnipeg by the Government of Manitoba was a unique phenomenon, which attracted Stephenson's attention, the more so as the example of Manitoba was shortly to be followed in Britain.

Late in 1922, the British Broadcasting Company was formed in London by the leading wireless manufacturers and traders in the country, and early in the following year the new company received a licence from the Postmaster-General which conferred upon it the exclusive right to broadcast programmes in Britain. The company as such neither manufactured, sold nor recommended apparatus, and its revenue, like that of the Winnipeg station, was derived from a share in the receiving licences levied by the Government. Nevertheless the British radio industry, then in its infancy, had an obvious interest in the success of the new venture; indeed it was to insure a ready market for their products that its leading firms had originally combined to form the B.B.C. The publicity manager of one of these firms was a young Canadian known to Stephenson, William Gladstone Murray, a daring combatant flier like himself in the war and a former air correspondent of the Canadian Lord Beaverbrook's *Daily Express* newspaper. Gladstone Murray now became the B.B.C.'s first Director of Public Relations—as well as a good friend to Stephenson.

It was with the primary aim of looking into the extended possibilities of radio manufacture and research created by these developments that Stephenson decided to revisit London. He planned only a short trip. In fact he was to remain in England for most of the next nineteen years and to make his home there, while his peculiar inventive and commercial genius transformed him into a millionaire.

### 3

What struck Stephenson most of all about broadcasting on his arrival in England in 1921 was the relatively slow response of the public to its attractions. The primary need was a complete range of wireless receiving apparatus for popular use at a moderate cost, which he now made up his mind to stay in England and provide. With a little capital which he had succeeded in raising, he now bought an interest in two companies, the General Radio Company Limited and the Cox-Cavendish Electrical Company Limited, both engaged in the manufacture and marketing of broadcasting and other electrical equipment including X-ray. Within an astonishingly short time the cheap and popular radio sets manufactured by the General Radio Company were in thousands of homes throughout Britain.

Stephenson now turned his attention towards the solution of an extremely important kindred problem of radio technology, namely the transmission by wireless of pictures, both still and moving. For the past thirty years, it had been possible to transmit a wireless photograph by splitting it up into small sections, each section being denoted by a letter of the alphabet or a number to indicate the appropriate degree of light or shade. But this method always remained unsatisfactory pictorially, although it had been subject to a number of improvements over the years. It was now borne in upon Stephenson that an actual photograph could only be sent over the air with absolute accuracy if the picture itself operated the transmitting installation. And this was precisely what Stephenson proceeded to invent.

The London *Daily Mail*, which then enjoyed the largest circulation of any national newspaper in the world, was naturally interested in wireless photography and in fact had been conducting research in the subject since 1908. This journal, whose dynamic founder Lord Northcliffe, shortly before his death, had had his attention drawn to Stephenson as a brilliant young scientist, now agreed to furnish Stephenson with assistance on the photographic side in the shape of a well-known research chemist, Professor T. Thorne Baker, who joined Stephenson in the General Radio Company's laboratories at Twyford. The results of this collaboration were to revolutionize pictorial journalism and also point the way to commercial television.

The element generally used at that time to convert light into electric currents which could be transmitted over wires or by wireless telegraphy was selenium. Unfortunately it had one great disadvantage, namely its relatively slow action. After long and detailed experiments Stephenson succeeded in producing a substitute for selenium in the shape of what he described as a 'light sensitive device', which greatly increased the rate of transmission while at the same time providing a completely faithful image. 'This photograph was transmitted by our method in twenty seconds', he said to a caller as he held up a small picture with a parallel line effect reminiscent of a fine half-tone reproduction on the cinema screen. The broadcasting of moving pictures, he went on, was now no longer a fantastic dream. 'It is only a question of speeding up the apparatus to reduce the twenty seconds to the time necessary for the persistence of vision.'

The *Daily Mail*, in publishing the first picture transmitted by this novel process in December, 1922, hailed the young inventor as 'a brilliant scientist' and his discovery as 'a great scientific event'.[1] It went on to describe its implications in the following words:

> Wireless photography is now an accomplished fact. That is to say, an actual photograph can now be made to operate a wireless transmitting apparatus in such a manner that the photograph is reproduced on a sensitive film at some distant

---

[1] *Daily Mail*, December 27, 1922.

station. One of the goals toward which inventors have been working for more than half a century, ever since the transmission of signals by the ordinary telegraph became possible, has been reached; and a new era in illustrated journalism is beginning. The wireless tape machine can now, automatically and without the intervention of a human operator, tick out an exact reproduction of a photograph at a distance.

As well as professional and business success, Stephenson was to experience deep personal happiness at this time. He became engaged to be married to a charming American girl from Tennessee, Miss Mary French Simmons, whom he had met on board ship and whose home was in Springfield, Tennessee. A woman of an innately sweet disposition, kind and gentle, Mary Simmons was the ideal wife for a man of Stephenson's restless energy, carefully watching over his health and sustaining him in his many-sided and arduous activities by her sympathy and forbearance. The marriage took place in the South Kensington Presbyterian Church in London on July 22, 1924.

Mary Simmons was comparatively well-off in her own right, since her father was a rich tobacco exporter in Tennessee. But Stephenson had no need of his wife's money. The patents which he took out to protect his wireless invention proved a gold mine. For the eighteen years of their duration they brought him an average sum of £100,000 annually in royalties. Thus by the beginning of 1926, when he celebrated his thirtieth birthday, William Stephenson was worth a million dollars. By the early nineteen-thirties he controlled a score of companies from an impressive office in St. James's Street and he had a house in fashionable New Cavendish Street as well as an attractive country place and farm in the Chilterns, in both of which he and his wife entertained on a generous scale.

While absorbed in scientific research and development in the field of electronics Stephenson was 'somewhat paradoxically' (to use his own words) boxing actively to retain his title of amateur light-weight world champion. Indeed, his career as an amateur boxer was most spectacular and when he finally retired from the ring in 1923, he was undefeated.

He also kept up his interest in flying, and incidentally his friendly rivalry with his former fellow Flight Commander in

73 Squadron, Captain Orlebar. In 1929, Orlebar won the Schneider Trophy for Britain breaking the world's previous speed record in the air with an average speed of 357.7 m.p.h. He did this in a Supermarine Special, the prototype for the military version which was to become the renowned Spitfire in World War II.[1]

In 1934 Stephenson won the King's Cup air race with a machine piloted by Captain H. M. Schofield which had been designed and built in one of his factories, General Aircraft Limited. This was the Monospar, a twin-engine low-wing monoplane. Its performance on this occasion made such an impression on Lord Londonderry, then Air Minister and himself an enthusiastic pilot—it could fly and climb on one engine, an unheard of achievement at that time—that he immediately ordered one for his private use, an incident well remembered by the present writer as he frequently flew in it with the Minister at the controls. One of the first objects which meets the eyes of any visitor to Sir William Stephenson's New York apartment today is the gold cup which he received at the hands of King George V as the winner of the classic contest of the air.

Another of Stephenson's companies was Sound City Films, which produced over half of the total output of British films at this period in its Shepperton studios. Then there was Earls Court Ltd., which was responsible for the erection of the world's biggest stadium and exhibition hall in the London district of that name; there was Catalina Ltd., one of the first manufacturers of plastics in the United Kingdom; and last but by no means least there was Pressed Steel, the Company which made ninety per cent. of the car bodies for such British firms as Morris, Humber, Hillman and Austin. With these and other concerns in which he was interested, such as Alpha Cement, he did business in five continents and was in touch with the world's leading bankers and financiers. He travelled widely in Europe and Asia meeting Prime Ministers, ambassadors and industrialists of foreign countries, and with the Aga Khan and the Nawab of Bhopal he helped to underwrite schemes for the development of backward areas and the raising of standards

---

[1] Orlebar was promoted Air Commodore and served as Deputy Chief of Combined Operations in World War II. He died in 1943.

of living among native peoples in the Middle East and India. This he regarded from every point of view as the most rewarding field for the investment of capital overseas.

In this context Stephenson headed a mission of highly qualified technical experts to India in 1934 to investigate the prospects for the development of local natural resources and industry. Besides Stephenson, the mission included Henry G. Acres, a fellow Canadian and internationally known hydro-electric engineer, the American geologist Eugene Dawson, the English chemical engineer Robin Edgeworth-Johnson, and another fellow Canadian, Colonel Beverley MacDonald, a civil engineer and expert on railway and docks construction. This high-powered mission concentrated its attention on Bhopal and Kashmir, two of the principal Muslim states in the sub-continent.

The Nawab of Bhopal was Chancellor of the Chamber of Native Princes in India at this time and as such was interested, along with the late Aga Khan, in promoting the prosperity of the whole country. He and Stephenson became close friends and were to correspond regularly until his death.[1] It began with the Nawab's openly professed admiration of Stephenson's skill with the rifle in the tiger and panther shoots, which the Nawab organized for the mission. After one of these shoots, the Nawab wrote to his friend, Lord Southborough in London: 'Stephenson is certainly the best shot I have ever had the honour to have as my guest. How the Begum would have loved to be with us on the shikaris!'

It was his connection with the Pressed Steel Company that first led Stephenson into the field of secret intelligence. In the course of the business trips which he made to Germany at this period in order to buy steel, he soon discovered that practically the whole of the German steel production had been turned over to the manufacture of armaments and munitions, although Germany had been expressly forbidden by the Treaty of Versailles to maintain any armed forces. Unfortunately this state of affairs was not appreciated in Britain either by Mr. Baldwin's

[1] Air Vice-Marshal H. H. Nawab Haji Sir Muhammed Hamidulla Khan (1894–1961) who succeeded his mother Begum Sultan Jehan on the latter's abdication in 1926, was the first male ruler of the state for more than eighty years, there having been a remarkable succession of female Nawabs of Bhopal since 1844. The last one was known popularly as 'the Queen Victoria of India'.

Conservative Government or by the general public. Almost alone among parliamentary back benchers, for he was in the political wilderness during these critical years, Winston Churchill harped unceasingly on what he knew to be going on in the new Reich of Adolf Hitler and his Nazi followers. As Churchill put it, 'my mind was obsessed by the impression of the terrific Germany I had seen and felt in action during the years of 1914 to 1918, suddenly again becoming possessed of all her martial power, while the Allies who had so narrowly survived gaped idle and bewildered. Therefore I continued by every means and on every occasion to use what influence I had with the House of Commons and also with individual Ministers to urge forward our military preparations and to procure Allies and associates for what would before long become again the Common Cause.'[1]

Not being in the Government, Churchill had no access to official information, so he decided to pursue various private lines of inquiry in order to obtain facts and figures in support of his arguments. Among them, indeed perhaps the most significant, were those provided by Stephenson through access he managed surreptitiously to obtain to the balance sheets of the steel firms of the Ruhr. In April, 1936, Stephenson reported to Churchill that the expenditure by Germany upon purposes directly and indirectly concerned with military preparations, including the strategic roads, amounted to the equivalent of eight hundred millions sterling.

The effect of this startling piece of information on Churchill was immediate and characteristic. He decided that the British public should know the facts. Accordingly he embodied Stephenson's figure of £800 millions in a parliamentary question to Mr. Neville Chamberlain, which he put to the then Chancellor of the Exchequer and future Prime Minister on the floor of the House, having previously given him private notice of his intention. Chamberlain replied that the Government had no official figures, but from such information as they had he had no reason to think that Churchill's figure was 'necessarily excessive' as applied to either 1935 or 1936, although, as Churchill himself would agree, the Minister added, 'there are elements of conjecture'. This answer, of course, clearly implied that the

[1] Winston Churchill. *The Second World War*. I, 176.

figure had been confirmed by the Government's own secret intelligence service.

For the next three years, that is until Churchill rejoined the Cabinet on the outbreak of the Second World War, Stephenson continued to feed him with detailed evidence of Hitler's rearmament expenditure. 'That', said Stephenson modestly, looking back afterwards, 'was my only training in espionage.'

4

It was inevitable that sooner or later Stephenson should come into contact with the Government's secret intelligence organization. The introduction was provided by an influential back-bench Conservative M.P., Ralph Glyn, later Lord Glyn, who had been Parliamentary Private Secretary to Ramsay MacDonald, when MacDonald was Prime Minister and later Lord President of the Council. Glyn was also a prominent figure in the City, where he was known to Stephenson as a director, among other companies, of the British Match Corporation, which obtained some of the raw material for its manufactures from Sweden, a country in which Stephenson's Pressed Steel was interested from the point of view of the mining of iron ore. Their common interest in Sweden's industrial potential led to meetings at which information was exchanged, information which from Stephenson's side covered the supply of Swedish iron ore to Hitler's armament factories. Glyn suggested that this information should be made available to the official Secret Intelligence Service (S.I.S.) and he arranged for Stephenson to meet a high-ranking member of that service.

The existence of the Official Secrets Act in Britain has always acted as an effective bar to the publication of factual details of this legendary body. Authentic information on the subject used not to go beyond the announcement of the sums of money which Parliament dutifully voted every year for its upkeep without asking any questions as to the precise manner in which this money was expended. Writers who had personal experience of the service and felt impelled to write about it, such as Sir Compton Mackenzie in his amusing *Water on the Brain* and Mr. Somerset Maugham in his more serious *Ashenden*, were obliged to do so in ostensibly fictional form, a device also employed more recently by Graham Greene in *Our Man in Havana* and Ian Fleming in his enthralling James Bond stories. When Mackenzie unwisely presumed to depart from this polite fiction and described some of the actual inner workings of the organization in his autobiographical *Greek Memories*, he was promptly prosecuted at the Old Bailey and severely punished, while the offending work was suppressed. One unfortunate result of the fictional approach was to invest the service with a wholly imaginary glamour in the public mind, which conceived the average British secret agent as a rather Kiplingesque figure wearing a monocle and spats, pursued across Europe by a ravishingly attractive version of Mata Hari who habitually attempted to steal the plans of the fort from his champagne-drugged person after a passionate seduction scene in a sleeping car between Vienna and Bucharest.

As Stephenson was to discover, the reality was far removed from the conventional picture, and the prosaic S.I.S. headquarters were very much like those of any other government department, such as the Board of Trade, except that their activities were largely screened from public view in spite of such an occasional slip-up as Compton Mackenzie's *Greek Memories*. For many years the chief of the service, always discreetly referred to by those in the know as 'C', had been a retired admiral. Indeed he had been in command at the time of the real-life exploits of Mackenzie and Maugham during the First War. But there was soon to be a new 'C' in the person of the admiral's principal assistant, a socially well-connected soldier (Life Guards, D.S.O. and M.C. in the First War), who had married twice into the peerage. It was to this distinguished officer that Ralph Glyn now introduced Stephenson. To disclose his identity would not in the ordinary course advance the purpose of this narrative. But as it was to be announced by the notorious William Joyce ('Lord Haw-Haw') in one of his early war-time broadcasts from Germany, not to mention various journalists after the war such as the American Joseph Alsop (in the *New York Herald-Tribune*) and the English Malcolm Muggeridge (in the *New Statesman*), there seems to be no particular point in withholding it here. He was Colonel Stewart Menzies, later Major-General Sir Stewart Menzies, K.C.B., whose brief biography as contributed by himself to *Who's Who* indicated that he was educated at Eton, that his regiment was the Life Guards and that his London clubs were White's and the St. James's.

The successful Canadian business man got on well with this under-cover representative of English upper-class society, although he could not understand why his name should be pronounced 'Mingiss' instead of as it was spelt phonetically. For his part Menzies was most grateful for the industrial and economic intelligence which Stephenson gladly undertook to provide free of charge, and Menzies immediately instructed one of the most experienced senior officers in his organization to act as liaison between them. Stephenson's reports were passed on to the Industrial Intelligence Centre (I.I.C.), which had been set up some years previously under Major (later Sir) Desmond Morton to study and report to the Committee of Imperial Defence on the state of industrial preparedness of foreign countries to make war. This able and far-seeing individual, who was to act as Winston Churchill's Personal Assistant throughout the whole of the latter's war-time Premiership, was also concerned with the preparation of strategic plans for economic warfare for the Chiefs of Staff, and his small centre provided the nucleus of the Intelligence Department of the embryo Ministry of Economic Warfare. Morton was to become a close friend and ally of Stephenson's, and their collaboration was to prove invaluable in sustaining Stephenson when the time came in America.

The adoption of the term 'economic warfare' in the pre-1939 planning period introduced a much broader and more positive conception of the role of economics in a future war, a conception with which Stephenson, like Morton, was in complete agreement. Incidentally it was Morton and his I.I.C. that coined the term, and led the authorities to reject the older conception of 'blockade' as out of date in the 'total war' of the future for which they were planning. In this, said Morton, many civilian elements would have to be taken into account, not only in defensive but also in offensive operations, and the Ministry of Economic Warfare, when it officially came into existence, must be regarded as a fighting department on a level with the three service departments. As Morton used aptly to point out in the lectures he regularly gave at this period to the Imperial

Defence College and the Staff Colleges, there were four horse-men of the Apocalypse and the one with the scales was neither the last nor the least of the four. Thus the new Ministry, Morton insisted, should concern itself not only with such overt activities as contraband control but also with a whole new offensive field of 'special operations' in the shape of subversion and sabotage to be directed against both the enemy country and those neutral countries from which the enemy drew his supplies.[1]

The German output of high-grade steel for armament manu-facture depended on the Bessemer process in which iron ore of high phosphorus content from the Gallivare mines in northern Sweden was used. Normally this was shipped in winter through Narvik on the west coast of Norway, and, in the spring and summer when they were free from ice, through Lulea and other Swedish ports on the Gulf of Bothnia. When Hitler launched his *blitzkrieg* against Poland at the beginning of September, 1939, Germany had about nine months' supply of ore, sufficient only for the short war on which the Nazis were gambling. With the immediate entry of Britain and France into the con-flict and the likelihood that it would be prolonged well into the following year, it became imperative for Germany that the Swedish supplies should continue and if possible be increased. Meanwhile Fritz Thyssen, the German industrialist, now a refugee in Switzerland, had let it become known in Allied circles that he had told Hitler and Goering that the war would be won by the side which secured control of the Swedish ores.

Mr. Churchill, who had joined the Chamberlain Government and occupied his old office in the Admiralty, immediately applied his mind to this question. The new First Lord of the Admiralty was informed that ore carriers sailing from Narvik to German ports would hug the Norwegian coast as far as the Skagerrak, and he accordingly proposed that mines should be laid in Norwegian territorial waters as a means of forcing the vessels into the open sea. No action on these lines was taken at the time, largely through Foreign Office scruples on the subject of Norway's neutrality. As it happened, hardly any German or Swedish ships were trying to take ore south from Narvik at this time, principally it appears on account of the reluctance of their crews to sail. Stephenson now learned through his

[1] W. N. Medlicott. *The Economic Blockade* (1952), I, 16.

Stephenson (*right*) on joining 73 Squadron, R.F.C. and (*below*) as a fighter pilot in France

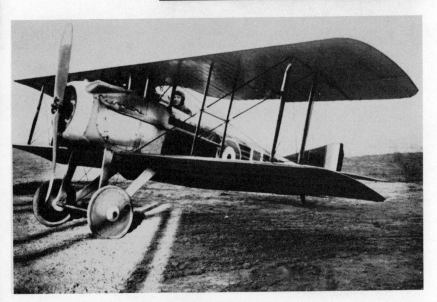

'. . . *never forgets the boys on the ground when things are hot.*'

Stephenson with the wireless photography transmitter which he
invented in 1922

'. . . a new era in illustrated journalism is beginning.'

Swedish correspondents that the Germans were accumulating ore at the ice-free Baltic port of Oxelsund, about sixty miles south-west of Stockholm, against the freeze-up in the Gulf of Bothnia. This information he passed on to Churchill who told the Cabinet that in consequence the Germans would be able to bring good supplies down the Baltic via the Kiel Canal to the Ruhr during the winter months.[1]

At the same time Stephenson proposed that ore shipments from Oxelsund and the other ports on the west coast of Sweden which might be used after the break-up of the ice should be sabotaged, and he volunteered to carry out the operation himself with the aid of his Swedish friends. Churchill from the Admiralty welcomed the idea enthusiastically, while continuing to press for the mining of the Norwegian waters since the Narvik shipments had been resumed on a modest scale. On December 16, 1939, he pointedly recommended in a memorandum which he placed before the Cabinet that the ore from Oxelsund 'must be prevented from leaving by methods which will be neither diplomatic nor military'.[2] Morton at the new Ministry of Economic Warfare was equally enthusiastic, although his Ministry had not yet assumed political responsibility for 'special operations'.

At this period, subversion (S.O.1) and sabotage (S.O.2) were regarded as off-shoots of the 'C' organization headed by Colonel Menzies and as such formed part of what was now officially referred to as M.I.6. In charge of the S.O. side was a sapper officer, Colonel Laurence Grand, known in the service as 'D', who had spent many years soldiering in India. As soon as Stephenson's project had been approved in principle, it was turned over to the 'D' section for the details to be worked out and then carried into execution. For this purpose one of 'D''s officers was specially attached to Stephenson as an assistant: his job was to collect supplies of high explosive in plastic form and convey them secretly to Sweden, where Stephenson would arrange for their distribution among his friends. These preparations were duly made, the explosives being introduced in diplomatic bags carried by the officer in question who travelled on a diplomatic courier's passport.

[1] Churchill. I, 424.
[2] Churchill. I, 431.

At this time plastic explosives were quite a novelty; these were the first of their kind to be produced at Woolwich Arsenal and the first to leave England. The bags, which each contained thirty to forty pounds of raw material, with accompanying detonators, were stored in a cellar of the British Legation in Stockholm, immediately underneath the Minister's office. This arrangement was facilitated by the Military Attaché, who was let into the secret and co-operated fully, although the Minister himself knew nothing about it. If he had had any inkling of what he was sitting on top of, the accustomed even flow of his despatches to the Foreign Office might have been somewhat disturbed.

More of the plastic was consigned to the studio of a Swedish friend of the Military Attaché, an amateur sculptor, who pretended to use it for his modelling. This was quite feasible since plastic explosive is indistinguishable in appearance from plasticene used by sculptors: the difference can only be detected by their smell.

For his part, the British Military Attaché took a considerable risk of being compromised, since two service attachés in other missions—the German Naval Attaché and the Soviet Military Attaché—had recently been expelled from the country for becoming involved in activities which the Swedes considered had endangered their neutrality. Furthermore, another member of the Legation staff, who had been informed of what was afoot by his military colleague, became so worried that he had a complete nervous breakdown. He slept with a hatchet by his bed and the door barricaded, and, in the Military Attaché's words, 'called us all at 2 a.m. to a "conference"!' He eventually had to be recalled to London. 'We got him off', the Military Attaché wrote to Stephenson's assistant, 'but he was as dotty as hell—largely your doing, and mine.'

The operation involved the two principal participants in considerable personal risk. There were plenty of German undercover agents in Sweden, and they were quite capable of kidnapping or murdering the two British agents if they should discover what they were up to, since their purpose was to blow up the cranes and other mechanical equipment used for loading the iron ore aboard the German ships. But Stephenson seems to have been much less concerned with possible danger from the enemy than from his travelling companion who insisted at all times on carrying a loaded revolver, even in bed. On one occasion he accidentally let it off in his hotel room in Stockholm, narrowly missing Stephenson's leg.

In fact, the operation was frustrated not by the Germans but by the Swedes. News of the saboteurs' plans reached the ears of King Gustav, and it threw the aged monarch into a state bordering on panic. He immediately sent a frantic telegram to King George VI, appealing to him to call off the operation, which he assured his brother monarch would undoubtedly result in the Germans invading Sweden. King George lost no time in informing Lord Halifax, the Foreign Minister, and Stephenson and his assistant were consequently ordered to take no further action.

The possibility that Sweden would be overrun by the Nazis had already been increased by the decision of the Allies at a meeting of the Supreme War Council in Paris on February 5, 1940, to send reinforcements to the gallant Finns in their struggle against the vastly superior forces of Soviet Russia. It was planned to despatch an expeditionary force to Narvik, which would have the effect of cutting off the iron ore as well as helping the Finns. But Germany made it clear that if Allied troops entered either Norway or Sweden, she would interfere, and so the project came to nothing, although Churchill was always in favour of taking the risk.

At this stage Stephenson, who had not yet left Stockholm, was asked to continue his journey to Helsinki and there discuss with the relevant Finnish authorities possible alternative means of helping them, either by subversion or sabotage. Among those whom Stephenson saw was the aged Field-Marshal Mannerheim, who had saved his country in 1917 from the Soviets and was responsible for the Mannerheim Line of defences which the Soviet forces had now breached. The Field-Marshal told Stephenson that it was now too late to do anything effective and that the only alternative to complete annihilation at Soviet hands was for Finland to sue for peace. She had already begun overtures to this end, and peace was in fact concluded on March 13, 1940, Finland being obliged to cede to Russia a considerable slice of her territory. Stephenson returned to London greatly disheartened, as indeed Churchill also was, by these fruits of allied indecision.

At the end of March, after seven months' maddening delay, the Supreme War Council agreed to the mining of Norwegian waters and the Cabinet authorized Churchill to carry out this operation. But it came too late. Twenty-four hours later the Germans attacked Norway, with cold-blooded treachery, landing ammunition and other military supplies in apparently empty ore carriers running into Narvik.

The Swedes had a good army and could enter Norway easily, and Churchill shared French desires that they could be brought into the war on the side of the Allies with general assurances that all help would be given to them and that British troops would be active in the Scandinavian Peninsula. 'It would be disastrous', he told Chamberlain two days after the German landings in Norway, 'if they remained neutral and bought Germany off with iron ore from Gallivare down the Gulf of Bothnia.' Hence, he added, 'our diplomacy should be active in Stockholm'.[1]

Stephenson would gladly have done anything he could with his Swedish friends to achieve this object. But it was not to be. Both Chamberlain and Halifax rejected Churchill's proposed method of approach to the Swedes. Once more a valuable opportunity was allowed to slip away, and Sweden remained neutral in the conflict, with the consequences that Churchill had predicted.

Meanwhile Stephenson had returned to London and reported to Intelligence Headquarters. He was thanked for what he had done in Scandinavia and asked if he would undertake another secret mission, this time to the United States. He immediately agreed and went home to repack his bags.

5

Stephenson travelled to America ostensibly as a business man engaged in promoting the interests of his various companies. His secret instructions were explicit but limited in purpose to furthering Anglo-American co-operation in one specific field. He was required to establish relations on the highest possible level between the British S.I.S. organization and the U.S. Federal Bureau of Investigation. Such contacts between the

[1] Churchill. I, 481.

two services as existed before the war were largely of a routine character and confined to information about wanted criminals and suspicious applications for British visas, which might be referred by the Passport Control branch of the British Consulate-General in New York to the local F.B.I. office. But with the outbreak of the war even these contacts, owing to the fact of Britain's belligerency and America's neutrality, had necessarily to be maintained on a tenuous and unofficial basis between the individual officers concerned. German intelligence and subversive activities in the United States at this time, which were directed against the allied war effort, did not threaten American internal security. But without the co-operation and good will of the F.B.I., the British intelligence and security services were powerless to take any effective countermeasures, nor could they really function at all.

Stephenson was informally introduced to the head of the F.B.I. by a mutual friend, Gene Tunney, the American world-champion boxer, as has already been noted. At this date John Edgar Hoover was forty-five years of age, a year older than Stephenson, and had been Director of the F.B.I. since 1924. An able lawyer and criminologist, Hoover had first been appointed Acting Director at a time when the Bureau was in low water through being involved in the political scandals of President Harding's Administration. He had proved an immediate success in spite of some ill-natured criticisms about his being too young for the job; his appointment had been speedily confirmed; and during the next fifteen years he had succeeded in building up the F.B.I. from a little known and poorly regarded federal agency into a renowned national institution, dedicated to the establishment of the conception that in America, at least, crime does not pay. Furthermore, he had been careful to keep free from party politics, serving the cause of law enforcement regardless of whether the occupant of the White House was a Republican or a Democrat, and his public relations were excellent. Hoover's 'G-men' (G for Government) were famous from coast to coast in their relentless pursuit of gangsters and hoodlums, and the Bureau's ambitious Director took good care to ensure that their exploits in the line of duty received the widest publicity. One F.B.I. agent, fatally wounded in a gun battle with two bank robbers, was said to have died with the heroic words on his lips, 'Tell Mr. Hoover I did my best'.

Hoover listened with polite attention, as Stephenson explained the purpose of his visit. Then he spoke out frankly. He told his caller that, while he himself would welcome the idea of working with British Intelligence, he was under a strict injunction from the State Department to refrain from collaborating with the British in any way which might conceivably be interpreted as infringing or compromising United States neutrality in the European struggle, and he made it clear that he would not be prepared to contravene this policy without a direct order from the White House. Further, he stipulated that, even if President Roosevelt could be persuaded to agree to the principle of collaboration between the F.B.I. and the British S.I.S., this collaboration should be effected initially by a personal liaison between Stephenson and himself, and that no other United States Government Department, including the Department of State, should be informed of it.

Stephenson agreed to this condition—indeed he had no alternative—and undertook to get one of the President's confidential advisers, with whom they were both acquainted, to put the matter before Mr. Roosevelt. The intermediary chosen for this purpose was Ernest Cuneo, a clever lawyer of Italian descent from New Jersey with a most engaging personality, then in his mid-thirties. Cuneo, who is now president of the North American Newspaper Alliance, had begun his career as legal assistant to New York's colourful Mayor Fiorello La Guardia, and then, like his first employer, became a successful international law practitioner, specializing in cases of Western European and Mediterranean interest, besides acting as standing counsel to the Democratic National Committee; this had brought him into touch with the White House. Stephenson accordingly lost no time in communicating with Cuneo, who promised to see the President as soon as possible.

A day or two later Cuneo reported that President Roosevelt had welcomed the idea enthusiastically. 'There should be the closest possible marriage between the F.B.I. and British Intelligence', the President had said. Later, by way of confirmation, Mr. Roosevelt repeated these words to the British Ambassador in Washington, then Lord Lothian.

That such an agreement was reached at all was a remarkable indication of the President's clarity of vision, while the fact that it had to be kept secret even from the State Department provided a striking illustration of the strength of American neutrality at this period. It was all the more courageous of Franklin Roosevelt to act as he did, since he was in the last year of his Presidential term and he had necessarily to behave with particular circumspection if he was to run again successfully for election. The isolationist atmosphere was strong throughout the country, the old anti-colonialist and anti-imperialist prejudices against the British died hard, and there were few Americans, in or out of Congress, who realized that the safety of their own country would be endangered by the collapse of Britain. Even pro-British sympathizers had become disheartened by the disastrous appeasement policy of the Chamberlain Government and the indecisions and blunders of what they called 'the phoney war'.

It was true that the Neutrality Act had been amended so as to remove the embargo on the sale of arms to the Allies, but these had to be paid for in cash and they could not be conveyed across the Atlantic in American ships. Hence the operation of supply was known as 'Cash and Carry'. The British Purchasing Commission, which had been established in New York to obtain these supplies, was under the charge of a hard-working and influential Scots-Canadian industrialist, Arthur Purvis, who like Stephenson enjoyed the confidence of the Americans to a remarkable degree and like him too drew no salary for his official labours. ('It always takes a Scotsman to pull England out of a hole', he used to say with a chuckle.) But Purvis and his assistants in the Cunard Building on Broadway were much too busy working out supply policy with Mr. Henry Morgenthau and the United States Treasury to attend to the security of the shipments for which they were in theory also responsible.[1] In any event, they had no means of instituting adequate safeguards at the various ports where the material was loaded on to British ships and where, in Stephenson's view, the risk of sabotage was most serious. For this purpose it was comparatively easy for the Germans to recruit dock labourers and stevedores from the local German, Italian and Irish communities, who

[1] Duncan Hall. *North American Supply* (1955), 72 *et seq.*

hated Britain, while the F.B.I. agents were unable to intervene so long as German subversive activities did not directly threaten American interests.

Upon his return to London, Stephenson reported these findings to S.I.S. headquarters. In the discussions which followed, he urged that any secret British organization which might be formed in the United States to assist the war effort, though necessarily founded on the liaison with Hoover and the F.B.I. for which he had laid the foundations, should cover a considerably wider field than the collection of secret intelligence by the old and well-tried methods; in other words it should comprise everything that was not being done and could not be done by overt means to assure sufficient aid for Britain, to counter the enemy's subversive plans throughout the Western Hemisphere, and eventually to bring the United States into the war. This included counter-espionage, political warfare and 'special operations'.

Colonel Menzies thereupon told Stephenson that, as far as the service for which he had responsibility was concerned, he would be grateful if Stephenson would accept the appointment of Passport Control Officer in New York, P.C.O. being then a convenient 'cover' for S.I.S. representatives abroad. Stephenson replied that he would like some time to think over this offer, as he had not envisaged an immediate return to the United States for what might well turn out to be a prolonged period. Anyhow he felt he had to consult others who might be interested in the conduct of secret activities.

Meanwhile big political changes were afoot in England. These were foreshadowed by the growing public discontent with the Chamberlain Government's conduct of the war, discontent which came to a head in the bungling of the Norwegian campaign. The latter has been well described by James Leasor in his book, *War at the Top*.[1]

> The British landing in Norway to defend that country against the Nazis was an example of how not to carry out such an operation. Almost everything was left to chance. They could not land their out-of-date heavy guns and tanks because of German air superiority; the Norwegians were hampered by

---

[1] James Leasor. *War at the Top* (1959), at pp. 73-4.

equipment of even greater age and uselessness. Barely twelve thousand British troops were put ashore—and these landed through their own skill, perseverance and determination, rather than through any feat of planning, to engage ten times as many Germans. Their commanders complained bitterly of the lack of accurate maps, or information about beaches and fjords. One transport sailed without either a barometer or chronometer and with the wrong charts. Several commanders were issued with plans based on woodcuts of Norwegian beauty spots dating back to 1860—which obviously bore no relation to the same places eighty years on. Some jetties had been described as possessing cranes and heavy tackle; other possible landing beaches were said to be suitable for small boats. In fact, the jetties had been abandoned half a century ago, and the beaches were strewn with great rocks, and were unapproachable by anything larger than a canoe. *This lack of topographical intelligence played a heavy part in the defeat. As a result of this débâcle, the Germans gained Norway as a most valuable air and submarine base on the North Atlantic coast, and also won control of the iron ore, for a loss of only 1,300 men. Most important, they now knew that Allied talk of welcoming attack was bravado; they knew how weak we were, and so did the rest of the world.* [My italics.]

On May 10, 1940, Hitler followed up his success in Norway by launching a lightning attack without previous warning upon Belgium, Holland and Luxembourg. Later that same day Chamberlain resigned his office of Prime Minister, and the King sent for Winston Churchill, who immediately set about forming his famous National Coalition Government. In the consequent reshuffle of posts, the key Ministry of Economic Warfare went to one of the most energetic and self-confident of the Labour Party leaders, Dr. Hugh Dalton, who was also put in charge of all 'special operations', the old S.O.1 and S.O.2 branches having been combined to form S.O.E. (Special Operations Executive), or, as the new Prime Minister jokingly called it, the Ministry of Ungentlemanly Warfare. Other appointments of particular interest to Stephenson were those of his old Canadian friend Lord Beaverbrook as Minister of Aircraft Production and his English friend and business associate Mr. Frederick Leathers, later Lord Leathers, as special adviser to the Ministry of Shipping. (Soon, under the stresses of the Battle of the Atlantic, the Prime Minister was to unite the Ministries of Shipping and Transport under the experienced direction of Leathers, who thus became the first Minister of War Transport.)

Stephenson talked to these people and to various others associated in one way or another with the new and dynamic direction of affairs. But he still could not make up his mind whether to go back to America. Finally he sought an interview with Mr. Churchill, and this decided him. The Prime Minister received him in his old room at the Admiralty since he had not yet had time to move into Downing Street. He spoke briefly of the United States and of their vital importance to the allied war effort, of the need of forty or fifty of their older destroyers on which he had already cabled President Roosevelt, and of the effective role of co-ordinated secret intelligence and special operations in the American theatre. Suddenly the Prime Minister looked Stephenson straight in the face. 'Your duty lies there,' he said. 'You must go.'

# CHAPTER II

## THE BIRTH OF B.S.C.

### I

STEPHENSON's return to New York, this time with his wife, coincided with the evacuation of the remaining British forces from Dunkirk and the drawn-out agony of the French military and political collapse. The new British Passport Control Officer found the atmosphere bleakly defeatist so far as Britain's chances of survival went. This was the view of many of the President's influential advisers, encouraged by the two principal American Ambassadors abroad, William Bullitt in Paris and Joseph Kennedy in London, the latter constantly and vehemently counselling the President against 'holding the bag in a war in which the Allies expect to be beaten'.[1] But it was not Stephenson's view. 'The arsenals of Britain are empty', he told Roosevelt when they met at this time, 'but she will win out. The British do not kneel easily.' Meanwhile Roosevelt, though continuing his intimate correspondence with Churchill, had been obliged to refuse the Prime Minister's repeated requests for American destroyers on the ground that this would require the assent of Congress and that the time was not opportune.

For some years the Passport Control Officer had been accommodated in a small room in the British Consulate-General in down-town Manhattan with a staff consisting of one assistant and a woman clerk and secretary. Stephenson took one look at this accommodation and saw that it was totally unsuitable for his own base headquarters and the kind of intelligence organization which he contemplated. It was his first and only visit to the cramped and depressing offices in Exchange Place. Until he could lease suitable office space in a more convenient part of the city, he decided to work from the

[1] Robert Sherwood. *The White House Papers of Harry L. Hopkins* (1948). I, 151–2.

apartment he had taken in Hampshire House overlooking
Central Park.

Next he flew down to Washington and reported his arrival
to Lord Lothian at the British Embassy. He found the Ambassador sympathetic and helpful and thoroughly familiar with the
local political scene, but also frankly worried. Lothian had just
received a cable from Churchill urging him to see the President
and impress upon him what would happen if Britain broke
under a German invasion and a pro-German Quisling type of
Government in Whitehall were induced by the prospect of
easier peace terms to surrender the British Fleet. 'You should
talk to him in this sense', Churchill had said, 'and thus discourage any complacent assumption on the United States' part
that they will pick up the *débris* of the British Empire by their
present policy. On the contrary, they run the terrible risk that
their sea-power will be completely over-matched. Moreover,
islands and naval bases to hold the United States in awe would
certainly be claimed by the Nazis. If we go down Hitler has
a very good chance of conquering the world.' [1]

On the night of June 16, 1940, Lothian was summoned to
the White House where he saw the President with Sumner
Welles, the Under-Secretary of State. The news had just come
in that the French Premier Paul Reynaud had resigned and
had been succeeded by the Pétain-Weygand Government which
had begun negotiations with the Germans for an armistice.
After saying he thought Churchill's telegrams to Reynaud,
urging that the French Fleet sail forthwith to British harbours
pending negotiations, were 'perfectly grand', the President went
on to express the hope that as many French airmen and others
would assist in carrying on the war in Algiers or with the
British, as also that, *if ever a similar crisis arose in Great Britain,
the war would be carried on overseas and that the British Fleet would
not be surrendered.* To this Lothian replied that Great Britain
could not be expected to transfer her Fleet across the seas and
associate it with any country that was not going to use it and
its own resources to the limit to rescue Great Britain herself
from conquest.

President Roosevelt then told the Ambassador that, so far as
he had thought out the position, he considered that, in the event

[1] Churchill. II, 355.

of Britain becoming useless as a naval base, the Fleet ought to be
withdrawn to Capetown, Singapore, Aden and Sydney, while
the main American navy reinforced the Atlantic and undertook
the defence of Canada and other British possessions. He added
that, if the crisis reached this point, the United States would
certainly allow British ships to use American facilities for re-
forming and supply, and that, while they might not have formally declared war on Germany because of constitutional
difficulties, they would in effect be a belligerent 'assisting the
Empire in every way and enforcing the blockade on Germany'.

This tremendous decision to back the seemingly hopeless
cause of Britain with all the material and moral encouragement
he could supply was entirely Roosevelt's own; it was taken
against the advice of the majority of the White House official
circle, and at a time when his position in the country in an
election year was far from secure. He immediately followed it
up by giving his Cabinet a new bi-partisan look, having anticipated over the past six months that the development of 'a real
crisis' in the shape of a German victory in Europe would justify
him in largely dispensing with what he called 'strictly old-
fashioned party government'. He accordingly dismissed the
isolationist Secretary of the Navy and his colleague in the War
Department, replacing them with leading Republicans who
were powerful advocates of American intervention in the
European struggle and strongly pro-British. Frank Knox,
Boston-born proprietor of the *Chicago Daily News*, whom Roosevelt considered of all the Republican leaders to 'have shown
a truer understanding of the effect which the international
situation will of necessity exert on our domestic future'—he
had been the Republican nominee for Vice-President in the
1936 election—became Secretary of the Navy, while the veteran
New York lawyer, Henry L. Stimson, who had been Secretary
of War under President Taft nearly thirty years before, returned
to that office at the urgent invitation of Roosevelt, because in
Stimson's words 'everybody was running around at loose ends
in Washington and he (Roosevelt) thought I would be a
stabilizing factor in whom both the Army and the public
would have confidence'.[1] At first the President seriously

[1] Henry L. Stimson and McGeorge Bundy. *On Active Service in Peace and
War* (1952), 144.

considered appointing another Republican, the fifty-seven-year-old 'Wild Bill' Donovan, to this important post, but after reflection decided to keep him for other duties. This was to prove a most fortunate decision for Anglo-American co-operation in the joint prosecution of the war.

William Joseph Donovan, whom Stephenson had first met during a visit to England and with whom he now lost no time in renewing acquaintance, was an Irish-American of truly dynamic character. He could be fairly described as a big man in every way, with great generosity of spirit, many enthusiasms and considerable breadth of interests. The son of a poor family of Irish immigrants in Buffalo and a Roman Catholic who neither smoked nor drank alcohol, Bill Donovan was entirely self-made, having risen by what is known in America as 'the hard way' to become a most successful New York City lawyer with offices in Wall Street, and Acting Attorney-General under President Coolidge. It was his service with the famous 'Fighting 69th' in the First World War which had earlier earned him the Congressional Medal of Honour and also the title of 'Wild Bill'. (This was to some extent a misnomer since he was by nature an extremely modest person.) It had been generally thought that Herbert Hoover, for whom he had campaigned actively in the 1928 Presidential Election, would make Donovan Attorney-General on reaching the White House, but the appointment was blocked by 'dry' elements in the Republican Party, to whom the idea of a member of a community with such 'wet' interests as the Catholic Irish-American was obnoxious, although Donovan himself was a teetotaller. After being defeated in the election for the Governorship of New York on the Republican ticket in 1932—he was successful in everything except politics—Donovan had returned to his law practice, which he would periodically leave in the hands of his partners to visit Europe, touring the battle fronts in the Italo-Abyssinian campaign and the Spanish Civil War where he viewed with alarm the rise of Fascist power. Although belonging to opposing political parties Donovan and Roosevelt were old friends from Columbia Law School, where they had been classmates together. 'Frankly I should like to have him in the Cabinet', the President had told Frank Knox at the end of 1939, 'not only for his own ability, but also to repair

in a sense the very great injustice done him by President
Hoover. . . .' [1] In fact, Donovan was now to become President
Roosevelt's roving ambassador in Europe and later chief of
all United States secret intelligence and 'special operations'
overseas.

Speaking many years later, in the privacy of his New York
apartment, Stephenson was to recall the vital significance of
initial contact with Donovan at this period. 'The procurement
of certain supplies for Britain was high on the list', he said,
'and it was the burning urgency of the attempt to fulfil this
requirement that made me instinctively—I don't think it can
be rated much higher than that—concentrate on a single
individual who, despite all my contacts in high places, might
achieve more than any widespread effort on the official or
sub-official levels which had so far been unproductive. My
assessment was proved correct in the event. Donovan, by
virtue of his very independence of thought and action,
inevitably had his critics, but there were few among them
who would deny the credit due to him for having reached
a correct appraisal of the international situation in the
summer of 1940.

'At that time the United States Government was debating
two alternative courses of action', Stephenson continued; 'one
was to endeavour to keep Britain in the war by supplying her
with material assistance of which she was desperately in need;
the other was to give Britain up for lost and to concentrate
exclusively on American rearmament to offset the German
threat. That the former course was eventually pursued was due
in large measure to Donovan's tireless advocacy of it. Immediately after the fall of France not even the President himself
could feel assured that aid to Britain was not to be wasted in
the circumstances. I need not remind you of the despatches
from the Ambassadors in London and Paris stressing that
Britain's cause was hopeless, and the majority of the Cabinet
here was inclined to the same conclusion, all of which found
vigorous expression in organized isolationism with men like
Colonel Lindbergh and Senator Wheeler. Donovan, on the
other hand, was convinced that granted sufficient aid from the
United States, Britain could and would survive. It was my task

[1] *The Roosevelt Letters.* Ed. Elliott Roosevelt (1952). III, 297.

first to inform him of Britain's foremost requirements so that he could make them known in the appropriate quarters, and secondly, to furnish him with concrete evidence in support of his contention that American material assistance would not be improvident charity but a sound investment.'

Donovan's immediate reaction on hearing from Stephenson was to arrange a meeting with Knox and Stimson, at which both he and Stephenson were present. At this meeting the main subject of discussion was Britain's urgent need of destroyers, and various ways and means were explored for a formula to cover the transfer of forty or fifty of the old 'four-stackers', then in cold storage, to Britain, without infringing the American neutrality law and without affronting American public opinion in which ships of the navy have a special sentimental value. Knox pointed out that under the present law such a transfer could only be made against a *quid pro quo* which represented such an obvious increase in American security that the Administration could safely transfer to a foreign power part of its naval forces. Even so, the transaction on a narrow interpretation of international law might be held to be a breach of neutrality. The only hope seemed to lie in being able to convince the President that he could sanction such an arrangement by executive decree, for in its present mood Congress if consulted would certainly reject it.

Besides the destroyers, Churchill had asked urgently for light naval craft, first line aircraft, including flying boats, and military equipment and supplies. Stephenson thereupon suggested that Donovan should pay a visit to Britain so that he would be in a position to give the President a first-hand report, having seen for himself what conditions were like and what were the country's chances of success against Hitler.

Donovan welcomed the idea, and with strong support from Knox it was referred to the President who immediately agreed that Donovan should make the trip and that he should travel as his unofficial personal representative.

2

Encouraged as it was by Stephenson, Donovan's visit to England, which took place between mid-July and early August,

1940, proved most fruitful. 'I arranged that he should be afforded every opportunity to conduct his inquiries', Stephenson recalled afterwards. 'I endeavoured to marshal my friends in high places to bare their breasts. He was received in audience by the King, he had ample time with Churchill and members of the Cabinet concerned. He visited war factories and military training centres. He spoke with industrial leaders, and with representatives of all classes of the community. He learned what was true—that Churchill, defying the Nazis, was no mere bold façade but the very heart of Britain which was still beating strongly.'

One person Donovan did not see in London was the defeatist Ambassador Joseph Kennedy who by a calculated snub was not advised by the White House of Donovan's tour. However, he did see a number of American naval, military and army air force observers, who were attached to the Embassy. The latter included Lt.-Colonel (later General) Carl Spaatz. 'The story goes that the naval and army observers, when asked what they thought of the British chance of survival, replied they had not got a hope. Lt.-Colonel Spaatz, on the other hand, said that he and the army air force observers were convinced that the British would pull through because the Germans could not beat the R.A.F. and they would not invade until they had. Colonel Donovan went back to the United States and reported these observations, recommending the transfer of the destroyers to Great Britain.'[1]

At the end of July, on the eve of Donovan's departure from London, Churchill made a final appeal to Roosevelt for the destroyers: 'Mr. President, with great respect I must tell you that in the long history of the world this is a thing to do *now*. . . . If the destroyers were given, the motor-boats and flying-boats, which would be invaluable, could surely come in behind them. I am beginning to feel very hopeful about this war if we can get round the next three or four months. The air is holding well. We are hitting that man hard, both in repelling attacks and in bombing Germany. But the loss of destroyers by air attack may well be so serious as to break down our defence of the food and trade routes across the Atlantic.'[2]

[1] John G. Winant. *A Letter from Grosvenor Square* (1947), at p. 35.
[2] Churchill. II, 356–7.

This brought matters to a head in Washington, where at a Cabinet meeting held in the White House on August 2, to quote the President's own words, 'it was the general opinion, without any dissenting voice, that the survival of the British Isles under German attack might very possibly depend upon their getting these destroyers'. Ways and means were discussed of conveying the destroyers to Britain by some form of direct or indirect sale. Roosevelt, who still felt that legislation was necessary for any such plan, thought that a British pledge that the Royal Navy would not fall into German hands, in the event of German success, but would sail for North American or Empire ports 'where they would remain afloat and be available', would greatly lessen opposition in Congress, and he proposed to sound out Mr. Wendell Willkie, who had just received the Republican Party nomination for President.[1] In fact, Willkie did give assurances that he would not make a campaign issue of the proposed transfer. Churchill, on the other hand, was reluctant to give any public pledge which, contemplating as it did the fall of Britain, would be most damaging to the morale of his people. Fortunately, with the return of Donovan and his reports to the President and Knox, the emphasis on the consideration for the transfer shifted to naval and air bases.

'Donovan greatly impressed by visit', Stephenson cabled London on August 8. 'Has strongly urged our case *re* destroyers and is doing much to combat defeatist attitude in Washington by stating positively and convincingly that we shall win.' As a lawyer Donovan argued that there was no need for the President to submit the plan to Congress, on the ground that it was, broadly speaking, an exercise of the traditional power of the Executive in foreign affairs, and in this he was vigorously supported in the Cabinet by Stimson and Robert Jackson, the Attorney-General, and outside by Dean Acheson, the future Secretary of State, and a group of influential New York lawyers. The President was soon converted to this view, and on August 13, at a meeting with Knox, Stimson, Welles and Morgenthau, he drafted the essential principles of the so-called destroyers for bases deal, which now belongs to history. 'I think the trick has been done', noted Lothian on August 16. 'At least the President

[1] Roosevelt. III, 326.

told me on the telephone this morning that he thought it was. Donovan helped a lot, and Knox.'[1]

Owing to what Stephenson described at the time as 'strong opposition from below and procrastination from above', three weeks were to elapse before the agreement was formally concluded. During this period the stage was principally occupied by discussions between Lothian, Welles and Knox, with Stephenson and Donovan playing strong supporting roles in the wings. On August 21, Stephenson informed London by cable: 'Donovan has urged upon President to see promised matters through himself with definite results. Donovan believes you will have within a few days very favourable news, and thinks he has restored confidence as to Britain's determination and ability to resist.' In fact it was at midnight on the following day that Stephenson was able to report that the figure of fifty destroyers had been agreed by the President and that forty-four were in commission for delivery. On September 3, legal effect was given to the deal by an exchange of notes between Lothian and Cordell Hull, the Secretary of State. 'The exchange is a big thing', said Lothian at the time. 'It really links U.S.A. and the British Empire together for defence.'[2] It provided for a ninety-nine-year lease of British bases in the Caribbean in exchange for the fifty destroyers, a similar lease of bases in Bermuda and Newfoundland freely granted, and a personal reaffirmation to the President of the statement which the British Prime Minister had already made to Parliament that the Royal Navy would not in any circumstances be surrendered to the Germans or sunk. 'Thus we obtained the fifty American destroyers . . . and both countries were satisfied,' wrote Churchill afterwards. 'The effects in Europe were profound.'[3]

In Stephenson's view, which he communicated to headquarters in London, this historic agreement could certainly not have eventuated when it did without Donovan's intercession, and in recognition of this fact Stephenson was instructed to

---

[1] Roosevelt. III, 327. J. R. M. Butler, *Lord Lothian* (1960), 297. For detailed accounts of the transaction, see Churchill, II, 353–68 and Hall, 139–45, on the British side, and Cordell Hull, I, 831–43, and Stimson and Bundy, 169–71, on the American side.
[2] Butler. 298.
[3] Churchill. II, 368.

thank him on behalf of His Majesty's Government. During the same period and by the same means, there were other essential supplies which Donovan was largely instrumental in obtaining for Britain at this time, among them a hundred Flying Fortresses and a million rifles for use by the Home Guard in the event of a German invasion. Moreover, when Donovan was in London, Lord Beaverbrook, the Minister of Aircraft Production, had asked for particulars of the secret American Sperry bomb-sight, which he wished installed on British bombers operating over Europe. On his return to Washington, Donovan had urged on the President and Knox that the bomb-sight should be made available. At first they objected, pointing out—with good reason—that if employed in the manner contemplated the bomb-sight would sooner or later be bound to fall into enemy hands. Fortunately Stephenson was able to overcome this objection by advising Donovan, on the basis of recent British secret intelligence, that the Germans already possessed details of the invention. (Drawings of the bomb-sight, or one similar to it, had been sold to German agents in 1938.) On September 24, 1940, Stephenson cabled London: 'President has sanctioned release to us of bomb-sight, to be fitted henceforth to bombers supplied to us.' In fact, the Sperry bomb-sight was released a few days later, and forty sights were immediately provided from stock.[1]

Stephenson has described his work with Donovan at this period as 'covert diplomacy inasmuch as it was preparatory and supplementary to negotiations conducted directly by H.M. Ambassador'. At first consideration it may seem that this work was far removed from the secret intelligence and special operations with which he had been primarily charged, and indeed that it necessitated, since it was strictly a personal undertaking, no organizational machinery of any kind. But the truth is that whatever he was able to accomplish in the way of obtaining certain essential supplies during the fateful summer of 1940 was largely assisted by his connection with both secret intelligence and political warfare activities.

For example, it would in all probability have been impossible for Stephenson to overcome the objections raised to releasing the Sperry bomb-sight to Britain, had he not had

[1] Hall. 191.

ready access to secret sources of information. Again, Donovan would certainly have found it considerably more difficult to achieve success in his negotiations if Stephenson had not had means at his disposal for influencing American public opinion. In fact, covert propaganda, one of the most powerful weapons which Stephenson and the organization which he was slowly building up employed against the enemy, was directly harnessed to this task. Thus, General Pershing had been persuaded through the good offices of an intermediary, a wealthy American business man named Albert Younglove Gowen, who was a friend of both Stephenson and the General, to come out with a strong speech early in August supporting the destroyers deal. Since Pershing was a national hero and was known to have no political ambitions or party affiliations, his voice carried great weight in the country.[1] Then, Donovan himself on his return from London wrote a series of articles in collaboration with a newspaperman, Edgar Ansel Mowrer, on 'German Fifth Column Tactics', based on material supplied by Stephenson from British secret intelligence sources. The articles, which created a great stir, were originally published in the influential *Chicago Daily News* owned by Frank Knox, the Secretary of the Navy, and reproduced in many other newspapers throughout the country, including the *New York Herald-Tribune*. They were also the occasion for a broadcast talk by Donovan over a nation-wide 'hook-up', the first ever afforded to a speaker other than the President. Finally Knox himself wrote an article summing up the series.[2]

3

The United States Government's conviction of the wisdom in principle of providing Britain with material aid was reflected in a telegram which Stephenson sent to Intelligence Head-quarters in London on September 14, 1940: 'Our American friends desire guidance as to what requirements in addition to Flying Fortresses they may assist to fulfil.' For the next few weeks President Roosevelt could give the subject little personal attention as he was engaged in the election campaign, which

[1] *New York Herald-Tribune*, August 5, 1940.
[2] *New York Herald-Tribune*, August 20–24, 1940.

resulted in his triumphant return to the White House for a third term at the beginning of November. However, once the election was out of the way, and he had taken a short holiday cruise, the President bent all his energies to the task of helping his British friends. Churchill had told him that Britain was coming to the end of her dollar resources with which to purchase supplies in America, and this prompted the President, at his first press conference on returning from his cruise, to put forward the conception of lend-lease, using the simple and homely analogy of lending a neighbour a length of hose with which to fight a fire. He followed this up with his famous 'fireside chat' on the radio, in which he told the American people that 'we must produce arms and ships with every energy and resource we can command' and that 'we must be the great arsenal of Democracy'. After a two-month struggle in Congress, the Lend-Lease Bill which empowered the President to 'sell, transfer, exchange, lend, lease or otherwise dispose of defence materials for the Government of any country whose defence the President deems vital to the defence of the United States', eventually became law, in spite of violent opposition led by Senator Burton K. Wheeler and other members of the 'American First' organization who claimed that its enactment would mean 'ploughing under every fourth American boy on foreign battlefields for the benefit of a decayed British Empire'.[1]

Stephenson's immediate task of helping with essential supplies was now accomplished, or rather it became inextricably a part of the broader purpose of promoting American intervention, to which in turn his intelligence and propaganda activities were initially directed. In pursuing that purpose Donovan's co-operation continued to be of inestimable value. Although some of the more important services which Donovan rendered Britain at this time were outside Stephenson's sphere of operations, nevertheless they deserve some mention here as one of the results of his liaison with Stephenson and also because they have not hitherto been described.

During the autumn and early winter of 1940, Mr. Churchill was especially concerned to secure the assistance of the United States Navy in convoying British merchant ships across the Atlantic. At this time there were two German armed raiders

[1] Churchill. II, 495.

and the pocket battleship *Scheer* roaming the seas and the resultant losses to British shipping were constantly mounting. In the five weeks ending November 3, 1940, as the Prime Minister told the President in a letter seeking this protection, the losses reached a total of 420,300 tons.[1] However, this was a measure of assistance which the Americans were at first reluctant to extend for fear that the Germans would regard it as an excuse for declaring war on the United States.

Stephenson discussed the problem at length with Donovan, whom he had little difficulty in persuading, first that it seemed unlikely on the basis of the evidence available that Germany would be provoked into a war with the United States by anything short of direct aggression, at least until she had defeated Britain, and secondly, that for the American Navy to participate in convoy duty should be regarded as an essential step in the United States policy of playing for time, that is to say, in the policy of enabling Britain to keep the enemy at bay until American preparedness was sufficiently advanced to meet the German challenge.

Donovan himself advanced these arguments at a conference with Knox, Stimson and Hull, who were impressed by them but felt they needed more concrete evidence before they could take action, particularly evidence supporting the contention that the necessity of agreeing to the British proposal outweighed the inherent risk in so doing. To obtain such evidence, Donovan proposed that he should pay another visit to London and go on to the Mediterranean, where the danger to British shipping and communications had recently been increased by the Italian invasion of Greece. This time it was agreed that Donovan should travel officially as representing the Navy Department. Before leaving, Stephenson, who flew as far as London with him, cabled Intelligence Headquarters that it was impossible to over-emphasize the importance of Donovan's visit. 'He can play a great role, perhaps a vital one, but it may not be consistent with orthodox diplomacy nor confined to its channels', Stephenson pleaded. 'You should personally convey to the Prime Minister that Donovan is presently the strongest friend we have.'

After being delayed by bad weather for nearly a fortnight

[1] Churchill. II, 495.

in Bermuda, they reached London about the middle of December. Here they had talks with Churchill and others who, in Stephenson's words, 'appreciated the significance and potentialities of this second visit of one who had justified my "build up" for him prior to his first visit'. The Prime Minister arranged for Brigadier Vivian Dykes, one of the Assistant Secretaries to the Cabinet and a brilliant military planner, to accompany Donovan to the Middle East.[1]

Then Stephenson got the Director of Naval Intelligence at the Admiralty to send a signal to Admiral Cunningham, the Commander-in-Chief, Mediterranean Fleet, on the subject of Donovan's tour, 'which made it abundantly clear to the Admiral and his staff that Donovan was the most important emissary that they were ever likely to meet in this world or the next', as Stephenson put it afterwards. 'I know', he added, 'because I dictated every word of it myself in the presence of the D.N.I. in his office.'

The following is an extract from this signal:

> Donovan exercises controlling influence over Knox, strong influence over Stimson, friendly advisory influence over President and Hull. . . . Being a Republican, a Catholic and of Irish descent, he has following of the strongest opposition to the Administration. . . . It was Donovan who was responsible for getting us the destroyers, the bomb-sight and other urgent requirements. . . . There is no doubt that we can achieve infinitely more through Donovan than through any other individual. . . . He is very receptive and should be made fully aware of our requirements and deficiencies and can be trusted to represent our needs in the right quarters and in the right way in the U.S.A. . . .

Donovan was greatly impressed by the reception which Stephenson had arranged for him, saying afterwards that 'he had never been treated in such royal and exalted fashion and that the red carpet had been thicker and wider than he thought it was possible to lay'. Among others he had talks with Admiral Cunningham and General Wavell, who commanded the British naval and land forces respectively in the area, and as a result he was convinced that American supplies must be made abundantly available if Britain's important strategic position

---

[1] Dykes was killed in an air accident in 1943.

was to be held. On January 28, 1941, Churchill sent a message to Roosevelt thanking him for the 'fine work' which Donovan had done in the Middle East.[1]

At Churchill's suggestion, Donovan with the President's approval agreed to extend his tour to Bulgaria and Yugoslavia. The Prime Minister was anxious to find some means of upsetting Hitler's timetable for the subjugation of the Balkan countries, which would have the effect of postponing even by a few weeks his contemplated attack upon Russia. This attack, which Churchill had learned of from intelligence sources, had been planned for May 15. As a result very largely of Donovan's actions it did not take place until June 22.

Donovan went first to Sofia. He could not dissuade King Boris and the Bulgarian leaders from their pro-German policy, but he did succeed in implanting in their minds a measure of doubt as to the wisdom of that policy. Consequently they hesitated before allowing German troops unrestricted passage through their country so as to prevent the British forces from obtaining a foothold in Greece. The British Prime Minister had intimated that he would be content with a delay of twenty-four hours. Donovan secured a delay of eight days.[2] During this visit Donovan was shadowed by German agents, who even followed him into the Royal Palace, where they relieved him of his passport and other papers, although they found nothing compromising.

When he reached Yugoslavia, Donovan found the pro-German Regent Prince Paul and his craven Government on the point of adhering to the Axis Powers. 'I think we should find some means of getting across to the Prince Regent and others that the United States is looking not merely to the present but to the future', Roosevelt had written to Belgrade, 'and that any nation which tamely submits on the grounds of being quickly overrun would receive less sympathy from the world than a nation which resists, even if this resistance can be continued for only a few weeks. . . . Our type of civilization and the war in whose outcome we are definitely interested, will be

---

[1] Churchill. III, 24.
[2] Bulgaria adhered to the Axis Tripartite Pact (Germany, Italy, Japan) on March 1, 1940, and German troops immediately began to occupy the country and to move towards the Greek border.

definitely helped by resistance on the part of Yugoslavia and almost automatically resistance on the part of Turkey—even though temporarily Yugoslavia and Turkey are not successful in the military sense.'[1]

Donovan did his best to get these views accepted, but he found that the Prime Minister, Dr. Cvetovic, and the Foreign Minister, Mr. Markovic, had already been summoned by Hitler to Berchtesgaden and committed their country to the Axis side. Only the Air Force General Simovic and a group of Serbian nationalist officers formed a clandestine opposition to German infiltration of Yugoslavia. Donovan accordingly visited Simovic at the Air Force Headquarters across the river from Belgrade at Zemun. The General asked him whether Britain could hold out against the Nazis and whether the United States would enter the war. After warning Simovic that he was merely expressing his personal views, Donovan answered both questions in the affirmative. As a result of this meeting Simovic was persuaded to organize the revolution which shortly afterwards led to the overthrow of Prince Paul and his treacherous Ministers and their replacement by a patriot Government led by Simovic.[2] Immediately Hitler heard this news, he countermanded an order moving three Panzer divisions from Roumania to southern Poland, and postponed the German invasion of Russia for five weeks, while he turned his immediate attention to Yugoslavia and Greece.[3]

Donovan returned to Washington on March 18, 1941. Next morning he had breakfast with the President, to whom he reported his findings. Roosevelt was delighted to see him, as he had just received another message from Churchill thanking him for the 'magnificent work done by Donovan in his prolonged tour of the Balkans and the Middle East'. ('He has carried with him throughout an animating, heart-warming flame.')[4] At his breakfast-time meeting Donovan particularly urged the importance of sending war materials direct to the Middle East if the British forces were to hold Egypt. The

[1] Roosevelt. III, 356 (memorandum dated February 20, 1941).
[2] The Yugoslav Ministers signed the Axis pact in Vienna on March 25. The revolution in Belgrade took over two days later, and on April 6 the German armies invaded both Yugoslavia and Greece.
[3] Churchill. III, 320, 323.
[4] Churchill. III, 97.

President instructed him to consult with the Government departments concerned 'to see what could be worked out'. He then promptly issued a proclamation to the effect that the Red Sea and the Persian Gulf were no longer combat zones from which American vessels were excluded by the Neutrality Act. Inside a week or two the ships were loading for Suez.[1] Convoy protection for British vessels in their hazardous Atlantic voyages followed soon afterwards.

At the President's request, Donovan again broadcast to the American people. His speech, which was widely publicized, was designed to create a favourable public atmosphere for the announcement of further measures of American intervention on the side of Britain. In essence it was a plea for the United States Government's policy of 'enlightened self-interest', delivered by a man who had had considerable share in shaping that policy—with a little help from his quiet Canadian friend.

4

While the task of building a secret organization in America had necessarily to be begun from scratch, Stephenson embarked upon it with four definite advantages. The first was his liaison with Hoover and the F.B.I., which he had previously arranged and which, as will be seen, was an essential pre-requisite of his work. The second was his acquaintance with a number of convinced interventionists, particularly Colonel Donovan, who were in a position to influence both United States public opinion and Government policy. The third was the goodwill of the Canadian authorities, who could give him considerable assistance which he needed. The fourth was the support which he enlisted immediately upon his arrival in the United States of the British Ambassador, Lord Lothian, who in the circumstances of the moment, when Britain was critically dependent upon American aid but could make no move to solicit it openly without playing into the hands of the isolationists, fully endorsed the need for an organization which, though independent of the Embassy, in effect constituted a covert counterpart of it.

Philip Kerr, 11th Marquess of Lothian, whom an educated

[1] Hull. II, 944.

American described at the time of his appointment in 1939 as 'the first British Ambassador since Bryce who has been any-thing but a diplomatic clerk', was a man of most attractive and brilliant personality, with fluent and persuasive gifts of speech, in spite of somewhat erratic religious beliefs—he was a Roman Catholic turned Christian Scientist.[1] Indeed it was his insistence on summoning to his bedside a faith-healer from Boston instead of the Embassy doctor when he was suffering from a relatively minor ailment that was generally thought to have killed him. His sudden and unexpected death, which took place in Washington in December, 1940, came as a great shock to those who, like Stephenson, worked closely with him, and he was mourned alike by Americans and his own countrymen. In the words of the U.S. Secretary of State, Cordell Hull, 'his outstanding ability, his willingness and readiness to grasp our point of view and to represent that of his own Government, and his pleasing personality, made him an unsurpassed medium through which to carry on relations between the two Govern-ments'.[2] The American Government accorded him burial in Arlington National Cemetery, a rare honour reserved for only one other British representative during the war.[3] Lothian was succeeded as Ambassador, after an interval, by Lord Halifax, with whom Stephenson worked amicably but neither so intimately nor so informally as he had done with Lothian.

The man whom Stephenson would have liked to see above all others in occupation of the handsome red-brick building in Massachusetts Avenue, Washington, which Sir Edwin Lutyens had recently designed as the new British Embassy, was his buoyant compatriot and friend Lord Beaverbrook. Indeed Stephenson did some quiet lobbying on his friend's behalf, and in 1941 he was to work hard in informal discussions with Mr. Averill Harriman, who had been sent to London as President Roosevelt's Special Representative with the rank of Minister, to further the project of Beaverbrook's appointment to the post; for, like Harriman, Stephenson was keenly aware, to quote his own words, that 'Max was likely to achieve more

---

[1] Dr. Abraham Flexner, cited by Thomas Jones in *A Diary with Letters* (1954) at p. 433.
[2] Hull. I, 874.
[3] Field-Marshal Sir John Dill.

with F. D. R. than Halifax, who was looked upon by the President as somewhat of a cold fish'.

Stephenson admired Beaverbrook with more than ordinary enthusiasm, and he would hotly denounce any of his detractors —and there were many—whom he happened to encounter during this period. 'Little Bill' was wholeheartedly on the side of what he called the 'war winners', a category headed in Britain by Churchill and Beaverbrook and in America by Roosevelt and Donovan. In Stephenson's eyes, as also in the Prime Minister's, Beaverbrook in the role of Minister of Aircraft Production was the great hero of the 'Battle of Britain', and his almost superhuman achievement in replenishing the fighter squadrons with new and repaired machines fully justified the place in the War Cabinet to which Churchill had appointed him at the beginning of August, 1940. 'This was his hour', as the Prime Minister afterwards wrote.[1] Or, as Stephenson was to put it in characteristic language to the author of these pages, 'but for the tremendous pressure that Beaverbrook exerted in his dynamic way, who could say whether the pitifully few aircraft that were flyable at the end of the battle in the air might not have been a minus zero force?'

As an old and experienced fighter pilot himself, Stephenson shared Beaverbrook's anxiety for the safety of his son Max Aitken in the battle, and also the father's pride in his son's record of conspicuous gallantry in the air. He particularly liked the tribute paid by a Canadian newspaper, which described them both as busily engaged in reducing the disparity between the British and German air forces. 'The father builds British machines, while the son destroys the German ones.'[2]

Another great war-time achievement of Beaverbrook, in Stephenson's estimation, was his 'personal triumph', in Washington in inducing President Roosevelt to 'paint with a very wide brush' at the commencement of the American war production programme. Indeed Stephenson considered this, at least as regards its long-term effects, to be even more important than his work at the Ministry of Aircraft Production in London, and Stephenson was to witness its execution at close quarters. 'It fairly took my breath away,' he was to remark on learning of

---

[1] Churchill. II, 287.
[2] Cited by Tom Driberg in *Beaverbrook* (1956), at p. 257.

the President's specific production objectives for the year 1942 in respect of planes, ships, tanks and anti-aircraft guns, to the tune of fifty billion dollars, which he knew must tax the country's productive capacity to the utmost. In this Stephenson agreed with Beaverbrook's biographer and former employee, Mr. Tom Driberg, M.P., who was to write that 'probably nobody else, with his North American big-business background—certainly no conventional, conservative Englishman—could have talked round the hardest-headed and highest-powered industrialists in the United States. It was a feat that may stand for ever to his credit.'[1]

As Stephenson well knew, the President liked Beaverbrook and much admired his direct and positive methods in the then desperate situation that required these methods. Thus Roosevelt would have given him a particularly cordial welcome, if he had been appointed as the successor of Lord Halifax in Massachusetts Avenue. But any prospects of such a move were frustrated by Beaverbrook's complete breakdown in health and his consequent resignation from the British War Cabinet early in 1942. Hence Halifax was to continue to serve as Ambassador until the end of the war.

Besides helping to obtain the essential supplies, as has already been described, Stephenson's three primary concerns were to investigate enemy activities, to institute adequate security measures against the danger of sabotage to British shipping and other property, and to mobilize American public opinion in favour of aid to Britain. It was to fulfil these purposes that his headquarters organization in New York was originally established by him on the thirty-fifth and thirty-sixth floors of the International Building in Rockefeller Centre (630 Fifth Avenue), opposite St. Patrick's Cathedral. At first it operated under cover of the British Passport Control Office, and was inevitably small, although it was to grow rapidly as necessity required and opportunity offered. Apart from an Assistant Passport Control Officer and a senior S.I.S. officer, who was sent out from London and whose assistance proved of great value, it was staffed exclusively by men and women whom Stephenson recruited after taking up his appointment. With one or two exceptions none of them had any previous experience of secret

[1] Driberg. *op. cit.*, 273.

work, but were chosen by virtue of having held responsible positions in private or professional life or of possessing special knowledge which fitted them to undertake the various tasks involved. A number of officers and virtually all the secretarial staff were recruited in Canada.

At the same time agents in the field were recruited, with the object of penetrating enemy or enemy-controlled commercial concerns, propaganda groups and diplomatic and consular missions, and Stephenson sent representatives to such key points as Washington, D.C., Los Angeles, San Francisco, and Seattle. But he was also quick to realize that the scope of his investigations could not logically be confined to the United States, for in the general purpose of obstructing Britain's receipt of American material assistance, the enemy could both attack and be attacked at other points in the Western Hemisphere. Accordingly Stephenson established the closest liaison with the British Imperial Censorship, which had just sent out a detachment from England to Bermuda, where the American mail-carrying Clipper aircraft and ships were now calling on their voyages to and from Europe, and where the examination of these transit mails was to provide most valuable information on enemy activities of all kinds throughout America, north and south.

Mr. (later Sir) Edwin Herbert, an energetic solicitor, had recently been appointed Director-General of the Postal and Telegraph Censorship in London, and he lost no time in visiting Stephenson in New York. Complete confidence was established between them, a relationship which was shortly afterwards extended by Stephenson to two of the most experienced officers in censorship, the late Charles des Graz, Chairman of Sotheby's and his assistant, William Hill-Wood, of the London banking house of Morgan Grenfell, when they took charge of all British censorship operations in the Western Hemisphere on Herbert's behalf and established their headquarters in New York. Similar liaison arrangements were made with the Canadian security authorities, notably the Royal Canadian Mounted Police. Finally, Stephenson was put in direct communication by London with the existing British secret intelligence network, such as it was, in Latin America. But he soon discovered that most of these agents were hardly better equipped for their work than the Passport Control Office in New York had been at the

time of his first arrival. Stephenson therefore proceeded to
reinforce the Latin-American organization by despatching
representatives of his own to all the important centres in Mexico
and Central America.

In these early days of their collaboration Edgar Hoover and
his F.B.I. could not have been more co-operative. Clearly
Stephenson's growing organization, employing as it did not
only its own intelligence agents but what amounted to its own
police force for the special protection of British property, represented an obvious threat to United States neutrality and could
not have existed at all without the F.B.I.'s tacit approval. But
Hoover was more than its licensor. He was in a very real sense
its patron. He suggested its cover name, British Security Co-
ordination. Furthermore, he placed at Stephenson's disposal
the F.B.I. wireless channel which for many months was to
provide B.S.C. with its only safe means of communication with
London headquarters. On a personal basis he worked very
closely with Stephenson to further what was then the wholly
unneutral purpose of protecting and furthering British interests
in the war against Germany and Italy, and he instructed his
officers to assist B.S.C. in every way open to them. In short,
Hoover led the F.B.I. into the fully fledged alliance with British
Intelligence that the President had urged. The results of that
alliance are described in some detail later in this book. Meanwhile one or two examples, which belong to the early period
of the Hoover-Stephenson collaboration, may conveniently be
given here.

In October, 1940, Hoover learned through his agents that
$3,850,000 worth of Italian funds, drawn from banks in the
United States by the Italian Embassy in Washington, were to be
sent to Latin America in Italian diplomatic bags. This information he discussed with Stephenson and they agreed that, while
it might mean nothing more than a precautionary measure by
the Italian Government against a possible 'freezing order' by
the U.S. Treasury, there was a likelihood that the transfer was
being made to finance subversive activities, particularly since
the money had been drawn in bills of small denomination.

Accordingly they planned joint counter-action. Hoover
arranged for the personnel of the Italian Embassy to be kept
under surveillance, and, when the couriers left by plane, for

J. Edgar Hoover

'... led the F.B.I. into the fully-fledged alliance with British Intelligence ...'

General William J. Donovan

'. . . *carried with him throughout, an animating, heart-warming flame.*'

F.B.I. agents to accompany them. There were three couriers in all, two consuls and an Embassy secretary. They travelled together as far as Brownsville, Texas, but there they separated. The consuls, who had $2,450,000 with them, went on to New Orleans, while the secretary, who had the balance of the money with him, boarded a train for Mexico City.

Stephenson now cabled this information to his representative in Mexico City for immediate action. The representative was able to arrange for the secretary's bag to be opened under the authority of the head of the Mexican Police Intelligence Department, and the money which was found inside confiscated. Such action was, of course, a violation of diplomatic privilege. When the Italian Minister protested, which he did with considerable vigour, the Mexican Government apologized politely for the stupid and unfortunate act of 'a new and inexperienced clerk'. However, it placed the money in a blocked account, thus rendering it useless for subversive activities. The incident was later used, both in Mexico and afterwards in the United States, as covert anti-Nazi propaganda.

Unfortunately the money being carried by the consuls escaped detention and control. British secret agents had made elaborate arrangements to purloin it at Pernambuco, but these were frustrated when the ship to which the couriers had transferred from New Orleans steamed on to Rio de Janeiro. Here the Brazilian Foreign Minister, forewarned of the arrival of the money, had agreed to give it his special protection; and, despite a subsequent assurance to an influential British contact in Rio that the money would be controlled, he kept his promise to the Italians by ensuring its safe delivery to their Embassy. This joint operation by Hoover's and Stephenson's men was, therefore, only partly successful. But it was sufficiently effective to discourage the Italians from any further attempts to transfer funds by covert methods to South America.

It speaks much for Hoover's courage and foresight that he was persuaded to co-operate so wholeheartedly with Stephenson. The very fact of his insistence upon knowledge of the liaison being kept secret from the State Department, as has been seen, showed that he was running a considerable risk when he agreed to it. That risk was the chance that his connection with British Intelligence would be exposed and would thus embroil him, as it would certainly have done if it had been detected, in a major political scandal with every isolationist and non-interventionist in the country after his scalp. At the same time he realized that the time must come sooner or later when the continued existence of the F.B.I. would depend not only on its success as a law-enforcement agency but on its record in the extended field of counter-espionage and security intelligence. It was in his necessary preparations to meet this public challenge that Hoover needed information and assistance of the kind that Stephenson with his unique resources was able to supply.

5

About the time Stephenson first met Hoover, the F.B.I. was entrusted by President Roosevelt with responsibility for collecting secret intelligence of subversive activities throughout the Western Hemisphere likely to endanger United States security, and for the preparation of adequate preventive measures against potential spies and saboteurs. It was a responsibility which Hoover welcomed, since it represented a considerable addition to the prestige and influence of the F.B.I., whose interests its ambitious Director was always most zealous in promoting. But he was severely handicapped in discharging this new responsibility by the Neutrality Act.

Unlike the British S.I.S., the American F.B.I. was obliged to operate in the fierce glare of the public scrutiny. To enable it to function as a secret intelligence organization Hoover needed the support of Congress, but this support was not forthcoming. Hoover had no legal right to employ any agents outside United States territory. As a result, he was forced to act surreptitiously without the knowledge of the State Department and the official United States missions in Latin-American countries. His legal authority was limited to counter-espionage in the United States, and even in this he was debarred from access to sources of information which were vital to his work. For example, there was no domestic censorship of mails or cables then in existence, and so F.B.I. agents were reduced to purloining letters from Post Offices. Had this illicit action been exposed, and proved unjustified in any particular instance, it

would have caused political repercussions of sufficient magnitude to place in jeopardy the continued existence of the organization or at least of Hoover as its Director. Another handicap
was reflected by a recent decision of the U.S. Supreme Court
declaring inadmissible in legal proceedings evidence obtained
through the unauthorized interception of telephone conversations or 'wire tapping' by F.B.I. agents, regardless of whether
the intercepted conversations endangered the national security.
Thus Hoover was caught between his anxiety to carry out the
President's directive in the light of the urgent need for American
military preparedness on the one hand, and the almost fanatical
insistence by a large proportion of the legislature in preserving
American neutrality on the other.

Stephenson helped Hoover to escape from this dilemma by
throwing open to him and his staff all the manifold resources
of British secret intelligence, which had been developed under
the impetus of war. He arranged for two of the Bureau's senior
officers to visit London headquarters, where they received a
detailed briefing in Nazi espionage methods, and subsequently
for one of Hoover's Assistant Directors to visit the various
British S.I.S. centres in Latin America and discuss with the
officers-in-charge the creation of an F.B.I. field organization in
that area. Through Stephenson's intimate relations with the
British Imperial Censorship authorities, it was possible for an
experienced F.B.I. agent to be sent to the Bermuda station and
instructed in the techniques of mail examination. F.B.I.
laboratory technicians were also made acquainted by one of
the Bermuda experts, a woman who had joined Stephenson's
New York staff, with the various methods of secretly examining
letters in such a manner that their recipients were not aware
that they had been opened. This highly secret process included
the unsealing and resealing of diplomatic and other privileged
mail so that the seals appeared absolutely intact and were
impervious to the ultra-violet ray and other chemical tests.

Recruitment of staff by the F.B.I. for this confidential and
delicate work led to an amusing incident. British experience
had shown that the work which demanded a high degree of
manual dexterity was best undertaken by women. Numbers of
potential female recruits were interviewed by an Assistant
Director at the Washington Headquarters of the Bureau, but

the details of the work obviously could not be explained to them at this stage in case they should be found unsuitable. Stephenson's Bermuda expert had given the Assistant Director a rough-and-ready rule, which was that a girl with neat ankles would be most likely to possess the required degree of manual dexterity for the job. The only thing that those interviewed were told was that the work involved was of a confidential character, and that they might be called upon to perform it in South America. Consequently several of them were considerably surprised when they found that the preliminary 'screening' consisted of a minute inspection of their ankles by an elderly G-man, and they began to speculate with some uneasiness as to the precise nature of the services expected of them in such places as Buenos Aires or Rio. Those who seemed particularly worried had their minds set at rest by being assured that it was not that kind of job!

Although Stephenson gave Hoover all the intelligence from secret sources that he was able to obtain at this period, not all of it was of direct interest to the F.B.I. Some of it concerned the intelligence branches of the Navy and War Departments, that is the Office of Naval Intelligence (O.N.I.) and the Military Intelligence Division (G.2). Hoover in turn passed on this particular information to O.N.I. and G.2, since Stephenson had no liaison with these service branches which at this time were opposed to the idea of collaborating with the British. In any event, Hoover was glad to do this, as it increased the Bureau's prestige and influence and gave its Director a commanding position in the existing framework of American intelligence. Hoover was also encouraged on occasion to invoke the help of the service departments on behalf of the British even when it ran counter to the State Department's strict policy of neutrality. The following incident, which took place in the autumn of 1940, provided a good example of such intervention.

Stephenson's representative in Mexico City reported that he had reason to believe that four German and twelve Italian ships, which were then lying in the Gulf ports of Tampico and Vera Cruz, were planning to run the British blockade. It certainly looked as if the Axis vessels might succeed in their intention, since the Royal Navy could not patrol Mexican

territorial waters. Stephenson passed this information to Hoover
for onward transmission to O.N.I. At the same time he informed
his London headquarters, who authorized the taking of any
action he might consider appropriate in the circumstances
provided the British Embassy in Washington was told what was
happening. Stephenson now sent his representative in Mexico
a quantity of 'limpet' bombs—small explosive charges to be
affixed to a magnetized frame which would adhere to the steel
plates of a ship's hull. However, while these provided a possible
means of causing sufficient damage to delay the vessels'
departure, it was only a temporary measure, and it was clear
that no really effective steps could be taken without the assistance of the U.S. Navy Department. Accordingly, after discussing the matter with Lord Lothian, Stephenson went to Hoover
and, having explained the position to him, begged him to
arrange for the despatch of a naval patrol to the area of the
Gulf ports. Hoover agreed, since besides helping his British
friends he considered it an excellent pretext for securing some
return from O.N.I. for the information he had been supplying
from British sources. After meeting with considerable difficulty,
he eventually won round the State Department which agreed
to the plan on the strict understanding that no act should be
committed which might conceivably be construed as a breach
of American neutrality. Four destroyers were accordingly
despatched to the Gulf with orders to lie off Tampico and
report by radio *en clair*—that is, not using code or cipher—any
movements which the Axis ships might make.

On the night of November 15, 1940, the four German
vessels steamed out of port into the Gulf of Mexico. The
American destroyers approached and trained the full battery
of their searchlights upon them. This was not in itself a
belligerent act, but it had the effect of making the German
captains think that it was the prelude to an all-out attack.
Panic ensued, in the course of which one of the German ships,
the *Phrygia*, either caught fire accidentally or was deliberately
scuttled. Anyhow her crew took to the boats and she was
abandoned as a total wreck. The others turned tail and
promptly put on full speed and steamed back to port. Intelligence reports subsequently revealed that the German captains
believed that they had encountered some of the old destroyers

which had recently been transferred to Britain; they had informed acquaintances in Tampico next day that they 'had been ordered to surrender by British warships'.

A fortnight later, two of the three remaining German ships sailed out to sea in broad daylight. The American destroyers shadowed them and, by transmitting position signals, enabled vessels of the Royal Navy to intercept them before they had got very far and to take them as prize. The one German and twelve Italian ships which had stayed behind were apparently too intimidated to make any further attempt to run the blockade. They remained impotent in port until they were eventually taken over by the Mexican Government in April, 1941.

This incident, which did not even indirectly concern enemy subversive activities, showed that Hoover was willing to carry his assistance well beyond what he might justifiably have regarded as the limits of his common interest with Stephenson at this time. Indeed it may fairly be said that he was in the war from the moment that they began their collaboration. He also undertook to 'plant' what was known in technical language as 'strategic deception material' in the German Embassy in Washington. One example of this, designed to deter Hitler from embarking upon any large-scale military campaign, read: 'From highly reliable source it is learned U.S.S.R. intend further military aggression instant Germany is embroiled in major operations.' A similar piece of information calculated to mislead the Germans was to the effect that in the event of their using poison gas Britain would retaliate by using their 'secret weapon'. This was said to consist of 'some kind of glass balls containing chemicals producing such terrific heat that they cannot be extinguished by any known means'.

Finally, as we have seen, Hoover suggested the cover name which was adopted by Stephenson's organization, when, to comply with American law, it was registered with the State Department as an official foreign agency in January, 1941. Its overt purpose was expressed as follows:

> Consequent upon the large-scale and vital interests of the British Government in connection with the purchase and ship-ment of munitions and war material from the United States, coupled with the presence in this country of a number of

British official missions, a variety of security problems has been created, and these, affecting closely as they do the interests of the British Government, call for very close and friendly collaboration between the authorities of the two countries.

Thus, for example, the presence in large numbers of British and Allied ships engaged in loading explosives and other war materials, and the existence of large quantities of similar materials in plants, on railways and in dock areas throughout the country, presenting as they do a tempting target to saboteurs and enemy agents, constitute in themselves a security problem of considerable magnitude.

With a view to co-ordinating the liaison between the various British missions and the United States authorities in all security matters arising from the present abnormal circumstances, an organization bearing the title *British Security Co-ordination* has been formed under the control of a Director of Security Co-ordination, assisted by a headquarters staff.

Such, in broad terms, was the nature and scope of the assistance which Edgar Hoover was persuaded to render William Stephenson and the British war effort at this period. But it should be remembered that this assistance, whilst willingly given, was always conditioned by Hoover's great ambition for the Bureau which he directed. Unhappily this was to lead him, after his country entered the war, into the untenable position of insisting in effect upon retaining for the F.B.I., among United States Intelligence agencies, monopoly of liaison with B.S.C. It was an untenable position, which Hoover was with some reluctance eventually brought to realize, because the F.B.I. was not recognized as a co-ordinating centre of American war-time intelligence and in its sphere of operations it was limited to the Western Hemisphere.

# CHAPTER III

# SPIES, SABOTEURS AND PROPAGANDISTS

## I

DURING the period before the Japanese attack upon Pearl Harbour brought the United States into the war at the end of 1941, and particularly before the passing of the Lend-Lease Act in the spring of that year, Britain was in the position of having a vast amount of her resources of production, supply, shipping and foreign investment situated in a country which was under no obligation to protect them. Yet it was vital to the British war effort that they should be protected, and it was for this express purpose that Stephenson's intelligence organization was officially recognized in the United States under the title of British Security Co-ordination. Some details of how these overt functions came about and how they were successfully carried out may conveniently be given here.

At this time there were six million German-speaking Americans and four million Italian-speaking Americans in the United States. Many of these American citizens were employed as workers in factories producing war material as the result of orders placed by the British Purchasing Mission in New York. Some of them were labourers in the freight yards or employees of the railways which transported the finished product, and others were stevedores engaged in loading it into British ships. Before B.S.C. took over its overt security job, there was little to prevent a wide-scale sabotage campaign in the private factories producing arms for the British account, or against a large proportion of Britain's twenty million tons of shipping which used American ports. Moreover, Stephenson had reason to believe, on the basis of the German sabotage record in the First War, that the resources of the enemy in the United States, coupled with the potentially subversive elements already

in existence there, were ample for this task. (He was not to
know, however, that these resources were in fact destined never
to be used on anything like the scale of the sabotage in the
1914–18 conflict.)

Enemy agents were scattered throughout the forty-eight
states, and each one knew well that he could rely upon the
assistance of many thousands of members of the German *Bund*
organizations. And there were others who were willing to help.
There were the isolationists; there were the business men with
European interests; there were the nationalist Indians, the
anti-British Irish and, in increasing volume, the Communist-
inspired left-wing propagandists who denounced the 'imperialist
war' while Soviet Russia was still apparently on friendly terms
with Germany. The Communist-dominated National Maritime
Union of America was bitterly attacking the despatch of United
States ships into the war zones and any form of American
intervention. The Union's lawyers had developed various
ingenious techniques of delaying the sailing of Allied vessels
from American ports by suborning members of Chinese and
other crews to refuse to sail without new and extravagant
equipment. All these groups and organizations were giving
help, either directly or indirectly, to the Nazis.

By the summer of 1940 the Purchasing Commission under
the direction of Arthur Purvis, had taken some tentative steps
to meet the threatened danger. It had appointed a Security
Officer in the person of an English business man, Mr. Hamish
Mitchell.[1] Also a Credit Investigation Section and a Shipping
Security Section had been formed within the existing staff of
the Commission. The former endeavoured to establish the
reliability of firms working for British account. The latter took
what measures it could to insure the safe loading of supplies
from wharf to ship. But their resources and facilities were meagre
and fell far short of what was required in the circumstances.
This was a security organization, distinct from Purvis's mission
but at the same time closely linked with it, which would be able
to advise on security and anti-sabotage precautions for factories,
railways, shipyards and docks; to investigate and report upon
sabotage and other subversive activities, Communist influence

[1] Mr. Mitchell later went as Stephenson's representative to Bermuda,
where he rendered valuable service.

amongst labour unions and the suborning and desertion of crews; to 'vet' the reliability of manufacturing companies and also of individuals applying for jobs in British missions in the U.S.A.; and finally, to establish the closest possible liaison with the American and Canadian security authorities, notably the F.B.I., Royal Canadian Mounted Police, the Customs and Immigration, and the local police and port officials.

Purvis was only too pleased to hand over these responsibilities to Stephenson. These were now assumed by the Security Division of B.S.C. which absorbed the old Credit Investigation and Shipping Security Sections of the Purchasing Commission. At the same time the Passport Control Office ceased to provide 'cover' for Stephenson's clandestine activities, which insofar as they concerned his headquarters staff were henceforth carried out by the Statistics and Analysis Division of B.S.C. in Rocke-feller Centre, although as a matter of convenience the ordinary functions of passport control relating to the granting of British visas to foreign applicants continued to be discharged on the same premises.

With Purvis's help, Stephenson was able to find accommoda-tion for the Security Division in the Cunard Building at 15 Broad Street, which also housed the Purchasing Commission besides the offices of various shipping companies. He was also fortunate in finding the ideal person to take charge of what came to be known as B.S.C.'s downtown office in Sir Connop Guthrie, a shrewd and genial English baronet with great personal charm as well as considerable shipping experience. There was something faintly suggestive of the Prussian officer in Guthrie's distinguished bearing and handsome appearance; in fact he had held a commission in the Grenadier Guards during the First World War. As head of the Security Division of B.S.C., he was a great success and deservedly popular on the New York waterfront as well as in café society. (He was a great diner-out, and it was while about to join a dinner party in Claridge's Hotel in London a few months after the end of the war in 1945 that he died as the result of a sudden heart attack.)

Another Englishman, also a baronet, who was a great help to Stephenson, and incidentally to Guthrie, in the work of the Security Division, was the Wall Street banker Sir William Wiseman, who had been in charge of the same security job a quarter of a century before in the First World War as a member of the Purchasing Commission of the British Ministry of Munitions. Wiseman's duties had also included intelligence and counter-espionage, so that Stephenson was able to draw upon his experience as well.[1] It is worth noting that Wiseman considered that Stephenson had a much more difficult task than he himself had had a quarter of a century earlier. 'The Germans were far better organized in World War Two', Wiseman recently recalled, not long before he died. 'I gave him what help I could.' As will be seen, Wiseman was to show that he had not lost his old touch.

Before America entered the war, British orders for war materials amounted to some $4,000 millions, of which about three-quarters were invested in plants and extensions of existing plants owned by the British Government. It was the duty of the Security Division to safeguard these assets in every way possible. The first step was to 'vet' the firms producing the war materials. In order to do this, the British Purchasing Commission, whenever any contract was in process of negotiation, would approach the Security Division and ask for a check to be made on the contractor from two points of view. First, was he financially reliable? Secondly, was he completely free from any connection with the enemy? The first check was made through credit agencies, banks and financial houses; the second through direct investigation and by obtaining all possible help from the F.B.I. and other U.S. Government agencies.

After the firm had been 'vetted' and the contract signed, it was necessary to make sure that the factory producing the war material was secure. Here advantage was taken of an existing clause in all British contracts with American firms, which provided for technical inspection of the product at various stages of manufacture and upon its completion. These inspections were carried out by the Inspection Board of the United Kingdom and Canada, with headquarters in Ottawa, an office, in New York, and a large technical staff in the field. Guthrie established liaison with this field staff and secured the assistance of one of the Board's administrative officers, who was later

---

[1] An interesting account of Wiseman's work in the First World War has been given by Sir Arthur Willert in *The Road to Safety* (1952). Wiseman died in 1962.

seconded to the Security Division. This officer's particular duty was to visit all factories working for Britain, to safeguard the welfare of the resident inspection staff and settle a large variety of other personnel problems. In collaboration with him, the Security Division prepared a standard form covering the security status of each factory, which was completed by the inspectors. At the same time independent reports were made on the efficacy of the protective measures. Thus the Security Division was able to make a complete survey of all British contracts placed with United States factories and to check the security conditions prevailing in each plant.

It must be remembered that B.S.C. had no legal authority to enforce any security measures in United States factories in United States territory, and before the passing of the Lend-Lease Act little or no assistance was forthcoming from the military authorities. B.S.C., therefore, approached the manufacturers on its own initiative, and although it was obviously necessary to exercise great care and tact, the Security Division eventually succeeded in persuading nearly all of them to co-operate in taking every possible precaution against sabotage in their plants. At the same time Purvis agreed to adopt a sabotage clause in the Purchasing Commission's standard form of contract. In this clause the manufacturer undertook to maintain all reasonable precautions against sabotage and to advise the Purchasing Commission of any actual or attempted sabotage in his factory. In this he was assisted by a list of recommendations which was issued by B.S.C. to all American plants working for British account, and which gave advice upon how to prevent the infiltration of potential saboteurs.

The next steps were to get the material safely from the factory to the wharf and then safely loaded on board ship. For the former purpose officers of the Security Division of B.S.C. kept a twenty-four hour watch, with the knowledge and approval of the local police and fire departments, port control officers and coast guards. For the latter purpose, which required particular skill in the handling of dockers and seamen who were apt to be 'difficult', Stephenson with Guthrie's advice recruited officers with wide experience of merchant shipping as well as knowledge of local conditions. These men, known as Consular Security Officers, were appointed in New

York, Boston, Philadelphia, San Francisco and a dozen other United States ports, at which 95 per cent. of British ships called. Their duties included the guarding against the entry aboard of saboteurs in the guise of visitors, repairmen, stevedores and ship-chandlers; the checking of anti-sabotage equipment, such as screens and nets; the protection of seamen from the attention of those anxious to learn their secrets, and the suppression of news of ships' cargoes, movements and convoys. In 1941, the system was extended to twenty-six of the principal ports in South America.

Probably the most exposed port area was in New York, where an enemy agent merely had to take a trip on the Staten Island ferry to see where British ships were berthed and when they sailed—as indeed one such agent testified at an espionage trial. The Consular Security Officer in New York, who had ten assistants, divided the harbour into three zones. A round-the-clock watch was kept on each of these zones by members of his staff who reported hourly by telephone to a central number. Continuous eight-hour watches were kept upon the two most important British merchant vessels, the *Queen Mary* and the *Queen Elizabeth*, whenever they were in port. In their case, as indeed in that of all other British ships in American ports, the closest attention was paid to the prevention of smoking and to the exclusion of unauthorized visitors and anyone under the influence of alcohol. A pass system was rigorously enforced; workmen and crew were searched both on embarking and going ashore; and all packages and tool kits were inspected.

At the height of the war B.S.C. was employing thirty-one Consular Security Officers with their staffs in the United States and forty-five in South America. Together they carried out approximately 30,000 anti-sabotage inspections a year aboard British merchant ships. In the result not a single British vessel was lost or seriously held up by sabotage in a United States port throughout the war. After the French liner *Normandie* caught fire and capsized in New York harbour in February, 1942—because sparks let fly by a welder ignited a heap of lifebelts filled with kapok—inquiry showed that of the Security Division's eight recommendations regarding welding practice, copies of which had been supplied to the

Captain of the Port of New York, no less than five were being ignored.

Second only to the preservation of the ships was the saving of tonnage time by effecting the quickest possible turn-round in the various ports of call. This was insured partly by the C.S.O.'s who were able to arrange with local police to return drunken seamen on board rather than hold them in jail (occasionally they organized this operation themselves), and partly by the excellent relations which Sir Connop Guthrie had established with the British National Union of Seamen, whose delegates in America helped to solve labour disputes and weed out trouble-makers among the crews. Seamen would complain that they were unfit for work, that their ship was dirty or unseaworthy, that their officers were harsh and so forth. The union delegate would investigate. If they were found to be malingering or exaggerating, he had the authority as their union representative to reject their complaint. On the other hand, if there was any justification for it, he reported it to the local C.S.O., who in turn informed B.S.C. headquarters, and action was taken to satisfy it. The fact that the Minister of War Transport in London, Lord Leathers, was a close personal friend of both Stephenson and Guthrie greatly facilitated the working of all these arrangements.

Occasionally there was a complaint from a local source, which caused an official protest to be made by the State Department. Mr. Sumner Welles, the Under-Secretary of State, was to relate an embarrassing incident at Baltimore concerning some vessels of the Danish Merchant Marine, which were under charter to the British Ministry of War Transport after the German occupation of Denmark, although they continued to be manned by their Danish crews. This is how he described it:

> When the ships were due to sail it was learned that a considerable number of Danish seamen were not to be found. They were scattered throughout the numerous taverns on Baltimore's waterfront. Thereupon some zealous officials of the British Intelligence hired a quantity of trucks, manned them with the necessary number of British naval shore police and, with a blithe disregard for the local American authorities, proceeded from bar to bar and by main force dumped all the

alleged Danish deserters they could find into the trucks for return to their ships. When the municipal authorities in Baltimore heard of this they promptly telephoned to me. I as promptly notified the British Ambassador. Lord Halifax, needless to say, had received no news of the occurrence, let alone any intimation that such action was to be taken. He was aghast at the reaction that might be provoked, even in war-time, if the American public learned of so flagrant a violation of American sovereignty, and one so painfully reminiscent of the British impressments of colonial days.

Neither Guthrie nor Stephenson was one to stand on diplomatic niceties at a period when Britain's Atlantic lifeline was so tenuous. However much Sumner Welles and his more apprehensive colleagues in the State Department may have been reminded of the press gang, the fact remains that valuable time was saved by the use of its unorthodox methods on this occasion, and the much-needed ships sailed with a minimum of delay and a near full crews' complement.[1]

By none perhaps was the success of the Security Division's efforts more appreciated than Arthur Purvis, whose Commission purchased the material protected. Unfortunately he barely lived long enough to see the results of these efforts in action. Recalled to London for consultation in the middle of 1941, he was suddenly summoned with Lord Beaverbrook to attend the historic meeting which took place between Churchill and Roosevelt in Placentia Bay, Newfoundland, in August, when the Atlantic Charter was formulated. The presence of Purvis and Beaverbrook at the discussions was required to cope with the delicate question of how supplies were going to be divided, now that Soviet Russia had become an active partner of the Allies.

What happened is best described in the Prime Minister's words. 'Beaverbrook and Purvis started from Prestwick in different aeroplanes within a few hours of one another. It was an even chance who went in either plane. Beaverbrook arrived safely at the Newfoundland airport, and joined me after a long train journey on the 12th. Purvis and all with him were killed by one of those sinister strokes of fortune which make a plane fly into a hill of no great height a few minutes after taking off.

[1] Sumner Welles. *Seven Major Decisions* (1951), at p. 61.

Purvis was a grievous loss, as he held so many British, American and Canadian threads in his hands, and had hitherto been the directing mind in their harmonious combination. When Max (Lord Beaverbrook) arrived I told him the shocking news. He was silent for a moment, but made no comment. It was war-time.'[1]

2

The German secret intelligence service, known as the *Abwehr*, was directed by a retired naval officer, Admiral Wilhelm Canaris. A certain air of mystery has always surrounded Canaris, and it has been suggested that he was really working for the British from the beginning of the war. The fact remains that he was a monarchist by conviction and consequently opposed to Hitler and the leading Nazis, particularly Gestapo Chief Himmler, who subsequently contrived his arrest and execution after torture in a concentration camp. However, although Canaris was an anti-Nazi, it is unlikely that a man with his traditional service background was anything other than a conscientious German patriot. At all events, he ran the *Abwehr* with skill and determination in spite of persistent interference from the Nazi high-ups.[2]

The *Abwehr* organization was divided into three sections, which were concerned respectively with espionage, sabotage and counter-espionage. The head of Section II (Sabotage), Colonel Erwin Lahousen, was an Austrian, who had previously been in charge of Austrian espionage and had worked with Canaris against the Czechs. It is now known from captured *Abwehr* documents that plans for sabotage in America were drawn up at the beginning of the war by Canaris and Lahousen which included the smuggling of explosives into British ships lying in American harbours. But Hitler, it appears, was opposed to carrying out these and similar plans, being of the opinion that the material advantage to be gained would not outweigh the political disadvantage in the circumstances of United States neutrality. In April, 1940, he ordered Canaris

[1] Churchill. II, 396–7.
[2] On Canaris, see Ian Colvin, *Chief of Intelligence* (1951) and Paul Leverkuehn, *German Military Intelligence* (1954).

to leave America alone; in the following month the order was repeated and at the same time instructions were given to recall the only experienced and reliable sabotage agent the *Abwehr* had in the United States at that time.

The Germans did possess one agent of dubious repute named Rekowski, who operated from Mexico under commercial cover—after the passing of the Lend-Lease Act he claimed to have blown up several ships 'by means of high connections he had' and to have set fire to a rubber dump in Ohio, whether or not with the consent of Hitler is unknown. But late in April, 1941, he was chased out of Mexico, where his relatively small-scale activities so alarmed the German Foreign Office, which thought that any further acts of sabotage might bring the United States into the war, that Canaris was again asked to lay off, this time by Ribbentrop. According to Canaris's German biographer, the chief of the *Abwehr* responded to this request with alacrity, arguing that if Nazi party fanatics were to reproach him in the future with 'having left the United States too much in peace', he would be able to refer to the arguments which the Minister of Foreign Affairs had himself employed.[1]

However true Sir William Wiseman's remark may be generally about the superior organization of German intelligence in America in the Second World War compared with the First, it would hardly seem to apply to the operations of the *Abwehr*'s Section II. Certainly the latter achieved nothing comparable, for example, to the famous 'Black Tom' explosion in Lower New York Harbour in July, 1916, when thirty-seven loads of high explosives, several warehouses, a dozen barges and ships and a whole railway station and yards were blown up in one terrific detonation. Had the Germans possessed a sabotage organization in America under the efficient direction of a man like Captain Von Rintelen as they did in the First War, the precautions taken by B.S.C.'s Security Division would have been much more hampered and less effective than they were proved to be in the event. Of upwards of 20,000 cases of suspected sabotage which the F.B.I. investigated during the Second World War, Hoover claimed that not a single case of

[1] Louis de Jong. *The German Fifth Column in the Second World War* (1956), pp. 214–5.

enemy directed sabotage was established. For the most part, they were industrial accidents caused by fatigue, carelessness, horseplay among the workers, and occasionally spite.[1]

The only attempt at active sabotage which the Germans made after America had entered the war was a complete fiasco. Early in 1942, Canaris received instructions from Hitler to cripple the American production of aluminium. Since no organization for sabotage existed in America at the time, agents had to be recruited and sent from Germany, an operation in whose success it appears that neither Canaris nor Lahousen had much faith. Nevertheless the Fuehrer's orders had to be obeyed, and accordingly on May 28, 1942, eight agents were landed by submarine in groups of four at two different points on the eastern American seaboard. Two of the prospective saboteurs promptly gave their comrades away to the F.B.I., thereby saving their own skins, while the remainder were rounded up and in due course sent to the electric chair. 'It was the biggest failure that ever occurred in my section,' General Lahousen recalled with a sigh after the war was over.[2]

As will be seen, the Germans had some success in the field of espionage and still more in other subversive activities, particularly propaganda directed against Britain and designed to frustrate projected American aid and keep the country out of the war. Some of these activities were organized under cover of the German Embassy in Washington by specially accredited high-grade agents such as Dr. Gerhard Alois Westrick, who arrived in New York from Japan in the spring of 1940, about the same time as Stephenson. Westrick held the diplomatic rank of Commercial Counsellor at the Embassy and as such was registered with the State Department. But he lived in an expensive rented house in Long Island, New York, where he entertained important American business men, particularly those in the oil industry. Stephenson, who began to investigate his activities in June, 1940, discovered that he was also visited by a number of comparatively obscure young Americans of German descent who were employed in strategic factories. Westrick was interested in a number of commercial concerns,

[1] Don Whitehead. *The F.B.I. Story* (1957), at p. 176.
[2] De Jong, 216.

including the International Telephone and Telegraph Company, and in one of them he was a partner with Heinrich Albert, who had been an active German propagandist in America during the First War.

One of Westrick's chief contacts was president of a certain oil company which was suspected of supplying the Axis with oil through the British blockade. It is significant that Westrick described himself as an employee of this company, and in applying for a driving licence gave its office as his business address. At a banquet given in Westrick's honour in New York to celebrate the fall of France, the company president was also present. It was evident that Westrick's purpose was to convince American big business that the war had already been won by Germany and to enlist its support for the isolationist campaign. The industrialists' rewards were to be commercial privileges in in Axis-dominated Europe.

These facts were passed by Stephenson, through an intermediary, to the *New York Herald-Tribune*, where they made a first-class news story and were expanded to form a series of articles. These in turn led to the publication of numerous editorials throughout the country on the dangers of a hidden Fifth Column, with particular reference to the fall of France which was attributed to German corruption of her business men and politicians.

The repercussions of these disclosures were immediate. Westrick was deluged with abusive letters and telephone calls. A hostile crowd gathered outside his house, and although he endeavoured to pacify it by playing 'God Bless America' and 'The Star Spangled Banner' on his gramophone, the F.B.I. had nevertheless to provide him with a twenty-four-hour guard. Eventually his landlord asked him to leave the house. His driving licence was revoked because he had described himself in applying for it as 'not crippled', whereas the *Herald-Tribune* had revealed that he had lost a leg. Finally the State Department, at the instigation of the F.B.I. prompted by Stephenson, requested the German Government to recall him for pursuing activities unfriendly to the United States, with the result that by the end of August, 1940 he was on his way back to Germany on a Japanese ship.

The *Herald-Tribune* was warmly congratulated on having

smoked out a dangerous emissary of Adolf Hitler, and there was even a proposal that the journal should receive the Pulitzer Prize for its good work. Meanwhile the shares of the oil company slumped sharply, and its president in alarm for his own future assured the press that he was thoroughly pro-British. Nevertheless he was forced to resign his office after a stormy stockholders' meeting; and, although he remained active in the oil business, he was henceforward closely watched and in consequence lost much of his capacity for doing harm.

The large numbers of Americans of German descent and citizens of German birth—there was over a quarter of a million of these *Reichsdeutscher* in the United States—provided a convenient channel for enemy propaganda. As early as May 16, 1940, when France was falling, President Roosevelt had warned Congress of the treacherous use of the Fifth Column by which 'persons supposed to be peaceful citizens were actually a part of an enemy unit of occupation', and ten days later he had followed this up with a fireside chat on the radio in which he had pointed out to his American listeners that the country's safety was not only menaced by weapons. 'We know of new methods of attack', he said, 'the Trojan Horse, the Fifth Column that betrays a nation uprepared for treachery. Spies, saboteurs and traitors are the actors in this new tragedy.'[1]

But the President's warnings had been largely unheeded by his countrymen. On the contrary, 'patriotic societies' had sprung up throughout the country devoted ostensibly to serving the interests of 'Americanism', of which the wealthy and powerful America First Committee became the most important. Dozens of these interlocking isolationist organizations held mass meetings, issued pamphlets and news-sheets, trained street corner speakers and organized 'educational' meetings under the auspices of existing clubs. In Detroit Lord Halifax was pelted with eggs and ripe tomatoes which were thrown with astonishing accuracy by isolationist women. ('We do not have any such surplus in England', said the Ambassador dryly, showing the Englishman's traditional stiff upper lip.) 'It is not freedom of the seas that England wants', an isolationist senator told three thousand people in Brooklyn while a similarly minded Congressman declared before an equally large audience that 'the

[1] De Jong. 105.

present war was brought upon the Third Reich by England and France'. Only a few months before Pearl Harbour, Colonel Lindbergh, one of the most prominent members of the million-strong America First organization, publicly stated that there were only three groups in the country which wished America to enter the war, namely the British, the Jews and the Roosevelt Administration.

Stephenson decided to concentrate on America First, and for this purpose he naturally enlisted the support of existing anti-Nazi societies such as the Fight for Freedom Committee and the Century Group. The latter, which rendered excellent service in mobilizing influential American opinion in favour of the destroyers-for-bases agreement, and was wholeheartedly on the side of intervention, was led by a member of the Virginia state legislature and a former Rhodes Scholar, Colonel Francis P. Miller, who was also a close friend of Colonel Donovan. Meanwhile Stephenson despatched agents to attend America First meetings in different parts of the country and to keep track of new members. One agent befriended the woman in charge of the America First lecture bureau in New York and procured from her a mass of information about its propaganda themes, its financing and its backers, particularly its German backers such as Ulrich von Gienanth of the German Embassy and Gunther Hansen-Sturm. The latter had paid Congressman Hamilton Fish a cheque, of which Stephenson managed to obtain a copy and pass to the press where it was published. When Representative Fish made a speech at an American First Rally at Milwaukee, Stephenson persuaded certain Fight For Freedom members to attend as well. Just before Fish concluded his oration, one of them handed him a card on which was written, 'Der Fuehrer thanks you for your loyalty'. At the same moment a photographer took a picture of the scene, and the picture with Hitler's message quoted in the caption made good copy for the newspapers. Stephenson also arranged for the meeting to be picketed outside the hall by the American Legion, while girls inside distributed Fight For Freedom literature.

Only once did a plan for harassing America First miscarry. That was at Madison Square Garden in New York on October 30, 1941, when Lindbergh was to address what was hoped would be a huge gathering. Stephenson had caused duplicate tickets for the meeting to be printed, and these were freely distributed to members of the various pro-British societies. The plan was for some of the holders of these spurious tickets to go early and be in their seats before the genuine ticket-holders arrived, while others would arrive late and start trouble by demanding the accommodation to which their tickets ostensibly entitled them. Thus it seemed there was a good chance of disrupting the whole proceedings. But unluckily, for some unexplained reason, there was a very small audience that night, much smaller than the organizers had anticipated. The duplication of the tickets was soon noticed and the ushers merely showed the would-be trouble-makers into the numerous vacant seats. The result was that Lindbergh addressed a considerably larger audience than he would have done without Stephenson's benevolent assistance.

While the campaign directed by Stephenson against America First throughout 1941 did not cause its disintegration, it did considerably reduce its usefulness to the Germans at a very critical period in Hitler's fortunes, and the way was paved for the great disrepute into which it shortly fell. Its last big meeting was addressed by a leading isolationist Senator on Sunday, December 7, 1941. Suddenly the chairman interrupted to say that the Japanese had attacked the American Fleet at Pearl Harbour. 'It's just what the British planned for us!' the Senator remarked without a moment's hesitation. A few days later the United States were in the war at Britain's side, and America First was no more than an ugly memory.

3

In April, 1940, the British Consul-General in San Francisco informed the British Embassy in Washington that he had been approached by an acquaintance of his German opposite number, who apparently wished to establish relations on a secret and confidential basis with some responsible representative of the British Government. Now the German Consul-General at this time was Captain Fritz Weidemann, who had been Hitler's superior officer when the Fuehrer was a corporal in the First War. For a time Weidemann had been close to

Hitler who had employed him first as a personal A.D.C. and then on a number of confidential missions as a special envoy, including one to London in the summer of 1938 when, unknown to Ribbentrop (who subsequently found out), he had tried without success to pave the way for a visit by Field-Marshal Goering. He was believed to have in some degree fallen from favour after Munich, an impression confirmed by his San Francisco appointment early in 1939, although the F.B.I. considered it a possible cover for the direction of Nazi espionage on the West Coast and in Latin America. According to Weidemann's acquaintance, a British subject of doubtful reliability, Weidemann expected to be ordered back to Germany and was afraid to return because of his quarrel with Ribbentrop; he had hinted that perhaps he might be allowed instead to come to Britain where he could help in negotiating peace with a restored Hohenzollern monarchy after Hitler and the Nazi régime had been overthrown.

Lord Lothian, who was then Ambassador, turned the matter over to Stephenson. Before taking any steps, Stephenson consulted the F.B.I., and he learned from Hoover that the Bureau had been monitoring Weidemann's telephone calls. In one recent conversation with the German Embassy, it appeared that the Embassy had adopted a 'domineering attitude' towards him, so that there seemed some grounds for believing that Weidemann's story might have some foundation in fact. As the result of further discussion between Stephenson and Hoover, it was agreed that contact should be made with Weidemann from the British side. For this purpose Stephenson invited the assistance of Sir William Wiseman.

At this point a woman entered the story—a clever, scheming Austrian who bore some resemblance to the glamorous spy of fiction. Born plain Steffi Richter, the daughter of a middle-class Viennese lawyer, she had married a Hungarian nobleman in London in 1914, divorcing him six years later but keeping his name and title, so that she continued to be styled Her Serene Highness Princess Stephanie Hohenlohe-Waldenberg-Schillings-furst. She moved freely about Europe between the wars, at one time living in the Schloss Leopoldskron across the valley from the Hitler villa in Berchtesgaden and at another in a flat in Mayfair, where she acted as hostess to Weidemann during his visit to England in the summer of 1938. (Ribbentrop always said she was Weidemann's mistress.) She entertained lavishly, but nobody knew where her money came from until a lawsuit she brought against the British newspaper magnate, the late Lord Rothermere, revealed that she had been employed by him as a kind of public relations agent with the top Nazis and that some of the money at least came from him. The rest no doubt originated in Nazi funds. On the writing-table of her Mayfair flat stood a photograph of Hitler inscribed in his own hand to 'My dear Princess', and presented to her with a letter in which the Fuehrer had conveyed his 'sincere thanks for the great understanding you have always shown for our people generally and for my work especially'. Forced to leave England shortly after the outbreak of war—she was described in the House of Commons as 'a notorious member of the Hitler spy organization'—she turned up shortly afterwards in New York where she announced that she had come 'to go shopping on Fifth Avenue'. However, it was observed that her old friend Fritz Weidemann had flown in from the West Coast to meet her, and the next that was heard of her was that she was staying as the guest of Weidemann and his wife at their house in San Francisco.

Since Sir William Wiseman had known the Princess slightly in London, Stephenson suggested that Wiseman should see her first and that the contact with Weidemann could best be made through her, particularly as this might also throw some light on the Princess's own position. Accordingly, with the knowledge and approval of the F.B.I., Wiseman invited the Princess to meet him in San Francisco. The first of several such meetings took place in Room 1026 of the Mark Hopkins Hotel on November 26, 1940. They began by discussing the possibility of the Princess's going to Berlin to place a peace proposal before Hitler and Ribbentrop, for the Princess was confident that 'she could make Hitler realize he was butting his head against a stone wall and that at the opportune time he should align himself with England to achieve lasting peace'. Wiseman listened attentively and undertook to relay her proposition to the appropriate British quarters and ascertain whether her mission could not receive the unofficial blessing of the British Government.

The following evening they were joined by Weidemann and

the conversation was resumed. But on this occasion the idea of negotiating with Hitler was pushed into the background and does not seem to have been seriously reconsidered. Instead, the trio discussed the possibility of re-establishing the monarchy in Germany with the support of the German army. Next day Wiseman returned to New York, and reports of the 'peace talks' duly reached both the White House and Downing Street. As might be guessed, nothing came of them, although Wiseman was asked to resume his conversations with Weidemann, this time alone.

During the next month or so, Wiseman had several long conversations with the German Consul-General in San Francisco; and, while the Englishman held out no promises, he encouraged the German to talk freely. The result was that Weidemann furnished a great deal of information about Germany, much of which was proved to be both accurate and valuable. He said that he himself had been opposed to the Nazi régime since the dismissal of General Von Fritsch from the command of the army on a trumped-up homosexuality charge towards the end of 1938. He claimed to be in communication with a number of high-ranking officers who felt that the only hope for Germany was a Hohenzollern restoration 'because the monarchists did not share Hitler's aim of world conquest and wanted only the security of their country'. He suggested that the Crown Prince, whom Princess Hohenlohe called 'Little Willie', would be the right person to head an anti-Nazi revolution, although Weidemann doubted if he would become Kaiser. Weidemann gave the names of several of the high-ranking officers, including General Franz Halder (later executed for alleged complicity in the bomb plot against Hitler's life in July, 1944), saying that they had conferred with the Crown Prince and that the latter, or one of his representatives, would be glad to meet an accredited British representative in Switzerland to discuss their plans.

In the course of these talks, Weidemann made some accurate prognostications concerning German strategy. Although he did not mention Hitler's intention to invade Russia, he did disclose that the Soviet Foreign Minister Molotov's recent visit to Berlin when he met Hitler had been a failure. In Weidemann's opinion, Molotov had been given instructions by

Stalin to discuss everything and agree to nothing. Furthermore, Weidem ann emphasized that 'Hitler had never liked or trusted the Russians and this fact should not be forgotten'. He also revealed that Hitler, who had expected Britain to be defeated by the beginning of October, 1940, was 'now off balance for the first time', and that the persons chiefly responsible for mis-leading him by confirming Ribbentrop's advice that 'England would not fight' were Lord Rothermere and Hitler's blonde English admirer, Unity Mitford, who had both reported in 1939 that England was 'on the verge of a Fascist revolution'. Weide-mann said that there had been a sound and detailed plan for invading England, drawn up by the Army Chief of Staff General Beck, but that it had been superseded by an impractical and amateurish plan which no one favoured except Hitler and Goering. When the General Staff told him that an attempted invasion of Britain by this means would be suicidal, Hitler had withdrawn into a state of deep gloom for three days. The latest plan for dealing with Britain, Weidemann continued, was to subjugate the country by heavy and persistent air raids, for Hitler was convinced that 'Britain could not withstand prolonged bombing'.

Perhaps Weidemann's most valuable piece of intelligence concerned future German strategy in the Balkans. In November, 1940, he told Wiseman that the German High Command planned to close the Mediterranean at both ends by persuading Spain to collaborate and by inducing Bulgaria and Yugoslavia to join the Axis. 'From the point of view of logistics', Weide-mann added, 'a movement through the Balkans would not be so difficult as some people think. The problem has been very carefully studied.' As has already been seen, this was an absolutely accurate forecast of what happened five months later when Hitler's Panzer troops swept through Bulgaria to invade Yugoslavia and Greece.

News of these conversations eventually reached the State Department, probably via the White House, and this caused the contact to be broken off, since it was feared that concerting plans for peace negotiations was an undesirable political activity, inconsistent with America's neutral status. Princess Stephanie was refused an extension of her residence permit and ordered by the U.S. Immigration authorities to leave the country. (There was even a suggestion that Wiseman should also be deported, until it was explained that his participation in the conversations had been known all along and approved by the F.B.I.) After many tears and entreaties the Princess was allowed to remain after she had volunteered some 'interesting information'. But when America eventually entered the war, she was interned for the remainder of hostilities. As for Weidemann, after the German Consular offices in the United States were closed, he was transferred to a similar post in Tientsin.

Stephenson did not forget the services rendered to the Allied cause by Hitler's former commanding officer in the Sixteenth Bavarian Infantry Regiment. Alone of all the German consular representatives, who were obliged to leave the United States in 1941, Captain Fritz Weidemann was provided with a safe conduct by the British authorities which enabled him to avoid Berlin and reach China by the comfortable and leisurely route he had chosen.

4

A few days before Stephenson and Donovan arrived in Bermuda on their way to London in December, 1940, the British censorship examiners intercepted a typewritten letter addressed to Mr. Lothar Frederick, 1 Helgolaender Ufer, Berlin. It bore a New York postmark and the contents consisted of a list of allied shipping in New York harbour which had been observed by the writer, who gave details of their arrivals and departures together with particulars of their armament. The letter was signed 'Joe K', and although written in English, it contained certain expressions, such for example as the use of the word 'cannon' for guns (German *kannone*), which suggested not only that the writer was German but that he was also a Nazi agent. This surmise was correct. Indeed the Berlin address turned out to be a cover address for Gestapo Chief Heinrich Himmler.

At this time the present author happened to be the Security Officer attached by M.I.6. to the British Censorship station in Bermuda. He showed the letter on his arrival to Stephenson, whom he had previously met while visiting New York on duty, and whose organization he was shortly afterwards to join; it was also shown to Donovan who happened to be present at the time. 'This might turn out to be a most important letter', said Stephenson when he had looked at it. The consensus of opinion was that it could lead to the revelation of widespread German espionage activities in the United States. 'Keep a look out for any more like it', Stephenson added. The Security Officer promised to do so.

The mail sorters were thereupon instructed how to recognize the mysterious Joe K's handwriting on the envelopes, and as a result a considerable number of letters from him to different addresses was picked out, mostly those to intermediaries in Spain and Portugal. The envelopes bore return addresses on the back to places in or near New York, which were fictitious, although it was noted that in each case the Christian name began with the letter J. This corresdondence purported to be from an ordinary commercial agent dealing with various commodities, but most of it contained a secondary meaning which was not very difficult to determine. The following example was taken from a letter addressed to Manuel Alonso, Apartado 718, Madrid.

> Your order no. 5 is rather large—and I with my limited facilities and funds shall never be able to fill such an immense order completely. But I have already many numbers in stock, and shall ship whatever and whenever I can. I hope you have no objections to part shipments. . . .
>
> Please give me more details about the merchandise to which our customers have any objections. Since they are paying for it, they are entitled to ask for the best. From the paying customers I take any time criticism—and I should also appreciate your suggestions for improving the quality and delivery.

In other words, a recent request for information called for a lot of work, which with the relatively small organization and little money at the writer's disposal it would take him some time to supply. Meanwhile he would send what he could and would like to know how exactly his reports have fallen short of what is required by Berlin.

The censorship examiner who had been working on the secondary meaning in the Joe K correspondence was a very determined young lady named Nadya Gardner. She thought that the letters might contain secret writing in addition to the clear text, and she sent them to the censorship laboratory for chemical tests to be applied. The results were negative. Nevertheless Miss Gardner was not satisfied. Fortunately she herself possessed a slight knowledge of inorganic chemistry, and she suggested that the old-fashioned iodine reagent, which was much used by the Germans during the First World War, should be tried. After considerable persistence by Miss Gardner in the face of the doubts voiced by the experts, this test was eventually made. This time the results were astonishing, since the secret writing which was brought out in every letter tested was seen to contain the latest information on aircraft production and shipping movements. Morever, it was established that the secret ink was a solution of pyramidon, a powdered substance often used as a headache cure and readily obtainable at any pharmacy or drug store.

Early in March, 1941, a letter in German to one of the cover addresses in Portugal was intercepted. It contained elaborate details of aircraft supplied to Britain by the United States and also of the U.S. Army training programme. It was signed 'Konrad' and was evidently the work of a trained military observer. This letter was also tested for secret writing which revealed that the writer's address was 'c/o Joe', and also that he was posting duplicate reports via China and Japan. 'Konrad' added: 'If further information on Puerto Rico is desired (see my report sent through Smith, China), please send Joe a telegram of good wishes.'

At the same time Joe's letters indicated that he was in touch with Konrad, whom he sometimes called 'Phil' or 'Julio'. Meanwhile, thanks to the lead given by the Bermuda censors through Stephenson, the F.B.I. had intercepted a report from Konrad to Mr. Smith of China giving exact details of the defences of Hawaii, with maps and photographs, notably of Pearl Harbour. 'This will be of interest mostly to our yellow allies', the report concluded. Nevertheless the F.B.I. was still no nearer discovering the identity of either Konrad or Joe.

Again it was the Bermuda censorship that provided the vital clue. On March 25, 1941, a letter written by Joe five days previously to Manuel Alonso in Madrid contained a most important piece of news. While attempting to cross Broadway at Times Square, New York, on the evening of March 18, it appeared that 'Phil' had been knocked down by a taxi and struck by another car as he lay on the ground. He had been taken to hospital where he had died the next day without recovering consciousness.

> As his condition was according to information received by telephone very critical, and I myself could not do anything, I notified 'his' consulate (through an old friend) which acted at once but it was impossible to save his life—the injuries were too serious.

This letter also contained secret writing which gave further particulars of the accident including the number of the car which had caused the fatal injury, and the name of the hospital, St. Vincent's, to which he had been taken, also the text of several cables which Joe had sent immediately after the accident. This part of the letter also stated: 'The Consulate mentioned is the Spanish.'

The F.B.I. soon followed up this information, which had been immediately passed to them by Stephenson. In fact, Hoover's men were already working on the accident from a different angle and had easily traced the victim from the Spanish passport he was carrying in the name of Julio Lopez Lido. They had been called in following the prompt action of the manager of the Hotel Taft, where Mr. Lido had been staying. After the accident Joe had managed to grab his brief-case but was worried about his luggage. The same evening he had telephoned the hotel and said that Mr. Lido had met with an accident and asked that his luggage should be taken good care of. When the voice at the other end began to ask questions, Joe became uneasy and hung up without giving his name. It was this incident which had aroused the hotel manager's suspicions. In the hotel register Mr. Lido had stated that his nationality was Spanish and that he had come from Shanghai. This seemed innocent enough, but the manager thought the anonymous telephone call rather queer. Anyhow he notified the police, who in turn informed the Public Administrator, who took possession of the dead man's luggage and effects and later turned them over to the F.B.I. Some letters were found among his effects addressed to him from a certain Carl Wilhelm Von der Osten from Denver, Colorado. This individual was already suspected by the F.B.I. of being a German agent.

Under interrogation he now admitted that the dead man was his brother, Captain Ulrich Von der Osten, who was attached to the German military intelligence, that is the *Abwehr*. But he could throw no light on any of his brother's acquaintances.

In his letters Joe had often referred to his uncle Dave and aunt Loney, who had a shop which they intended to sell. Later he wrote that 'Mr. H. sold his store', and in the letter of March 20 giving the details of Ulrich Von der Osten's fatal accident, Joe stated:

> As mentioned in one of my cables my aunt sold her store recently, and so it is not advisable to send her any more mail, but my other friends and relatives are still in business.

Among the effects of the dead Von der Osten the F.B.I. found a telephone number which they traced to a shop in a New York suburb. They then discovered that its owner had recently bought it from a couple named Dave and Loni Harris. Further inquiries revealed that the couple had a nephew named Fred Ludwig who was living somewhere in New York. The next problem was to find him among the city's millions of inhabitants.

It was Stephenson's organization which provided the missing link in the chain of investigation. London headquarters reported that in early March a German agent in Lisbon had telegraphed a code message to 'Fouzie' in New York, and they asked for identification of 'Fouzie'. The F.B.I. were requested to help, but they replied that, since 10,000 cablegrams were filed every day in New York, identification was impossible. Stephenson then obtained the information from a contact in the cable company's office, which was that 'Fouzie' was the code name for Fred Ludwig, who lived in a suburb of New York. The name and address were passed to the F.B.I., who replied two days later: 'Investigation has disclosed that Joe K is identical with one Fred Ludwig.'

Further investigation revealed that the spy, whose full name was Kurt Frederick Ludwig and whose age was forty-eight, had been born in Fremont, Ohio, and taken to Germany as a child where he grew up, married and had a wife and three children living in Munich. He had visited the United States several times in the nineteen-twenties and thirties, and when he finally returned to organize a spy ring in March, 1940, he had entered the country on an American passport, posing as a salesman of leather goods. He had then proceeded to gather a number of willing helpers from among the members of the German-American Bund. It must have been love of his work which kept him at it, as he was certainly not overpaid, his remuneration consisting of sums ranging from $50 to $500 which from time to time would be surreptitiously passed to him in an envelope by a member of the German Consulate in New York at some pre-arranged meeting place such as Child's Restaurant on 34th Street. From the time of Von der Osten's arrival, Ludwig had been acting under his orders.

Ludwig was not arrested immediately, as the F.B.I. wished to get on the trail of as many of his confederates as possible. Instead he was kept under careful surveillance, while his acquaintances were being investigated at the same time. Eventually he discovered that he was being watched. In June, 1941, the F.B.I. uncovered another spy ring and made a number of arrests. This was effected through the co-operation of a 'double agent' named William Sebold, a naturalized American citizen of German birth who ostensibly ran a secret radio transmitting station for the Germans while really working for the F.B.I. who fed him with appropriate information. (The story of this operation, which was an exclusively American one, was later recorded in the film, *The House on 92nd Street*.) Some of the agents arrested in this case were actually with Ludwig when they were picked up. Consequently he decided that it was time for him to get out of the country, and he left New York, driving his car west. He was followed and eventually apprehended in the state of Washington near Seattle, which he was making for in the hopes of catching a ship for Japan. When arrested, he was found to have several bottles of pyramidon in his possession. Asked by the F.B.I. why he had so many, he replied that he suffered from chronic headaches. But the headaches could not explain the contents of another small package in his possession—namely a lotion eyebath and several toothpicks slightly brown at the ends where they had obviously been dipped in some solution.

Other arrests quickly followed, among them a particularly interesting agent named Paul Borchardt, a scholarly ex-officer of the German Army, who (as Stephenson was able to tell the

F.B.I.) had taught young Nazi officers the science of 'geopolitics' under the direction of the celebrated Professor Haushofer in Munich, and had later spent a year in Britain apparently as a refugee, since he was of Jewish extraction. His job was to assess the military value of the information which Ludwig and the others collected. Some of the documents incriminating Borchardt had been obtained through the initiative of an American employee of the German Consulate in New York, who was in charge of the furnace and had managed to retrieve them largely intact by throwing them into the furnace in such a way that they choked off the draught.

Ludwig and eight of his confederates were tried in the United States District Court in Brooklyn, New York, and convicted. (The documentary evidence put in by the prosecution consisted of three hundred exhibits.) Much of the evidence which secured their conviction was supplied by the testimony of two British witnesses, Mr. Charles Watkins-Mence, the Chief Censor at Bermuda, and his indefatigable assistant Miss Nadya Gardner, who identified the more important examples of Ludwig's correspondence, which were produced in Court. Commenting on their evidence at the time, the *New York Herald-Tribune* drew attention to the fact that this co-operation between British and American officials was the first such instance publicly recorded in the period immediately before and during the present war. 'Although the Federal Bureau of Investigation did not really get on the trail of the alleged spies until one of them was accidentally killed by a taxi in Times Square last March', the *Herald-Tribune* continued, 'the letters turned over by the British dovetailed neatly with what the F.B.I. uncovered here.'[1]

On March 13, 1942, Judge Henry W. Goddard, who had tried the case, imposed sentences varying from twenty years imprisonment, in the case of Ludwig, Borchardt and another of the defendants—René Froelich who had passed over to Ludwig important military intelligence from Governor's Island, New York, where he was stationed—to five years in the case of Ludwig's secretary, an eighteen-year-old blonde named Lucy Boehmler, who pleaded guilty and was the principal witness for the prosecution. All the defendants were

[1] *New York Herald-Tribune*, February 18, 1942.

released after the war and in the circumstances were fortunate, since, of course, had their acts of espionage occurred after instead of before Pearl Harbour, most of them would have gone to the electric chair.

Immediately after the trial, Mr. Mathias Correa, the District Attorney, who had led the prosecution, wrote to the liaison officer in Stephenson's organization whose duty it had been to assemble the evidence from the British side and produce the key witnesses from Bermuda in court.

> Department of Justice,
> United States Attorney,
> Southern District of
> New York,
> New York, N.Y.
> *March 16, 1942.*

Captain H. Montgomery Hyde,
British Security Co-ordination,
Room 3801,
630, Fifth Avenue,
New York, N.Y.

Dear Captain Hyde,

Now that the Ludwig case is finally and successfully concluded, I wish to take this opportunity of expressing to you my appreciation of the most friendly and helpful co-operation and assistance which you and your associates rendered us in that case.

In my opinion the testimony and exhibits furnished by Mr. Watkins-Mence and the other members of the Imperial Censorship stationed at Bermuda contributed very largely, in the case of some of the defendants almost wholly, to the successful outcome of the case.

Finally, I wish to thank you for the friendly spirit of co-operation in which you helped us at all stages of the case with which you were concerned. I look forward to a continuance of that pleasant relationship, however our official paths may cross.

> With kindest personal regards,
> Sincerely,
> Mathias F. Correa,
> United States Attorney.

Thus ended the first case of espionage to be tried in the United States after that country had entered the war. For reasons of policy the part played by the two British agencies, Stephenson's B.S.C. and the Bermuda censorship, was deliberately 'played down'. It is well that the record should now be put straight.

5

Members of the United States Congress (unlike British Members of Parliament) have long enjoyed the privilege of sending letters through the mails without paying for the postage, using envelopes which are 'franked' with the signature of the sender. This privilege is constantly and quite legally used by Senators and Representatives to distribute to their constituents copies of their own speeches, poems, or anything else which in their opinion their constituents should read. It is, however, illegal to employ the Congressional 'frank' for the benefit of clubs or societies. Early in 1941, a friend of Stephenson, who was in the advertising business, drew his attention to the fact that certain isolationist Congressmen were using the 'frank' for distributing free through the mails not only their own isolationist speeches but others which had been specially written by Nazi propagandists. Moreover this material was being sent to people throughout the United States regardless of where they lived. It almost seemed as if Congress was being converted by some sinister means into a distributing house for German propaganda.

A little inquiry by Stephenson disclosed that the material was going to all persons on the mailing list of the German Library of Information in New York. This fact was checked by one of Stephenson's staff who was able to arrange for certain names and addresses to be inserted into the Library's list. Very soon the same names began to appear on 'franked' isolationist mail from United States Congressmen. It was remarked that this mail was not confined to New York, but also originated in Washington and elsewhere. Next the envelopes were compared, and it was found that, while the 'franked' envelopes emanated from different Senators and Representatives, they were all addressed in the same hand. For instance, in one month an American of German descent in New York received 'franked' mail from five different Congressmen, although these isolationist Congressmen represented widely separated states. This obviously suggested that there was one single centre of distribution.

Examination of a certain Senator's 'franked' envelopes posted in New York revealed that the names and addresses were stencilled in a peculiar blue ink by a distinctive type of addressing machine. Further investigation showed that the machine was an out-of-date Elliott, of which there were only three specimens in New York, and that it belonged to a German 'cultural' organization called the Steuben Society, which had an office in Lexington Avenue. Samples of the Steuben Society's literature were then procured and found to have been stencilled on a similar machine in the same peculiar blue ink and in the same distinctive style. Furthermore, the address plate bore the same code number as the one used for the Senator's envelopes. The literature sampled urged members of the society to attend certain meetings at which reprints of the Senator's speeches would be available in 'franked' envelopes for mailing to their friends.

In May, 1941, Stephenson began his counter-offensive. His friend in the advertising business published an open letter to the Senator, accusing him of misusing the privilege of the Congressional 'frank', and supported his charge with choice quotations from the evidence which Stephenson had collected. This open letter, of which 100,000 copies were reprinted and widely distributed throughout the country, was sensational in its public effect. The Senator raised a somewhat feeble protest in the Senate, in the course of which he admitted that the America First organization had purchased a million of his 'franked' postcards. The immediate result was that the Steuben Society was fined for violation of the postal regulations, while the Senator lost considerable prestige.

Although the German Consulates and other official German agencies in the United States were closed shortly afterwards by Presidential executive order, the abuse of the Congressional 'frank' continued. Indeed the volume of Nazi propaganda distributed through this medium seemed if anything to increase. Stephenson now shifted his inquiries to Washington, where they eventually led to the office of Representative Hamilton Fish on Capitol Hill. Fish, a fifty-one-year-old lawyer and Harvard graduate from New York, was an extreme Republican isolationist. But, in spite of his pro-German sympathies, he does not appear to have been guilty of any crime under American law. It was his clerk, an insignificant bureaucrat named George Hill, who was the real villain behind the scenes.

Hill, who was also the local commander of the Order of the Purple Heart, the American wounded war veterans' organization, used his position to get isolationist and pro-German propaganda inserted in the Congressional Record. It was not necessary for this material to be read out on the floor of the Chamber. Any Congressman had merely to rise in the House or Senate and obtain formal permission for a document of virtually any length to be incorporated in the official proceedings, and he would then hand it to the Government Printer. Fish could usually be relied upon to oblige in this respect. Other Congressmen were persuaded to sign an order to the Government Printer for so many reprints in the belief that they were helping the Order of the Purple Heart. Hill paid the government price for the printing, which was about one third of the normal retail price. He would then sell the reprints with appropriate 'franked' envelopes to America First and isolationist organizations at the retail price, pocketing the difference for himself.

One of these other organizations, the Make Europe Pay War Debts Committee, was run by a friend of Hill called Prescott Dennett. One day Dennett received a *subpoena* to attend before a Grand Jury, which was investigating the distribution of German propaganda, in terms which suggested that he was known to have been misusing the Congressional 'frank'. Dennett took fright and in a panic telephoned Hill asking him to remove the bags of 'franked' mail which Hill had given him to despatch. Hill ordered a government truck to collect the bags and deliver them to a storeroom in the Congress building used by Hamilton Fish. The lorry duly collected the bags, but by mistake delivered them to Fish's office. Fish's girl secretary, who was somewhat taken aback by this unwelcome consignment, kept a few of the bags in the office; the remainder, about a dozen, she sent over to the office of America First, a move which was observed by one of Stephenson's agents who had been keeping watch. Stephenson lost no time in informing Hoover, and suggested that the America First office should be raided by the Federal authorities. The raid took place, and the bags were found.

Called before the Federal Grand Jury investigating German propaganda activities, Hill swore that he had not given orders to hide the mail bags. He also denied that he knew the ace German propagandist George Viereck. He was promptly indicted on a charge of perjury and duly convicted. (It was proved that his employer, Representative Fish, had introduced him to Viereck.) He was sentenced to a term of from two to six years' imprisonment. Hamilton Fish, after unsuccessfully attempting to get the House of Representatives to grant him immunity from testifying, only escaped the ordeal of questioning by hurriedly rejoining the army. But he had to take the stand at Viereck's trial. ('I have been in Congress for twenty-two years and not a piece of Nazi propaganda has gone out of my office with my knowledge or consent.')

Hill's paymaster Viereck, who later admitted that between September, 1939, and America's entry into the war he had received over $100,000 from German sources for his propaganda activities, was arrested in October, 1941, and charged with failure to comply with the Foreign Agents Registration Act. Described at the time of his arrest by a Government spokesman as 'the top-ranking German propagandist in the world and a menace to security', George Sylvester Viereck, who was a naturalized American citizen, had been known as a pro-German publicist since before the First War. His father Louis Viereck, a former Socialist member of the Reichstag, was said to have been the illegitimate son of the German Emperor William I by an actress, and George himself was always a fervent admirer of the Hohenzollern dynasty. Among the counts in his indictment was one charging him with having arranged for the wholesale distribution of speeches attacking the Administration's foreign policy under the Congressional 'frank' with the collaboration of George Hill.

In the course of Viereck's trial, which opened in the Federal District Court in Washington on February 4, 1942, Mr. William Maloney of the Attorney-General's office, who was in charge of the prosecution, learned from the F.B.I. that a letter had been intercepted by the Bermuda censors from Viereck to Dr. Hans Heinrich Dieckhoff, former German Ambassador to the United States and at that time Chief of the Foreign Propaganda Division of the German Foreign Office. This letter contained proofs of a book entitled *Who's Who Among the War Mongers* by Senator Rush Holt with corrections in Viereck's handwriting. By a fortunate coincidence the examiner who had dealt with this letter was Miss Nadya Gardner, who was actually in New York at the time giving evidence in the Ludwig spy trial. Stephenson immediately arranged for the letter to be made available and for Miss Gardner to attend the court to prove it in evidence. As a surprise witness in the case, her testimony caused a considerable sensation, since it was the only evidence that the prosecution was able to establish as proof of Viereck's connection with the Propaganda Division of the German Foreign Office. It was also conclusive proof of his guilt. He was convicted on three of the five counts on which he was charged. 'I am passionately devoted to the United States and all that she stands for, and she is the only country to which I owe allegiance', he declared indignantly. 'I deplore the cruel war that has come between the land of my birth and the land of my choice.' He added that he had one son in the United States Army and another about to enlist. But this declaration did not save him from a sentence of from two to six years' imprisonment and a fine of $1,500.

The Supreme Court, to which Viereck's lawyers successfully carried his appeal, set aside the verdict of the lower court and ordered a new trial on the ground that the jury had been misdirected by the trial judge and that Viereck had been called upon to supply more information than was required by the statute, since he was not obliged to disclose propaganda activities carried out on his own account. Chief Justice Stone also described some of Prosecutor Maloney's remarks to the jury as 'highly prejudicial' to the course of justice. Consequently at the new trial, which began on June 25, 1943, Mr. George A. McNulty, Special Assistant to the Attorney-General, appeared in charge of the prosecution, and undertook to establish that all the acts proved in the first trial had been committed by Viereck as an agent of the German Government and not merely for himself.

Miss Gardner of the Bermuda censorship again took the witness stand and testified that she had intercepted a weekly news-letter from Viereck to Dieckhoff, which frequently went through a Lisbon intermediary, Hoynigero Hueneras, an alias for Baron von Hoyningen-Huene, former German Ambassador to Portugal. George Hill was brought into court from prison to give evidence which earned him a remission of his sentence— he described how he had mailed speeches written by Viereck under Congressional 'frank' and that the expenses had been paid partly by Viereck and partly by Prescott Dennett. Finally, Dr. Paul Schwarz, a former German Consul in New York, related how Viereck had been engaged by the Consulate as a public relations adviser and had agreed to influence American public opinion in his writings. Incidentally, Viereck's cash book, which the prosecution produced, showed that for the first six months of 1941 he had received $32,000 from the German Library of Information, although his agreement with that organization only provided for $500 a month.

Viereck was again convicted, and this time the sentence was one to five years. In fact, he served four-and-a-half years in various federal penitentiaries and was released shortly after the end of the war. He went back to propaganda, choosing the safer but equally congenial theme of the seamier side of American prison life which he dealt with no less effectively. 'You seem to have stood it with extraordinary spirit', Bernard Shaw wrote to him on his release. 'Most martyrs are duds.'[1]

When the trial was over, Stephenson's liaison officer with the Department of Justice—the same one who had helped the federal authorities with the Ludwig spy case—was invited to visit the Department's headquarters in Washington where he was personally thanked by the Attorney-General, Mr. Francis Biddle. The chief prosecutor in charge of the case likewise sent him an official letter of thanks. 'I want to express our thanks and the thanks of the Department to you and the British Security Co-ordination for the assistance which you have rendered in the Viereck case', wrote Mr. George McNulty. 'I am sure that you must be gratified that the material intercepted by the British Censorship has been put to such effective use. Miss Gardner deserves great credit both for the quality of her work and her shrewdness as a witness.'

Justice also caught up with Congressman Hamilton Fish.

[1] G. S. Viereck. *Men into Beasts* (1952), at p. 8.

The details of the malpractices of his clerk Hill and his friend Viereck, not forgetting their abuse of the Congressional 'frank' in his office, were suitably recorded in print and the result distributed by Fish's opponents to the voters of the 26th New York District before the elections of November, 1944, at which he was a candidate. Hamilton Fish was not re-elected. He attributed his defeat to Reds and Communists. He might— with more accuracy—have blamed William Stephenson and B.S.C.

CHAPTER IV

# THE VICHY FRENCH
# AND OTHERS

I

No action of President Roosevelt in the diplomatic field divided American public opinion so sharply, or was more severely criticized at the time, as his decision to maintain relations with the Government of Unoccupied France which had been established on an avowedly authoritarian basis at Vichy with the aged Marshal Pétain as Chief of State. The Canadian Premier Mackenzie King was similarly under fire in his country for keeping a representative at Vichy. Judged in the light of subsequent events, there can be no doubt now that the action of these two statesmen was fully justified, since, as Mr. Churchill later put it, 'here at least was a window upon a courtyard to which we had no other access'.[1] Nevertheless it was widely misunderstood in many quarters, particularly where there was sympathy with General de Gaulle and his Free French Committee who were carrying on the struggle against the Nazi victor overseas. The feeling was intensified when it was seen that behind the degrading Fascist façade of Vichy lurked the sinister figure of Vice-Premier Pierre Laval, the arch-collaborationist and Pétain's designated successor, who arranged the meeting between the Marshal and Hitler at Montoire and openly prayed for Britain's defeat.

In September, 1940, Gaston Henry-Haye, the Vichy Government's first Ambassador, arrived in Washington to take up his appointment. When Henry-Haye called to pay his respects at the State Department, Cordell Hull received him coolly, since the Secretary of State knew that this little man with the ruddy cheeks and the truculent moustache bore the taint of association with Laval and his group. The Ambassador's first effort with

[1] Churchill. II, 450.

94

Hull was to try to exonerate himself from the recently published charges that he was anti-British and pro-German. 'It is due to you to know', Hull commented tartly, 'that your Government is anti-British and pro-German when it goes beyond the spirit of the letter of the armistice agreement.' The Secretary of State had in mind Hitler's designs on the French fleet, and he was not in the least deceived by the Ambassador's assurances that all plans had been made to send the fleet away or scuttle it if the Germans attempted to gain possession of it.[1]

Although the Vichy Ambassador attempted to dissemble in front of Secretary Hull, he made himself perfectly clear when he called together the staff of the Embassy and addressed them on their duties. 'Our prime objective is to establish the fact that Britain betrayed France and is therefore her real enemy', he said. 'Every means at our disposal must be used to convince American officialdom and the American public that this is true.' (Stephenson learned of this speech, which was of course confidential, from a contact he had established inside the Embassy.) At this time there were many influential Americans who had social connections or investments or both in France and who were inclined to support Marshal Pétain. They and their French friends felt bitterly towards the British for refusing to send any more planes in the last days of the fighting, and they felt still more anti-British by reason of the attack on the French fleet at Mers-el-Kebir and Oran, which had resulted in the disabling of several naval vessels as well as in considerable loss of life. Henry-Haye exploited these feelings assiduously. At the same time he organized a kind of Gestapo in the Embassy to report upon the activities of supporters of the former French Government and in particular those who had responded to General de Gaulle's patriotic call. Every means was employed to prevent them joining the Free French movement, their families in France were threatened with reprisals, and their names were sent to Vichy where they were published in a decree depriving them of their citizenship.

At first, according to a report received by Stephenson, this Gestapo was directed by Count René de Chambrun, whose wife José was a daughter of the infamous Laval. Towards the end of 1940, José de Chambrun returned to France by Clipper.

[1] Hull. I, 847–8.

The British Embassy at Washington issued instructions not to detain her at Bermuda where the aircraft was due to call, since she was travelling on a diplomatic passport which Britain, not being at war with the Vichy Government, was bound to respect. Her safe-conduct also covered any documents she might be carrying provided that they were destined for Unoccupied France. On being asked by the passenger control at Bermuda to produce any letters in her possession, she exhibited several sealed envelopes which were examined and found to be addressed to the Minister of Foreign Affairs in *Paris*. Of course, this was intended for Vichy, but they were old printed envelopes from the Embassy stock in Washington and in preparing them the clerks in Henry-Haye's office had not (as they should have done) crossed out the word Paris and substituted Vichy. On this pretext the Security Officer, who was the present writer, relieved the Countess of the envelopes, having informed her that His Majesty's Government did not recognize any Government in Paris and regarded any address there as being in enemy occupation. The enraged Countess protested in vain. Later the contents of her packages were examined and seen to contain several letters actually destined for Paris, including one to Hitler's personal representative Otto Abetz. This latter letter was from an employee of the Embassy in Washington named Jean-Louis Musa, who was a personal confidant of the Ambassador's, and handled all covert propaganda on behalf of the Vichy authorities in America. When René de Chambrun followed his wife back to France shortly, afterwards, Musa took over the work of the Embassy Gestapo.

Interesting facts of which Stephenson had knowledge concerned another seizure at Bermuda at about the same time, in which the Vichy Government was implicated. In October, 1940, the famous Vollard collection of impressionist paintings worth hundreds of thousands of dollars was consigned by the Vichy authorities to a French art expert in New York named Martin Fabiani. There was reason to believe that Fabiani was acting on German instructions and intended to sell the collection to secure dollar exchange for Hitler. The consignment, which consisted of 270 paintings and drawings by Renoir, thirty paintings by Cézanne, twelve by Gauguin, seven by Degas and also some by Manet, Monet and Picasso, had been in various Paris museums, whence the British Ministry of Economic Warfare feared that they had been abstracted.[1]

The pictures were shipped from Lisbon for New York in the American Export Lines' *Excalibur*, which was brought into Bermuda by the British Contraband Control. Meanwhile instructions had been received from London to remove the contraband cargo. It fell to the writer of these pages to carry out this operation in defiance of the vessel's master who refused to open the strong-room where the precious packing cases reposed. This was eventually accomplished by blasting a way in with oxy-acetylene flame burners, and the pictures were removed. So as to avoid the effects of the Bermuda climate, they were sent to Ottawa, where they were kept for the duration of the war in the Canadian National Gallery, having in the meantime been condemned as prize.

It was the successful execution of this operation which drew the present writer to Stephenson's attention, thus beginning a stimulating association of which this book has been the eventual outcome.

2

As a first step towards exposing the under-cover activities of the Vichy Embassy, Stephenson instituted some inquiries about the Ambassador's henchman Jean Musa. He discovered that Musa, although he had been born in Switzerland of a French mother by an Italian father, had been a United States citizen for more than twenty years—he had once worked as a waiter in the Hotel Lafayette in New York where he was called 'Nino', a nickname by which he was still known in the Vichy Embassy. In the earlier part of 1940 he had returned from France to New York, hoping to negotiate contracts for the sale of armaments for the French Government on a commission basis. The armistice suddenly put an end to this business, at the same time leaving him extremely short of cash. He was delighted when he heard that Henry-Haye was coming as Ambassador, since they had had business dealings together in the past, and so he got into touch with him as soon as he arrived. In the result Musa became Henry-Haye's personal secretary and *homme*

[1] The collection was formed by Ambrose Vollard. See his *Recollections of a Picture Dealer* (1936).

*d'affaires.* A tall, swarthy man in his early fifties with dark fluid eyes and a fondness for bow ties, Musa soon made himself extremely useful to the Ambassador and to the Embassy generally. As Henry-Haye himself said, he was exactly right for the job.

At the outset Musa was paid a salary of $300 a month, with an additional $200 as expenses, a sum quite inadequate for a man of his extravagant tastes, especially when his wife and children joined him. Indeed, he confided to one of Stephenson's agents, who had deliberately cultivated his acquaintance, that the Ambassador paid him 'a perfectly ridiculous sum'. As cover for the operation which he planned, the agent took offices in New York where he ostensibly ran a trading company. He now suggested to Musa that they should go into business together and he offered to put an office and a secretary at Musa's disposal. Musa accepted readily and at once settled down in his new office, where Stephenson had microphones conveniently installed. In the result all Musa's conversations, whether on the telephone or otherwise, were recorded, his papers were examined daily and where necessary discreetly photographed; and the contents of his safe were regularly inspected, since Musa's 'business partner' had no difficulty in learning the combination. In fact there was little that went on in Musa's business and private life that Stephenson did not immediately know. He knew, for instance, all the details of Musa's plan to buy the controlling interest in a company which had the exclusive rights to manufacture the Bren gun in the U.S.A. Musa succeeded in interesting the French motor manufacturer, Emil Mathis, to whom he posed as a supporter of General de Gaulle, in the project; but, when at last it seemed likely to mature, and that Musa might obtain blueprints of the weapon, Stephenson informed Purvis of the British Purchasing Commission, who stepped in and stopped the deal.

A more ambitious scheme, and a more dangerous one had it materialized, was the Vichy Government's plan to erect, in conjunction with the Western Union Cable Company, a powerful wireless station in the French island of St. Pierre, situated off the south coast of Newfoundland. Western Union had five cables running into St. Pierre from its 34,000 offices in the United States, and the proposed new station which the company envisaged building on land provided by the French colonial government would be capable of communicating with anywhere in the world by radio-telegraph, while at the same time avoiding all the British censorship controls. For this privilege Western Union were to pay the Vichy Government a fixed royalty. 'I hope that you will give the necessary instructions', Musa wrote from his New York office to the Ambassador in Washington, 'so that this project of the greatest interest takes shape and progresses as fast as possible.'

Fortunately Stephenson was in touch with one of the directors of Western Union, Vincent Astor, head of the Astor family in America and a confidential adviser of President Roosevelt; in fact Astor had recently been appointed to act as special liaison between the White House and Stephenson. Astor was not aware of the details of the scheme, but as soon as Stephenson had put him in possession of the relevant facts he brought up the matter at a company board meeting, outlining the dangers from the point of view of the British war effort. Knowing the confidential relationship in which he stood to the President, Astor's colleagues on the Western Union board assumed he had the President's backing for his statement. Anyhow it was decided to drop the whole business, and Western Union's European general manager, Maurice Cartoux, who had been working on the negotiations from the company's side, was consequently instructed 'in view of certain circumstances which have arisen concerning our proposed arrangements at St. Pierre' to 'discontinue all your activities in this connection'.

The watch which was kept on Musa's office revealed many other characteristic activities. For instance, he assisted the Embassy Military Attaché, Colonel Georges Bertrand-Vigne, in evading both the American freezing regulations and the British blockade by paying dollars on the Colonel's behalf to Louis Arpels, the New York jeweller, while Arpels's company paid the equivalent in francs to the order of Bertrand-Vigne in France. He likewise conducted a regular business in remitting money to a Portuguese intermediary in Lisbon for the purchase of food parcels for transmission to the German Occupied Zone of France. He dabbled in the passport racket and some of the visas he obtained were for known German agents. He also sold exit permits from Unoccupied France for considerable sums, and on one occasion he endeavoured to work out a scheme whereby

French vessels would carry Spanish refugees to Mexico and would return to Marseilles fully laden with cargo, incidentally earning $150,000 for himself from each voyage. (Needless to say this scheme did not come off.) He collected information from French girls, former employees of the French Purchasing Commission, whom he had placed in various French and American business firms. And he succeeded in persuading a French language newspaper in Montreal not to engage Pierre Lazareff, the French journalist and editor, whom he suspected of supporting de Gaulle.

Stephenson arranged that a comprehensive report should be prepared of Vichy French activities in the United States, including transcripts of Musa's telephone conversations and photostat copies of his letters and other documents. The report was given to President Roosevelt who read it as 'a bed-time story', describing it as 'the most fascinating reading I have had for a long time' and 'the best piece of comprehensive intelligence work I have come across since the last war'. Stephenson thereupon asked the President's permission to publish a suitably edited version in the American press. The President agreed, provided that the State Department had no objection. In the event the State Department proved amenable, but emphasized that the operation of discrediting Vichy policy in the United States must not be such as to cause a break in diplomatic relations between the two Governments. While Under-Secretary Sumner Welles had some reservations, Secretary of State Cordell Hull, who regarded Henry-Haye as a most contemptible Ambassador, let it be known that he hoped Stephenson would go ahead and 'blow Vichy sky high'.

3

On August 31, 1941, which was a Sunday, the *New York Herald-Tribune* came out with the following headlines in large type splashed across three columns of the front page:

### VICHY EMBASSY IN U.S.
### SHOWN AS HEADING CLIQUE
### OF AGENTS AIDING NAZIS

Underneath there were smaller captions such as 'Jean Musa, Ex-Waiter, Called Chief Aid in N.Y. in "Information" Work' and 'Henry-Haye Cited As Guiding Hand'. The story which followed bore a Washington date line and had been written by one of the *Tribune*'s reporters, Ansel E. Talbert, who had been supplied with carefully selected extracts from the anti-Vichy material collected by Stephenson's agents. It bluntly accused the Vichy Embassy of operating a secret intelligence organization inside the United States with funds blocked by the U.S. Government with the object of assisting the Nazis to make France a vassal state of Germany. The three men in charge of this underground work under the general direction of the Ambassador were stated to be Colonel Bertrand-Vigne, the Military Attaché, Captain Charles Brousse, the former Press Attaché, and Jean Musa. An accompanying photograph showed the Ambassador walking with Musa and Bertrand-Vigne in the garden of the Embassy.

Besides the Gestapo activities already described, the story gave an interesting example of intelligence in the broader military field. It revealed how the Vichy authorities were able to thwart General de Gaulle's plans to capture Dakar in the previous year. Apparently the plans for the ill-fated Free French expedition to the west coast of Africa were smuggled into the United States for the transmission to Vichy in the fuel tank of a motor car which was shipped from London to Hoboken on board the Greek steamer *Nea Hellas*. Also in the tank were lists of French army and naval officers and air force pilots who had joined the Free French movement.

During the same week three more articles appeared with similar headlines such as VICHY AGENTS SOUGHT PLANS OF BREN GUN with the sub-heading: 'Tried to Get Blueprints of Weapon Defending Britain From Invasion.' All the articles were reproduced in over one hundred newspapers in the United States and Canada, including the *Washington Post*, the *Baltimore Sun* and the *New York Daily Mirror*. Mr. Henry Morgenthau, the Secretary of the Treasury, voiced the general acclaim when he expressed a desire to meet the *Herald-Tribune* reporter who had produced such a brilliant series of articles. He said he wished to compliment him personally on such an outstanding journalistic feat.[1]

It was, of course, a tremendous 'scoop' for the *Herald-Tribune*,

[1] *New York Herald-Tribune*, August 31, September 2, 3, 4, 1941.

since the articles were widely discussed throughout the country and provided the substance of numerous newspaper editorials. Henry-Haye reacted by summoning a press conference and stating that he was going to protest to Secretary of State Hull. 'As a matter of fact I am very sad', he told the newsmen. 'It will be just one year tomorrow that I left France to come to your country to represent a defeated nation—but still a very proud nation. The sacrifices we have made are greater than anyone else. And still here I am being obliged to give you an explanation of a campaign which is in no sense justified. What is the aim of this campaign? The aim is to try to realize the ambition of certain Americans and certain Frenchmen to break up or deteriorate diplomatic relations between the French government and the United States. I say the French government because there is no other French government than the one I represent.' The Ambassador then held up a copy of the *Herald-Tribune* of two days previously, adding as he did so, 'I saw the proof in the editorial of the paper which is just giving such a large hospitality to their wonder stories'.

Stephenson arranged that a pro-British reporter should attend this press conference and had him primed with embarrassing questions to put to the Ambassador. This resulted in more unfavourable publicity for the Vichy representative and his staff, since Henry-Haye's feeble and evasive explanations were completely unconvincing. 'The Ambassador speaks as a representative of the French people, a friendly power', wrote the *Herald-Tribune* in a further editorial; 'yet the government he represents has repeatedly done everything it could to promote the German victory, which the United States has declared to be profoundly inimical to its vital interest, and to embarrass the British resistance to which the United States is pledged to render every aid in its power.'

The effect of this concerted newspaper campaign was altogether to discredit the Vichy régime's representation in the United States. The Free French were naturally jubilant. Not the least satisfactory result was that the Musa's Gestapo largely ceased its activities, although Musa himself was kept on by the Ambassador at a small salary. As for Henry-Haye, he made no further public attempt to explain away the attacks upon himself and his staff and declined to answer any more questions on the painful subject. But in private he was reported by a source of Stephenson's inside the Embassy to be 'not a little annoyed'. Indeed in a particularly violent outburst he described the whole affair as 'de Gaullist-Jewish-British-F.B.I. intrigue'. But he never really suspected the British at any time. Nor for that matter did S.I.S. headquarters in London. Some weeks after the articles had appeared, Stephenson received a communication from his London office to the effect that they expected he had seen reference in the *New York Herald-Tribune* to the exposure of Vichy French activities in the United States, and concluding: 'Please comment.' Stephenson's comment has not been recorded. It would probably be unprintable anyway.

The actions of prominent Vichy French outside the Embassy did not go unnoticed. One of these was the former Popular Front Prime Minister Camille Chautemps, who had helped to pave the way for Pétain by intriguing against Reynaud for an armistice in May, 1940. For his services he had been rewarded with the post of Vice-Premier in the first Pétain Government, but he had been ousted by Laval when the Marshal reconstructed his Cabinet two months later. During the period of Laval's temporary eclipse, he had persuaded Pétain to send him to America to attempt to keep faithful to Vichy those politically confused Frenchmen who, while being pro-Pétain, were nevertheless opposed to collaboration with the Germans and were consequently beginning to flirt with de Gaulle and the Free French. For his services Chautemps received a monthly allowance of $2,000 from France's blocked dollar funds, but this was later withdrawn on orders from Vichy apparently because he was a Freemason. He was exposed on Stephenson's initiative in an article which depicted him as hoping to capitalize on the State Department's dislike of de Gaulle, Marshal Pétain's prestige and the apprehensions of some Frenchmen who wished to reinsure against a German defeat.

While Chautemps got a five-year prison sentence from the French Purge Court after the war, other less conspicuous Pétainists in the United States emerged comparatively unscathed. They included the writer André Maurois, whose activities formed the subjects of reports by Stephenson to London.

Maurois, whose enthusiasm in the cause of Anglo-French goodwill had earned him an honorary K.B.E. from King

George V in 1938, abruptly changed his tune after the fall of France; on arriving in New York (where he established himself in the luxurious Ritz Towers), he let it be known that in his view Britain had no hope of survival against Germany and that his own country's downfall was due in great measure to the failure of Britain to honour her pledges to France for adequate military support and assistance. Nor was his open hostility to Britain at this period without its pusillanimous side. When a French refugee published, under the pseudonym André Simon, an attack on the men of Vichy under the title *J'Accuse* (originally used by Emile Zola in vindicating Captain Dreyfus), Maurois feared that the book might be attributed to him, as his first name was André and his wife's Simone. Accordingly he went to great pains to explain that not only was he not the author, but that in no way did he share the views expressed therein. Stephenson later learned that in May, 1941, Henry-Haye had cabled Vichy praising Maurois for his loyalty ('*action loyale*') to Marshal Pétain's government. 'By his numerous writings and lectures', the Ambassador added, 'M. Maurois has contributed to inform American opinion on the true facts of our situation.' The result was that Henry-Haye received instructions from the Government at Vichy restoring Maurois's French citizenship and renewing his passport for two years. Colonel Bramble had been conveniently forgotten.

Prior to the press revelations, Americans had tended to regard the Vichy French with sympathy and in some cases admiration. Now they realized that Henry-Haye and his henchmen deserved neither pity nor praise. They were not proud men trying to put a bold face on defeat, but potential enemies of the United States. A few months later the mask was torn off when Laval rejoined the Vichy Cabinet as 'Chief of the Government', taking charge of the Ministries of Foreign Affairs, Interior (including secret police) and Information. 'Monsieur Laval and I are one', the Marshal declared on this occasion. The surrender to Hitler was complete.

4

While preparing the exposure of the Vichy Embassy's under-cover activities in the United States, Stephenson determined to penetrate the Embassy itself. Credit for the successful accomplishment of this objective belongs in large measure to a woman agent, whom he recruited to the B.S.C. organization in its early days. As a product of British intelligence, her achievement was to prove of incalculable value to the allied war effort. For sheer bravado it probably has no equal in the records of espionage during the last war. Not only did she secure the texts *en clair* of nearly all the telegrams despatched from and received by the Vichy Embassy, but she was also instrumental in obtaining the key to both the French and the Italian naval ciphers, which enabled the British Admiralty to read for the remainder of the war all the relevant cablegrams, radiograms and fleet-signals which were intercepted in code or cipher.

As her story unfolds, it will become apparent that her peculiar feminine charms were the real instrument of her success. And yet, remarkably enough, she had no very obvious sexual allure. She was neither beautiful nor even pretty in the conventional sense, although she had pleasing blonde hair. She was tall, with rather prominent features, and always appeared well dressed. There was certainly nothing about her which suggested that her virtue was easy. She was a pleasant companion, for she was intelligent and talked well—or rather listened well. She had a soft, soothing voice which doubtless in itself inspired confidences. It may be that her appeal to her victims was in the first place intellectual, and that the discovery of her bodily charms came later as an intoxicating realization. That she was physically very attractive cannot be doubted, since the powerful hold which she exercised over the diplomats whose secrets she succeeded in obtaining was clearly based on sex. But she had many other qualities. She was widely travelled and understood well the psychology of Europeans. She possessed a keen, incisive brain and was an accurate reporter. She was extremely courageous, being often willing and even anxious to run risks which her British employers would not permit. Her security was irreproachable and her loyalty to her employers complete. She was not greedy for money, but greedy only to serve a cause in which she believed. In fact she was paid a small salary which represented little more than her living expenses. The worth of her services could not be assessed in monetary figures. In the event it was priceless.

For the purpose of this narrative she is called Cynthia, which was not her real name. And lest anyone reading these lines should think that she is in any sense the product of the present author's imagination, he must make it clear that he himself had the pleasure of her acquaintance at this period, but not in the manner enjoyed by some of her professional clients. For example, he still retains a vivid recollection of walking along Madison Avenue, New York, with her one afternoon in late August, 1941, and seeing the announcement on the news posters that Laval had been shot and wounded in an attempt on his life in France. Having bought a newspaper with the details, we adjourned to the hotel nearby, where she was living, and discussed the question of what might happen should Laval succumb to his injuries. However, Laval recovered and was destined to die, not from the bullets of an assassin but from those of an official firing party in the country that he had betrayed to France's traditional enemy.

Cynthia's first major assignment, in which she won her spurs during the winter of 1940–41, was to obtain the Italian naval ciphers from the Italian Embassy in Washington. She began by securing an introduction to the Naval Attaché, Admiral Alberto Lais, whom she lost no time in cultivating assiduously. He responded to her charms in the manner she desired, and soon—within a few weeks of their first meeting— he imagined himself deeply in love with her. As a result she was able to do with him virtually what she pleased. In retrospect, it seems almost incredible that a man of his experience and seniority, who was by instinct, training and conviction, a patriotic officer, should have become so enfeebled by passion as to be willing to work against the interests of his own country to win a woman's favours. But that is what happened.

As soon as she had him where she wanted, Cynthia came straight to the point. She told the Admiral that she wished to have copies of the naval cipher. Astounding as it may appear, he agreed without apparent demur to assist her. He put her in touch with his cipher clerk, who produced the cipher books after a suitable and satisfactory financial understanding had been reached. Photostatic copies were made by one of Stephenson's experts in Washington, and the results immediately despatched to London.

In spite of the blow it received from the British Fleet Air Arm in its main base at Taranto in November, 1940, the Italian naval force in the Mediterranean at this period was considerable, consisting of six battleships, including two mounting 15-inch guns, nineteen modern cruisers and 120 destroyers and torpedo-boats, besides over a hundred submarines. Numerically it was far superior to the British Admiral Cunningham's Mediterranean Fleet, which was based on Alexandria. There is no doubt that Cunningham found the intelligence of the Italian fleet movements obtained from the naval ciphers of immense advantage in making his own fleet dispositions. For example, the major movement of the Italian fleet towards the Aegean in the latter part of March, 1941, was correctly anticipated with the aid of the ciphers, and resulted in a resounding British naval victory off Cape Matapan which put the greater part of the Italian fleet out of action for the rest of the year.

For some time after securing the ciphers, Cynthia continued to meet Admiral Lais and was also able to learn details of other Axis plans in the Mediterranean. Finally Cynthia was responsible for the Admiral's enforced departure from the United States. This came about in the following way.

In the spring of 1941, there were numbers of Italian merchant ships lying in American ports, since their masters did not feel that it was either prudent or possible to attempt to get through the British blockade to Europe. Realizing that sooner or later America would enter the war and that these vessels would then be taken over by the Allies, Admiral Lais devised a plan to sabotage them. Fortunately he revealed to Cynthia how he had directed that the machinery of five of the ships at Norfolk, Virginia, should be put out of commission, and she immediately reported what she had learned. Stephenson thereupon caused the information to be conveyed to the United States' Office of Naval Intelligence, which passed it on to the State Department. Although it was too late to stop most of the vessels from being damaged, further serious sabotage was prevented. All the ships were then seized by the American Government, as well as a number of German vessels which had likewise been sabotaged by their crews. Both the Italian and German Governments protested at the American action, but on April 3, 1941, the

State Department returned strong replies, pointing out that the crews, in damaging their vessels to the detriment of navigation and the safety of United States harbours, had committed felonies under United States law in disregard of the hospitality that had been extended to them. At the same time Cordell Hull informed the Italian Ambassador, Prince Colonna, that his Naval Attaché was *persona non grata* and requested his immediate recall. The Ambassador had no alternative but to comply.[1] Admiral Lais never suspected Cynthia. As he was about to go on board the vessel which was to take him back to Italy, two parties were on the quayside to bid him farewell. One consisted of his wife and children—the other merely of Cynthia, who stood alone some distance away. The lovesick Admiral spent his final minutes with her and ignored his tearful family entirely.

In the following month, Cynthia was instructed to concentrate her attention upon the Vichy Embassy in Washington. Posing as a newspaperwoman and accompanied by a female assistant, she called at the Embassy to keep an appointment which she had made for a press interview with the Ambassador. At first the two ladies sat for a time with a senior member of the Embassy staff who talked to them while they were waiting for Henry-Haye. For the purposes of this narrative he will be called Captain Bestrand. He talked to the two visitors for nearly an hour, and by the end of that time Cynthia knew that she had achieved her first objective. As the gallant Captain escorted them to the Ambassador's office, he expressed the wish to see her again.

The two newspaperwomen had a long 'off-the-record' discussion with the Ambassador. He was an excitable man in the best of circumstances, but on this day he appeared quite overwrought as he had just had a particularly unpleasant interview with Secretary of State Hull. Nevertheless he did his best to explain for the benefit of his discreet and appreciative audience the very difficult mission with which he had been entrusted. On the subject of Franco-German relations he spoke very frankly. 'France's future requires co-operation with Germany', he said. 'If your car is in the ditch, you turn to the person who can help you to put it on the road again. That is why we will work with Germany.'

[1] Hull. II, 927.

The Ambassador was neither reticent nor unduly cautious. The occasion seemed to be a useful one in which to communicate to the American public some of the anti-British feelings he had expressed at his first staff meeting. He talked on and seemed in no hurry to finish the press conference, perhaps as a result of Cynthia's soothing influence. When at last the ladies rose and he showed them to the door, he told Cynthia that he would be glad to see her again at any time she cared to call at the Embassy.

Both the Ambassador and his staff officer did see her again. The Ambassador saw less of her than he would have liked. The officer saw more of her than was good for him. Very soon Captain Bestrand was completely infatuated and under her control, just as the Italian Admiral had been. Bestrand was married, but was at an age perhaps when the chance of a new conquest beckoned strongly. What is more, he was in every respect an emotional man. He felt especially bitterly towards the British for their action at Mers-el-Kebir. While he enjoyed the confidences of the Ambassador possibly more than any other member of his staff, nevertheless Bestrand despised Henry-Haye as a *parvenu* and a *bourgeois*, and thought that he himself, with his superior culture and family connections, would have made a better and more appropriate Ambassador. Like many Frenchmen at this time he expressed a hatred of Laval, and in so doing gave Cynthia an opportunity of which she made good use. Gradually, under the guidance of her employers, she stimulated Bestrand's feelings against Laval, and as her personal influence with the Captain increased, she persuaded him to talk more and more about Vichy affairs. Soon he was answering prepared questions and giving valuable information about Vichy's underground activities in the United States.

In July, 1941, the Vichy Government decided to abolish Bestrand's post in the Embassy. However, Henry-Haye retained Bestrand as a member of the Embassy staff, since he found him useful, and he paid him a small salary out of his secret funds. This substantial cut in Bestrand's income occurred at a psychologically opportune moment. Cynthia made a 'confession' to her lover. She told him that she was an agent of the United States Government and suggested that, in return for a cash consideration, Bestrand should pass her information about Embassy affairs. She pointed out that this was the only possible course for a patriotic Frenchman like himself and the only way to defeat Laval, and the Germans.

Bestrand agreed, and from then on information flowed into Stephenson's office from the Vichy Embassy. This eventually embraced every happening of importance and every current outgoing and incoming telegram, together with those of older date. Acting on instructions Cynthia also asked Bestrand to write a daily report of what went on in the Embassy, and these detailed reports filled in many gaps by supplying necessary background and enabling certain telegrams to be more easily understood. This daily news-letter related the particulars of all the Ambassador's appointments and the results of the interviews he gave.

The telegrams indicated what Stephenson had long suspected, namely that the Ambassador and his Naval Attaché were engaged in collecting intelligence to the detriment of the British war effort for transmission to Vichy. For example, on June 15, 1941, the Naval Attaché despatched a telegram, counter-signed by Henry-Haye, to Admiral Darlan, the anti-British Minister of Marine in Vichy, giving him information (for which he had apparently asked) of the location of those British warships which had come into American dockyards for refit. The Naval Attaché stated that he had learned 'from a reliable source' that the aircraft carrier *Illustrious* was at Norfolk, Virginia, the battleship *Repulse* was at Philadelphia, and several cruisers were in New York in addition to the *Malaya*, news of whose presence there he had already signalled. 'All these warships are undergoing extended repairs', he added. 'The first to be ready will undoubtedly be the *Malaya*, which will be immobilized for at least another month.'

Like all the other telegrams, the above signal was handed over in its deciphered form. Cynthia was shortly to be asked to obtain the naval cipher in which the signals were sent. This was to prove the biggest challenge and the most spectacular feat in her career as an intelligence agent.

5

In working against Vichy, Stephenson co-operated as far as he could with the Free French delegation and its leader Count

Jacques de Sièyes, who was General de Gaulle's chief personal representative in the United States. This liaison had necessarily to be conducted with circumspection since the State Department made it clear that, while sympathizing with de Gaulle's stand, it could not consider recognizing officially his right to speak for the French people as a whole. The Free French were naturally interested in the fate of France's colonial possessions in the Western Hemisphere which had now come under the control of Vichy, particularly the island of Martinique in the West Indies. This island was under the dictatorial rule of Admiral Georges Robert, who was fanatically loyal to Marshal Pétain. He had charge of the Vichy gold reserve valued at $245 millions, which had been sent to the island in the cruiser *Emile Bertin* and was closely guarded in an old stronghold, Fort Desaix, near Fort-de-France, the capital. Besides the *Emile Bertin*, there were several other French warships including the aircraft carrier *Béarn*, several merchant vessels and over one hundred fighter planes, mostly of American manufacture, which had been on their way to France at the time of the collapse.

Towards the end of August, 1940, Stephenson cabled London that there was a possibility of organizing a scheme to be carried out by 'a reliable Frenchman' for a *coup* in Martinique, 'which would release to ourselves gold, ships and aircraft', and he asked whether there were any objections. In due course he was informed that, 'provided you are not implicated and the scheme is entirely organized by the French, it is viewed favourably'.

The 'reliable Frenchman' was a huge, swashbuckling character from Martinique named Jacques Vauzanges, who had two sons living on the island and who knew many of the French officials and naval officers stationed there. Vauzanges planned to organize the anti-Vichy elements in the colony and to endeavour to alter the outlook of the others by propaganda. Should the *coup* prove successful and result in Martinique and the neighbouring island of Guadeloupe transferring their allegiance to de Gaulle, the warships would be sent to a Canadian port, probably Halifax, where they would join the British fleet, while the gold would be placed at the disposal of the Free French.

On his arrival at Fort-de-France, Vauzanges found the

situation less encouraging than he had supposed. While the local population seemed on balance to favour de Gaulle, feeling generally in the islands was apathetic and more interested in improving living conditions, alleviating unemployment and obtaining essential products such as fuel oil, of which there were severe shortages owing to the British blockade, than in any schemes for overthrowing Admiral Robert's government.

The date chosen by Vauzanges for putting his plan into execution was September 23, 1940. Unfortunately that was the very day on which the Anglo-Free French expedition to Dakar was beaten off by the Vichy defences and de Gaulle suffered a striking set-back. Had Dakar been taken, things might have turned out differently in Martinique. As it was, the officers who were designed to form the backbone of the projected *coup* drew back and refused to play the part expected of them. Public opinion in the islands swung away from the Free French movement and the unlucky Vauzanges had to abandon his project altogether.

Vauzanges stayed on in Martinique for several months and spread as much anti-Vichy propaganda as he could before eventually returning to New York where he made a detailed report to Stephenson on conditions in the islands. He recommended that the blockade should be tightened, since there was a very real danger that the islands might be used as a base for refuelling German submarines so long as they remained under Vichy's control. Meanwhile the United States sent Admiral John W. Greenslade on a special mission to Martinique in an endeavour to persuade the Governor to hand over the planes for transfer to Britain. But Admiral Robert remained obdurate and the much-needed fighter aircraft were allowed to rust away.

On May 16, 1941, Mr. Churchill sent the following minute to General Ismay, his Chief of Staff, as Minister of Defence:

> What is the situation at Martinique? Are the 50 million pounds of gold still there? What French forces are there? What French vessels are in harbour? I have it in mind that the United States might take over Martinique to safeguard it from being used as a base for U-boats in view of Vichy collaboration.[1]

---

[1] Churchill. II, 682.

The answers to these and similar questions were provided by Stephenson's organization, supplemented by copies of Admiral Robert's telegrams which were obtained from the Vichy Embassy in Washington, as well as information gained from inhabitants who had escaped to the nearby British island of St. Lucia.

The United States declined to act on the British Prime Minister's suggestion that they should occupy the islands, but they did send another mission to Martinique which eventually reached an understanding with Admiral Robert that the islands should not be used in the manner that Churchill had feared. But the Admiral raised so many objections to carrying out the agreement that eventually, in 1943, the State Department withdrew its Consul-General from Fort-de-France and adopted Vauzange's suggestion of imposing an economic blockade. Shortly after this Admiral Robert resigned and the islands came under Allied control, relief supplies were despatched to the civilian population and the previously immobilized naval and merchant vessels made available to the anti-Axis war effort.

Stephenson's co-operation with the Free French movement bore better fruit in the matter of two other Vichy-controlled islands. These were St. Pierre and Miquelon, off the Newfoundland coast, which were also under Admiral Robert's jurisdiction. Both the British and Canadian Chiefs of Staff had urged that the islands should be taken over, preferably by Free French forces, since there was reason to believe that Vichy agents were tapping the Western Union transatlantic cables which passed through St. Pierre and also passing information on allied convoys to the enemy by means of fishing boats which made an excellent cover for this type of espionage. The Canadian Department of External Affairs considered that any British participation in the proposed venture, such as had taken place at Dakar, might inflame anti-British feeling in the French-speaking provinces of Canada, and suggested that the Free French should be allowed to occupy the islands 'under Canadian supervision'.

Meanwhile, in order to avoid a repetition of the Dakar fiasco, de Gaulle's representatives in the United States requested Stephenson's assistance in ascertaining the precise political feelings and aspirations of the inhabitants of St. Pierre and Miquelon. Accordingly Stephenson sent a number of agents into the islands and their investigations revealed that 97 per cent. of the population were for the Free French. These findings were embodied in a comprehensive report which was sent to London in the autumn of 1941 and shown to General de Gaulle. The latter now determined to liberate the islands on his own without Canadian or any other supervision, which the Free French naval forces were quite capable of doing. While the Foreign Office in London had no objection, both the State Department in Washington and the Department of External Affairs in Ottawa were opposed to any move which might result in an embarrassing political situation. With the latter view President Roosevelt agreed. In these circumstances the General was asked to refrain from taking any action, and according to Churchill, he certainly said he would do so.[1] At the same time de Gaulle's 'shadow' Minister of Marine, Admiral Emile Muselier, who had been sent to Ottawa, was officially informed of the Canadian and American views. Acting in complete disregard of these views, de Gaulle peremptorily ordered Muselier to take over the two islands. This the Admiral was reluctantly obliged to do. Muselier's Free French expedition landed on Christmas Eve, 1941, and met with an enthusiastic reception from the local people.

Secretary Hull reacted sharply in Washington, doubtless fearing that otherwise Marshal Pétain might retaliate by granting the Nazis bases in North Africa. On Christmas Day he issued a statement from the State Department, which had been drafted by one of his senior assistants, condemning the action taken by the 'so-called Free French ships' as arbitrary and contrary to the agreement of all parties concerned. Hull's singularly ill-chosen reference to the Free French brought coals of fire upon his venerable head and was indeed widely resented. The American press was soon full of scornful remarks about 'the so-called State Department' and letters of protest were addressed to 'the so-called Secretary of State'. The British

[1] Churchill. III, 590–1. On December 17, 1941, the Foreign Office told the State Department that President Roosevelt's view had been communicated to de Gaulle 'who agreed that the proposed action should not now be undertaken'. Sherwood. I, 456.

Prime Minister was spending Christmas with the Roosevelt
family at the White House, where the irate Secretary of State
turned up and asked Churchill to get de Gaulle to withdraw
his forces. When Churchill demurred to this request, Hull
accused him of being behind the whole operation, which of
course was not true. The President, who thought the Department's statement ill-advised and flatly said so, was inclined to
shrug off the affair as a 'teapot tempest'; but Hull refused to be
mollified and went off in a huff to Florida where he seriously
contemplated resigning and for a time refused even to talk to
the President on the telephone. Eventually a compromise was
reached by which a semblance of Vichy sovereignty was
restored in the islands while the radio station was placed under
strict allied supervision so that it could be of no possible aid to
the Germans. Meanwhile a plebiscite was held in St. Pierre and
Miquelon. The result showed that 98 per cent. of the people
were against Vichy and for freedom from an obnoxious régime.
It also showed that the estimate formed by Stephenson's
agents was only 1 per cent. out—and that was on the conservative side.

6

In March, 1942, Stephenson received a message from
London asking him to endeavour to obtain the French naval
cipher, which was used not only by Vichy naval attachés
serving in foreign missions but also by the fleet commanders.
Plans were beginning to take shape for an allied invasion of
North Africa, and it was of the utmost importance for the
British Admiralty to be able to follow the signals sent by the
Ministry of Marine in Vichy to the fleet in Toulon and the
North African ports, so that those concerned could be kept
informed of the ships' intended movements.

Cynthia was instructed to approach her friend Captain
Bestrand. She promptly did so, and Bestrand was flabber-
gasted by her suggestion. He said it was an impossible task, and
that the only persons who had access to the code room were the
Chief of Codes, a man named Benoit, and his assistant, Count
de la L——. Furthermore, the room was always locked and
the telegrams were taken by the Embassy Counsellor in person
to the code room.

'Do you mean that even you haven't access to that room?' Cynthia asked.

'Nobody has,' Bestrand said. 'At one time the Naval Attaché used to go to the code room more often than seemed necessary, just out of curiosity which was second nature with him. The Ambassador himself—how do you say it?—ticked him off. In fact he sent him a note forbidding any more visits to the code room.'

'What about night time? Do they work all night?'

'No, but the room is carefully guarded at all times. The Foreign Affairs Ministry recently sent instructions that a permanent watchman should be on duty at nights and on holidays to guard the whole of the Embassy premises.'

'How big are the cipher books?' continued Cynthia.

'So big,' Bestrand answered, 'that if anybody could smuggle them out their absence would be noticed at once.'

Cynthia then asked about Benoit.

'He is a bear who has lived for the past twenty years with his work,' said Bestrand. 'He has no needs, no ambition and no imagination. He arrives in the Chancery, says good morning to no one and goes straight to the code and cipher room.' He added that 'no arrangement could be made with Benoit'.

Nevertheless, although Benoit was utterly loyal to Marshal Pétain, he became confused and unhappy when Laval returned to power in Vichy, as he did at this time, and began to pursue a policy of open collaboration with the Nazis. This was too much for old Benoit, and he resigned his job.

Thereupon Cynthia went to him and told him that here was a chance to serve France. 'Our desires and aims are the same as yours,' she said. 'We want to help France because we know that by doing so we will also be helping the allied war effort.'

The old man's eyes filled with tears. 'I am very confused,' he said, 'I have had no time to think. Everything has happened so quickly.'

'The ciphers could provide the key to show how much the traitors in the French Government are helping the Germans,' Cynthia quickly came to the point. 'To turn them over to us would be the greatest service you could perform for your unhappy country.'

'But I cannot do that,' Benoit replied. 'Everything is so

Secret naval cipher taken from the Vichy French Embassy in Washington

*'Twenty-four hours later the photostatic reproduction . . . reached the Admiralty in London.'*

LINEE AERIE TRANSCONTINENTALI ITALIANE S.A.

Roma, 30 ottobre 1941 XX

Caro Camerata,

ho ricevuto la Vostra relazione che è giunta cinque giorni dopo essere stata spedita.

La relazione è stata portata subito a conoscenza degl' interessati i quali la considerano di grande importanza. L' abbiamo confrontata con altra ricevuta dal Praga Del Arete. Le due relazioni prefigurano un quadro analogo della situazione che esiste laggiù tra la Vostra è più dettagliata. Desidero esprimerVi il mio compiacimento. Il fatto che, in questa occasione, noi abbiamo ottenuto informazioni più complete di quelle che abbiano S. ed i suoi, mi ha riempito di soddisfazione.

Non vi è dubbio che il grossoccio sta cedendo alle lusinghe degli Americani e che soltanto un intervento violento ca parte dei nostri amici verdi può salvare il paese. I nostri collaboratori di Berlino, in seguito alle conversazioni avute con il rappresentante a Lisbona, hanno deciso che tale intervento deve aver luogo al più presto. La Voi conoscete la situazione. Il giorno in cui si verificherà il cambiamento, i nostri collaboratori si preoccuperanno assai poco dei nostri interessi e la Lufthansa raccoglierà tutti i vantaggi. Per impedire che questo si verifichi dobbiamo procurarci al più presto altri amici influenti tra i verdi. Fatelo senza indugio. Lascio a Voi di decidere quali sarebbero le persone più adatte: forse Fadilha o E.F. de Andrade

sarebbero più utili di S.E. il quale, per quanto attivo, conta poco.

I fondi di cui avrete bisogno saranno messi a Vostra disposizione. Non importa se i verdi hanno bisogno di somme cospicuevoli: le avrete. L' importante è che i nostri servizi si avvantaggino di un cambiamento di regime. RiforateVi di chi vogliono nominare Ministro dell' Aeronautica e cercate di guadagnarne la simpatia.

S. dovrà essere tenuto al corrente di quanto avviene ma abbiamo convenuto che le trattative rimarranno completamente nelle mani della LATI la quale agirà nella sua capacità di ditta brasiliana che cerca di estendere e di migliorare i propri servizi.

Nel aspetto da Voi la massima discrezione. Come Voi dite nella relazione concernente la Standard Oil, gl' Inglesi e gli Americani si interessano di tutto e di tutti. Ed anche se è vero che - come giustamente affermate - i Brasiliani sono una nazione di scimmie, non bisogna dimenticare che sono scimmie disposte a servire chiunque tiene le redini in mano.

Saluti fascisti,

Comandante
Vicenzo OLIVCA
Linee Aeree Transcontinentali Italiane S.A.

The 'Lati Letter', fabricated by Station M, which caused President Vargas to close the Italian airline

*'There is no doubt that the fat little man is falling into the hands of the Americans . . .'*

confusing,' he kept repeating. 'Everything has happened so quickly.'

'Your loyalty should be to the French people,' said Cynthia. 'Not to a government of traitors.'

Benoit thought hard. At last he reached a decision, difficult and painful for him as it was disappointing to Cynthia. 'I cannot,' he said finally. 'I have a long record of loyalty to my chiefs. All of them have written me letters. The codes and ciphers have been my responsibility, my personal responsibility. To guard them has been my duty.'

Regretfully Cynthia had to abandon her attempt, having told her employers that here at least was one among the traitorous Vichy crew who remained faithful to his principles. Indeed Benoit stands out as a man who deserved to serve a better cause than the one he refused to betray.

On Benoit's resignation, Count de la L—— took over the charge of the code room. He was a young man with a wife and growing family, and there was good reason for believing that he was short of money. Cynthia, whose energy and persistence were boundless, did not have to be told what to do next. She at once began to cultivate him, though she was careful not to let Bestrand know what she was doing. De la L——'s wife was having her second child at the time and he himself was a little bored and glad to find such a *sympathique* companion as Cynthia.

Soon she was telling him her views about Laval and expressing astonishment that any loyal Frenchman should associate himself with such treacherous policies. Gradually she worked round to the subject of the naval cipher, and she stressed the immense assistance that its possession could render the enemies of Germany. As a further inducement she offered him a lump sum of money immediately if he would procure it for her, and a monthly retainer thereafter if he would keep her advised of any changes in it that might be made.

De la L—— appeared to be torn by doubts, but in the end he refused. In fact, his apparent doubts were pretended. He went straight to the Ambassador and told him the whole story. He somewhat exaggerated the sum Cynthia had offered him, and added that she was in the employ of the United States Intelligence Service.

This sensational account immediately spread round the Embassy. Naturally Bestrand heard of it, but he refused to believe it. He went to Henry-Haye and protested that it was untrue. He told him that de la L—— was unreliable. Had he not been spreading rumours about the Ambassador's supposed affair with an attractive Baroness? Obviously the man was a liar, said Bestrand, and having circulated such a malicious and damaging tale about the Ambassador, he was doubtless addicted to spreading equally untrue stories about other people. Henry-Haye heartily agreed. He immediately sent for de la L—— and soundly reprimanded him, ending up by telling him that he was to be withdrawn from the code room.

Cynthia had been extremely lucky. She had also been most astute in concealing her association with de la L—— from Bestrand. Now she devised a new plan for obtaining possession of the naval cipher. This involved Bestrand's co-operation, but his part was to be relatively simple as well as thoroughly congenial. When he heard the details, he agreed to co-operate without demur. In the event he did so most willingly. First of all, he supplied a floor plan of the Embassy, and with the aid of this the final dispositions were made.

One evening Bestrand arrived with Cynthia at the entrance to the Embassy. The watchman was on duty, and Bestrand took him aside, speaking in confidential undertones. He explained that he had nowhere else to go. Washington was crowded, he said, and anyway it would not do for a member of the Embassy to be seen in a hotel. The watchman's assistance was facilitated by a generous tip. He told Bestrand that he and his *amie* could spend the night on the divan on the first floor. A night or so later they came again, and the visit was repeated on several subsequent nights. Thus the watchman became accustomed to their comings and goings.

Then, one night in June, 1942, a cab drove up to the Embassy and deposited Bestrand and Cynthia. They appeared to be in festive mood, and the watchman noticed that they had brought several bottles of champagne with them. They invited the watchman to join them in a glass, and he gladly accepted. But the watchman's drink had been doctored with a powerful sleeping draught, and soon he was fast asleep. Cynthia then admitted the cab driver, who had been waiting for their signal in his taxi outside. This man was also an expert locksmith, and he immediately set about his appointed task. First he removed the lock from the door leading to the Naval Attaché's office. Then he worked out the combination of the safe in the code room. It took him three hours to complete the job, which had to be done silently and without leaving any trace of his presence. This meant that there was insufficient time in which to deal with the cipher books. But the most difficult part of the undertaking had been accomplished, and it only remained to put the knowledge thus obtained to the required use on the next occasion.

Two nights later Bestrand and Cynthia paid another nocturnal visit to the Embassy. They did not consider it advisable to drug the watchman again, since he might realize that the fact of his falling asleep for a second time was something more than a coincidence and so report the matter to his superiors next morning. Also Cynthia sensed that he was already a little suspicious and was probably intent upon finding out whether she and Bestrand were up to any 'funny business'. It was therefore essential that some effective method should be used for keeping him well out of the way. The expedient to which she now resorted was very simple. It was designed to satisfy the watchman's curiosity in a totally unexpected manner.

As soon as she and Bestrand were alone, she prepared herself for a surprise entrance on the part of the watchman. Sure enough he appeared about twenty minutes later—to find Cynthia completely undressed. He hastily withdrew in considerable embarrassment but perfectly reassured that the visitors had no other purpose for spending the night in the Embassy than the mutually agreeable one which Bestrand had originally intimated. The watchman's behaviour made it clear that he would not trouble them again with his presence.

The locksmith was now admitted through a window and lost no time in utilizing the knowledge that he had gained on his previous visit. Within a matter of minutes he was able to reach the safe and open it. The naval cipher books were instantly removed and handed through the open window to another of Stephenson's agents who was waiting outside. They were then rushed by car to a convenient house nearby where a photostat was made of each page. By 4 a.m.—well within the time limit —the books were back in the Embassy safe, and there was no sign that they had ever been abstracted. Twenty-four hours later the photostatic reproduction of the Vichy French naval cipher reached the Admiralty in London.

Those who participated in the successful landings in North Africa a few months afterwards would have been surprised to know how much the preparations for the elimination of Vichy naval resistance on that occasion owed to the determination of a quiet Canadian allied with the courage of a clever woman, who took off her clothes in the French Embassy in Washington in circumstances which are hardly likely to be repeated. Incidentally, Cynthia and Bestrand are now happily married.

# CHAPTER V

## SPECIAL OPERATIONS

### I

In a press interview which he gave in London shortly after Congress had passed the Lend-Lease Bill, Dr. Dalton, the Minister of Economic Warfare, told American correspondents that the United States could now best help Britain by the 'freezing of enemy assets, co-operation in "blacklisting" enemy commercial firms, and co-operation in the control of ships' bunkering'. He went on to name certain American firms which he said had 'traded with the enemy'. These included the General Aniline and Film Corporation, the Schering Corporation of Bloomfield, New Jersey, and the Pioneer Import Corporation of New York, all of which were really subsidiaries of German industrial or commercial concerns. In the same connection Dr. Dalton also mentioned the Chase National Bank.

This statement provoked strong reactions when it appeared in the American press. While the firms in question hotly denied the charges, Secretary of State Hull was said to have been 'made very angry' by them and to have expressed the belief that in one of the cases at least, that of the Chase National Bank, they were unfounded.[1] The facts on which the Minister based his statement had, of course, been supplied by Stephenson. They had also been brought to the attention of the U.S. Treasury, where they met with a very different reception from that accorded them by the State Department. In fact, Mr. Henry Morgenthau, the Secretary of the Treasury, asked the British Embassy in Washington to send a message to Dr. Dalton expressing warm approval of his action, which Mr. Morgenthau described as 'very friendly to the United States'.[2]

For a considerable number of years before the war the large

[1] The Chase National Bank was criticized for its dealings with the Reichsbank which apparently benefited the German Treasury.
[2] Medlicott. II, 33–4.

German industrial corporations, such as I.G. Farbenindustrie and Schering A.G., had been methodically consolidating their interests in the United States. This was done in two ways: first, through the branches and subsidiaries in the U.S.A. of German-owned companies which were usually camouflaged by neutral ownership in Sweden or Switzerland; and secondly, by the secret cartel agreements of German parent companies with their American subsidiaries. When Germany went to war in 1939, this vast and intricate network of companies became the backbone of the German intelligence and propaganda systems in the Western Hemisphere, and its existence endangered the security and the economy of both Britain and the United States. To devise a means of combating and if possible of liquidating it was one of the most urgent problems confronting Stephenson on his first arrival in New York.

Since most of these disguised German subsidiaries were registered as American companies and staffed by American employees, Stephenson had to achieve his objective without offending sensitive public opinion, particularly as represented in Congress. To begin with, he had to obtain absolute proof of the existence of direct connections between Germany and the German subsidiaries operating under cover in the United States. So long as the United States remained neutral, this was not in itself an offence under federal law. So it was necessary to go a step further and provide evidence which would justify the United States authorities taking action on technical grounds, such as the violation of the anti-trust laws, by showing the existence of cartel agreements between the German parent companies and the subsidiaries.

The first such parent company to attract Stephenson's attention was Schering A.G., the Berlin chemical firm, which had developed into one of the largest exporters of German pharmaceutical and medicinal products between the wars. Its president, who had devised its extremely efficient export system, was a Jew named Julius Weltzien, whom the Nazis had consequently transferred to the United States. The Schering Corporation of Bloomfield had been established in 1939 as a small facsimile of the parent Berlin company in such a manner that it could operate if necessary on its own. Weltzien was its president; its vice-president was an American physician called

Dr. Gregory Stragnell, and its secretary was an American naturalized German named Ernst Hammer. It owned all the parent company's patents and trademarks in the U.S.A. After the outbreak of war and the advent of the British blockade, it had taken over, by agreement with Berlin, the task of supplying the Schering subsidiaries in Latin America which had formerly been supplied by Schering A.G. For this purpose, the Bloomfield corporation had been supplied with German-type packages, labels, prescriptions and full instructions, which varied from country to country. The Bloomfield corporation, it should also be noted, was nominally a subsidiary of two holding companies controlled by the Swiss Bank Corporation of Basle, through which in fact the subsidiary was financed. Stephenson first learned of these facts from a worried employee of the Bloomfield corporation, who was a German citizen awaiting American naturalization. When he had discovered that the firm for which he was working was in reality a subsidiary of Schering A.G., Berlin, and that the professed Swiss ownership was merely a blind, he had gone to the State Department, where he had succeeded in obtaining an interview with Assistant Secretary Adolf Berle, who listened politely to what he had to say and remarked: 'Very interesting.' Mr. Berle subsequently wrote a confused report on the subject which began: 'From a source—the reliability of which is not confirmed —I have learned the following. . . .' When the Schering employee discovered that the State Department was really not interested, he went to the Department of Justice, only to be informed that there was no legal action which they could take. He was advised to get into touch with the British, and in due course met one of Stephenson's agents through the former manager of the Berlin branch of an American bank. He was advised to go back to his job in Bloomfield, N.J., for the time being and to try to collect documentary proof of his story.

Gradually he began to accumulate the necessary evidence. He would bring the files to Stephenson's agent in a hotel in mid-town Manhattan; they would then be photographed and the originals returned next morning. However, this material did not furnish conclusive proof of the German connection, since the Bloomfield corporation's directors were extremely careful in wording their correspondence with the dummy

Swiss holding companies, which they knew was liable to be intercepted by the British censorship in Bermuda. Consequently it was decided to manufacture evidence of the facts which had been ascertained but which could not otherwise be proved. Stephenson's agent persuaded the Schering employee to procure some of the Bloomfield corporation's letter-heads. These were brought to Stephenson's office where incriminating letters were written for the signature of the employee, who was a senior member of the Bloomfield corporation's staff. Whenever these letters were despatched to their Swiss addresses, Stephenson would advise Bermuda where they would be intercepted and scrutinized by the censorship examiners who would send them back to Stephenson as 'submissions'.

The dossier when complete revealed that the Berlin company retained its hold on many important world markets; that a constant flow of contraband was reaching Germany in spite of the British blockade; and further that half the considerable cash turnover of the American Schering concern found its way to Berlin through Switzerland. The total amount of foreign currency transferred in this way during the year 1940 was estimated at over two million dollars a month. Finally, the Bloomfield corporation's participation in cartel agreements contrary to the Sherman Anti-Trust Act was established beyond doubt. Both the Department of Justice and the press were supplied with full particulars by Stephenson's organization. The press campaign was taken up throughout the country by more than a thousand newspapers as well as by many magazines and radio commentators.

In the result, the Schering Corporation of Bloomfield, N.J., was fined $15,000, and its president and vice-president $2,000 and $1,000 respectively on being convicted of 'conspiracy to restrict trade'; the company's board was purged of all its members of German origin except Weltzien; the practice of mis-labelling goods for Latin America was stopped; and the Swiss Bank Corporation was ordered to divest itself of all stock held in the Bloomfield corporation within three months.

Meanwhile Stephenson had learned that Dr. Stragnell, the vice-president, had been trying to obtain control of the Canadian Schering company for the Bloomfield corporation. He thereupon caused the Custodian of Enemy Property in Ottawa to be advised to sell the Canadian subsidiary to the Bloomfield corporation. This was done and the purchase price being $150,000 was paid over. Twenty-four hours later the Custodian was supplied by Stephenson's organization with evidence of continuing German control which enabled him to seize the whole of the company's assets. Thus the Bloomfield corporation lost its $150,000 and Dr. Stragnell and the other remaining directors were discouraged from making any similar deals in the future.

After Pearl Harbour, the U.S. Treasury took over the entire control of the Schering Corporation of Bloomfield, N.J. All its common stock was acquired by the American Government and henceforward the business was conducted under the supervision of federal officials. But long before that time, thanks to the energetic measures of Stephenson and his assistants, its Nazi wings had been effectively clipped.

2

A much more formidable target for attack than the Schering concern was the colossal German dye trust commonly known as I.G. Farben, or to give it its full name, *Interessen Gemeinschaft Farbenindustrie Aktiengesellschaft*. With a capital of 900 million reichsmarks, it was probably the largest corporation of its kind in the world. An official of the Anti-Trust Division of the U.S. Department of Justice described it as 'an agglomeration of monopolies and an aggregation of cartels'. Its principal United States subsidiary was one of the companies denounced by Dr. Dalton, namely the $62,000,000 General Aniline and Film Corporation of New York (known until the outbreak of the war as the American I.G. Chemical Corporation). It had also strong links with Sterling Products Inc., the largest drug company in America, and the Bayer group which Sterling controlled, as well as with the Standard Oil Company of New Jersey and the Ford Motor Company of Detroit. (The Ford Company of Cologne was a wholly owned subsidiary of I.G. Farben.)

Stephenson's exposure of the I.G. Farben empire in the Americas was embodied in an anonymously written booklet called *Sequel to the Apocalypse*, which was put on sale for 25 cents and told the American public the 'uncensored story' of 'how your dimes and quarters helped pay for Hitler's war'. Besides explaining the various ingenious ramifications of the German trust, it contained several disturbing rumours calculated to deter the American public from buying Farben's pharmaceutical products. One was that the archives of the trust's head office in Berlin had been hit by British bombing aircraft and the formulae destroyed with the result that many deaths had been caused by wrong prescriptions. The publication aroused widespread interest at the time. The managing director of Standard Oil of New Jersey, whose relationship with I.G. Farben was clearly indicated, told an American contact of Stephenson's that he would give $50,000 to know who was behind this publication.

One of the results of the campaign was that William vom Rath, the German-born director and secretary of the General Aniline and Film Corporation, was obliged to resign his offices. (Vom Rath, whose father was in I.G. Farben, was a relative of Ernest vom Rath, secretary in the German Embassy in Paris, whose assassination by a young Polish Jew, Herschel Grynzspan, in 1938 was the excuse for one of the worst Nazi pogroms.) Another result of *Sequel to the Apocalypse* was that Sterling Products, which had given I.G. Farben an undertaking not to sell any of its manufactured goods in Britain, Canada, Australia, or South Africa, was prosecuted together with three subsidiary companies, each being fined $5,000.

Another American firm, which traded secretly with Germany, was the German-controlled Pioneer Import Corporation, which was headed by Werner von Clemm, a former German army officer, who had married the daughter of a rich Anglo-American banker and had himself become a United States citizen. He had close family as well as business relations with Germany, two of his sisters being married to army officers and his cousin being the wife of Foreign Minister Ribbentrop. His company dealt in a variety of commodities, including hops, tulips, glue, synthetic stones and diamonds and carried on an extensive correspondence with Germany in an intricate plain-language code. He was known to have imported diamonds, looted from Belgium and Holland, on false certificates of origin, which in due course were exposed in the press through Stephenson's intervention. In due course von Clemm was convicted and sentenced to two years' imprisonment and a fine of $10,000; in addition his ill-gotten personal funds were seized, as well as semi-precious stones to the value of $400,000 belonging to his company. During his trial the U.S. Treasury representative went out of his way to thank his 'newspaper friends' for their assistance in the investigation.

Information proving the German ownership in all of over one hundred German-owned subsidiary companies in the United States was furnished by Stephenson to the United States authorities. After the entry of America into the war it enabled the Alien Property Custodian to seize the assets of these subsidiaries amounting to some $260 millions.

Stephenson also kept a weather eye open for any secret economic agents whom Germany might despatch on special missions. We have already seen what befell Dr. Gerhard Westrick. In March, 1941, there arrived in Brownsville, Texas, on a visitor's visa from South America, a particularly notorious German. This was Dr. Kurt Heinrich Rieth, whose father had made a fortune as Standard Oil's representative in Antwerp and who was himself a former member of the German diplomatic service. At the time of Austrian Chancellor Dollfuss's assassination in 1934, Rieth had been German Minister in Vienna, where he had so conspicuously involved himself with the murderer of the unfortunate Chancellor that Hitler was obliged to recall him to Berlin in disgrace. On his arrival in New York, Rieth settled in to a $600-a-month apartment in the Waldorf-Astoria, where he proceeded to meet various German officials and also to make free and frequent use of the name of Standard Oil's chairman Walter Teagle as a business reference. Rieth's movements were carefully shadowed, and Stephenson soon discovered that the main purpose of his visit was to negotiate the sale to Germany of the Standard Oil Hungarian subsidiary company known as M.A.O.R.T. (short for *Magyar Amerikai Olajipari Resveny Tarsasag*). He also discussed with Standard Oil representatives the question of patent agreements between his company and I.G. Farben. Then he was in touch with the Inter-American Abstention Committee, an Axis inspired body which had recently been formed with the avowed purpose of hindering all types of American aid to Britain, with particular emphasis on lend-lease.

Stephenson lost no time in initiating action on the already familiar lines. On May 24, 1941, a detailed account of the facts of Rieth's secret mission appeared in the *New York Herald-Tribune* beneath the following headlines:

NAZI AGENT IS HERE
ON SECRET MISSION
SEEKS OIL HOLDINGS

Rieth, Figure in Dollfuss
Case, is after Standard
Properties in Hungary

Used Teagle's Name
To Win Confidence

Oil Man Denies Knowing
Him; Secondary Errand
Is to Fight British Aid

The story was repeated in other newspapers and caused the expected furore. While Standard Oil said they had never heard of Dr. Rieth, the gentleman in question shut himself up in his hotel apartment where he told press reporters on the telephone that he was in the United States 'on purely personal business'. Eventually the F.B.I. arranged with the Immigration Department to arrest him for giving false information in his visa application, since he had ostensibly entered the country as a tourist. He was removed to Ellis Island where he was held until he was eventually deported along with the German and Italian consular officials who left on the s.s. *West Point* when their offices were closed by President Roosevelt in July, 1941.

Professor Medlicott, the official war historian of the British economic blockade, has paid a warm tribute to the manner in which 'some of the British Security officers'—his euphemism for Stephenson and B.S.C.—in conjunction with the British censorship authorities and Mr. R. J. Stopford, the shrewd Financial Counsellor at the British Embassy in Washington, helped to prepare American public opinion to meet the consequences of the President's orders 'freezing' Axis assets and other measures affecting American financial and commercial interests before Pearl Harbour. 'These had all worked for nearly a year in close but discreet harmony with the United States

Treasury, the Department of Justice, the F.B.I., and other authorities, and had given much-needed information about Axis financial interests and activities in the United States and Latin America. As a result the United States Government was ready when the time came to expose any protest against active measures of economic warfare that might be made by Americans acting in the Axis interest.'[1]

3

Another aspect of secret economic warfare, with which Stephenson and his organization were closely concerned, was the prevention of smuggling, particularly contraband of small bulk but high value.

The professional smuggler often displayed great ingenuity in attempting to get his illicit possessions through the British economic blockade. Preventive measures consequently had little chance of success unless they were equally ingenious and well organized. With the smugglers, sea-chests and lockers with false bottoms were commonplace. A special wireless transmitter was smuggled into Buenos Aires after three trips across the Atlantic disguised as a piano. The Spaniards in Venezuela placed diamonds inside their tubes of toothpaste. One report sent to Stephenson stated that platinum was smuggled in the drinking cups of canary cages; another showed that this commodity was conveyed in the form of thin wires placed behind postage stamps on ordinary letters. One man was caught by the Argentine customs carrying twenty pounds of the metal in powdered form inside a belt next to his skin. Another man, who was arrested in Gibraltar for carrying shipping intelligence, had a camera loaded with platinum concealed inside the vessel's radio installation. Platinum was also smuggled out of Argentina hidden in tins of peaches, and once a quantity was found in the stock pot in the cook's galley. Smugglers melted down gold coins and, having fashioned them into the semblance of brass buckles, fitted them to their trunks. In short, smuggling to beat the blockade was an art.

Neutral shipping was the main medium which the smugglers used, and before Pearl Harbour this included not only Spanish,

[1] Medlicott. II, 45.

Portuguese and Vichy French vessels, but also ships of the United States merchant navy. Since it was nearly always the small but valuable items in which the smugglers were interested, many members of ships' crews became regular couriers who regarded the business as a useful means of increasing their normal income. In 1941 particularly, the classified advertisement columns of newspapers in both North and South America were full of notices inserted by seamen who were willing to 'serve as a contractor' or 'undertake important confidential commissions, etc.'

It was with the object of combating this growing threat that Stephenson conceived a scheme of ships' observers. The essence of the scheme was this. One or more observers would be appointed among the crew of every neutral ship sailing from the United States and Latin American ports. The observer would be met by a British intelligence agent in all the principal ports at which the ship called. He would report any suspicious events he had observed on the voyage, Nazi or Communist talk among the crew, evidence of smuggling, possible Axis agents among passengers or crew, radio messages sent out after a British ship had been encountered, possible German supply vessels or raiders and similar matters. The reports would be despatched at once to Stephenson in New York for action. In some cases the ship-owners themselves offered their assistance, because the scheme increased the security of their vessels and they also knew that their co-operation facilitated the passage of their ships through British control points. By May, 1941, there were 145 such observers operating in ships on regular Atlantic, Caribbean and Pacific routes.

Many of the observers were masters of their vessels, and they often provided valuable intelligence which extended beyond the field of smuggling with which they were primarily concerned. The captain of one Portuguese steamer, for instance, became adept at extracting mail from unsuspecting passengers. 'We may soon be intercepted by a British cruiser', he would announce over the ship's public address system, 'so anyone with mail for safe keeping should hand it in to the Captain's office to avoid its being seized by the British.' On one voyage no less than eighteen letters with important information were obtained in this way and subsequently turned over to Stephenson's New

York office for examination before being sent on. Some of the Vichy French agent Musa's letters were obtained in this way and used by Stephenson in his campaign against Vichy's undercover activities in the United States. Another alert observer, on board a Spanish vessel, succeeded in obtaining surreptitiously the sealed sailing orders which had been given to the captains of all Spanish ships by the Chief of the Naval General Staff in Madrid and were to be opened only in the event of Spain going to war. These elaborately sealed orders were secretly opened, photographed, the seals replaced apparently intact, and the documents replaced without the knowledge of the captain or anyone else on board except the ship's observer.

Many of Stephenson's observers were able to report upon events in neutral and enemy countries which their ships visited. They were employed to spread rumours and disseminate anti-Axis propaganda literature. They provided information on seamen suspected of carrying contraband or verbal messages from one port of call to another for Axis agents. Thus the reports regularly furnished by the ships' observers enabled a complete list of suspect seamen to be compiled in Stephenson's office. The list was made available to various shipping agencies in the United States and resulted in many undesirable seamen being paid off and not signed on again by the owners.

Since it involved the use of agents by the British in U.S. ports and U.S. ships, the Ships Observer Scheme was inevitably a cause of friction with the American authorities. Eventually, towards the end of 1941, Stephenson agreed to hand over the operation of the scheme, so far as concerned United States vessels and ports, to the U.S. Office of Naval Intelligence, while retaining the observers on neutral vessels calling at Latin American ports. This arrangement provided for the exchange of the information gained and on the whole worked satisfactorily for the remainder of the war.

Brazil and Venezuela were the principal South American sources of industrial diamonds, used in the armament, aircraft and machine tool industries. In 1943, Stephenson's agent in Rio caused the arrest of a large diamond smuggling ring and, although its members were subsequently released on payment of stiff penalties to the Brazilian authorities, the incident caused a sharp fall in the price of diamonds throughout Brazil and did something to check the business. But it could never be completely controlled. In Venezuela it likewise flourished, but probably not to the same extent as in Brazil owing to the more co-operative attitude of the Venezuelan police and customs. There the prompt action taken by Stephenson's agent in Puerto Cabello on one occasion, when he flew in advance of a suspect passenger travelling by sea to Trinidad, resulted in the British authorities in that port seizing diamonds to the value of $30,000 and eliciting information which implicated the Spanish Minister in Caracas in the diamond smuggling racket to such an extent that his government was obliged to withdraw him at the request of the Venezuelan authorities.

Although never carried out on such a large scale as the smuggling of diamonds, platinum was very much the most important commodity involved in these activities, since Germany needed it badly for aeroplane magnetos and other war purposes and was obliged to rely on the mines in Colombia and Ecuador after the Russian supply had been cut off following Hitler's invasion of the Soviet Union in June, 1941. Considerable quantities of the commodity were carried on the Italian L.A.T.I. planes and could not be prevented until the airline, as will shortly be seen, was closed down as the result of Stephenson's action. Otherwise platinum was carried by sea mainly from Buenos Aires, Rio and Caracas to Lisbon where German agents paid £30 an ounce (later rising to £80) for it as against the official market price of £9 in the United States. Here is a typical report from Stephenson's agent in Buenos Aires:

> Our observer on s.s. *Cabo de Buena Esperanza* reports Muricia Abaroa Aldecoa carries considerable quantity of platinum in his cabin . . . Metal in tins of biscuits hidden inside panelling at head of Aldecoa's bunk.

A few days later another message reached New York to the effect that the platinum had been removed by the would-be smuggler and was now hidden in barrels of manzanilla wine in the Captain's cabin. The platinum was stated to have been previously stored in the apartment of the mistress of the ship's chandler in Buenos Aires.

Action was always taken on such reports as this. Sometimes it was successful, sometimes not. Besides platinum and diamonds, the principal articles smuggled were essential oils, which were used by New York perfumiers such as Madame Schiaparelli. Determined attempts were made by west-bound passengers from Lisbon to get supplies through the blockade. On one occasion, due to prior information from Stephenson, a Vichy Frenchman named Pierre Massin was interrogated by the security control at Bermuda and admitted having 750 grammes in his possession. The information from New York suggested that Massin was carrying considerably more, but he strongly denied this suggestion, pointing to his Legion of Honour ribbon in his coat and declaring: 'I give you my word as a French officer that this is all I have with me.' However a rigorous search of his cabin and personal belongings revealed three canisters each containing 750 grammes hidden in a bag of golf clubs, and six more in a box behind his trunk.

Other suspicious articles were lighter flints, radium, postage stamps and butterfly trays. The latter, which were made in Brazil, provided a constant puzzle for the British authorities, with their brightly coloured butterflies' wings arranged in variegated patterns underneath the glass tops of the trays. The Germans bought them in vast quantities, but neither Stephenson, nor for that matter anybody else, was ever able to determine whether their interest in them was economic or merely aesthetic. On several occasions suspects were reported to be handling these trays, and one of Stephenson's reliable agents reported that he had seen some women employees in the German Embassy in Rio taking the trays to pieces and putting them together again. Thus it looked as if they were possibly being used as a means of communicating secret messages. After much difficulty, and after many trays had been smashed in transit, some specimens reached London intact and were examined with great care. But nothing of any consequence was discovered and the mystery of the butterfly trays remains unsolved to this day.

Ultimately the problem of smuggling merged with the problem of counter-espionage and in the long run had to be solved by one and the same method. The Germans were as anxious to obtain shipping information as they were to procure strategic materials, and in their endeavour to achieve these aims they used parallel organizations which were sometimes controlled by the same agents. Eventually, after the United

States had entered the war and all the principal Latin American states except Argentina and Chile had either declared war against the Axis powers or else broken off diplomatic and commercial relations with them, Stephenson's organization was able to co-ordinate all the information on the subject both from American and British sources through regular shipping summaries of all Argentinian port traffic. The final result would be cabled to London, Buenos Aires and any other interested stations, so that before the ships reached Trinidad a decision could be taken as to their interception, search and interrogation and detention of suspect passengers and crews. This system proved so effective that by the middle of 1944 there was no longer much chance of smuggled goods reaching Germany from South America.[1]

4

The 'special operations' branch of Stephenson's organization was established early in 1941 with particular reference to Latin America. At that time every American republic was neutral in the war with the Axis powers, who were seeking to extend their influence by every means in that part of the hemisphere. In 1941, Congressman Martin Dies, chairman of the House Committee which had been appointed 'to investigate un-American activities', declared that Germany had about one million potential soldiers in South America 'organized in companies and battalions'. The danger of a German invasion of South America could not be ignored. Already, in June, 1940, a plot had been discovered in Uruguay, headed by a German citizen named Arnulf Fuhrmann, to take over the country in fifteen days and to mobilize a thousand 'combatants' from Argentina for further operations. Fuhrmann had pretended that he had written the outline plan of his projected *coup* as a joke, but the Uruguayan authorities paid no attention to this excuse and had locked him up. The American Ambassador, who was informed of the details, had immediately cabled President Roosevelt that 'unless the United States acted effectively and without delay there was genuine danger that countries like Uruguay might fall under Nazi domina-

[1] Further details will be found in Medlicott, II, 160–9, 427–35.

tion'.[1] The President did not feel that he could spare any warships to patrol the coast as the Ambassador would have liked, but he did empower Edgar Hoover and the F.B.I. to organize a secret intelligence service in Latin America to be responsible for the collection of all non-military intelligence, in other words counter-espionage. In this work, particularly in its initial stages, Hoover's men were greatly helped by Stephenson's agents, and the two organizations worked together most harmoniously in the field.[2]

The F.B.I. had no authority to engage in 'special operations', so that in this sphere Stephenson operated exclusively. Among other devices which he created at this time was a small establishment within the framework of his existing organization for the purpose of fabricating letters and other documents. It had a laboratory in Canada which was set up, with the aid of the R.C.M.P., under cover of the Canadian Broadcasting Corporation, whose general manager at this time was Stephenson's old friend Gladstone Murray. It was staffed by one or two experts and was called Station M. This name may have been suggested by the first letter of the surname of the officer who played a leading part in the station's nefarious activities. This was Eric Maschwitz, better known as a lyric writer ('The Nightingale sang in Berkeley Square') and the author of several successful musical comedies (*Balalaika*, *Carissima*). 'The operations with which I was concerned under a genius known as "Little Bill" were many and curious', Maschwitz has written in his autobiography, briefly and discreetly alluding to this strange interlude in his theatrical career. 'In them I was associated with . . . an industrial chemist, and two ruffians who could reproduce faultlessly the imprint of any typewriter on earth. I controlled a chemical laboratory in one place, a photographic studio in another. My travels took me to Canada, Brazil and Bermuda. . . .'[3]

For the fabrication of letters Station M needed, first, technical facilities in the form of special inks and paper; secondly, a certain amount of accurate information about individuals

---

[1] De Jong. 112, 118. Fuhrmann and five of his associates received prison sentences ranging from five to twelve years.
[2] Whitehead, 181-2, 189.
[3] Eric Maschwitz. *No Chip on My Shoulder* (1957) pp. 144-5.

derived from a variety of sources; and lastly, planned inventive-
ness which had to be based on a sound appraisal of political
conditions in the various target areas. In helping to fulfil these
requirements the various British censorship stations rendered
invaluable service, particularly Bermuda. They agreed to unseal
and reseal bags of transit mail in order to insert suitable propaganda matter. They forwarded such relevant raw material as
inks and the private papers carried by passengers on ships and
aircraft which had been impounded by the Travellers' Censorship. They supplied specimens of the epistolary paraphernalia
used by government departments, banks and other official and
quasi-official bodies in various countries, such as writing-paper
and rubber stamps, and also specimens of private stationery
which might be useful for purposes of reproduction. And they
reported fully on individuals whom they considered possible
subjects for propaganda or personal incrimination.

For example, three letters signed 'Anna' and posted in
Santiago, Chile, provided the evidence which caused a Nazi
military court to condemn to death a notorious Czech traitor
and collaborator in German-occupied Czechoslovakia. In
these letters truth and fiction were nicely blended. They
mentioned facts about the man's private life which he was
unable to deny, such as the 'strange death of your brother Jan'
and references to his former wife who was half-Jewish. On the
other hand they contained palpably incriminating statements
which he was unable to explain—indeed they were genuinely
incomprehensible to him—such as 'I looked after the marks
but could do nothing with the zlotys', 'Father caught 75 fish on
Wednesday the 17th, Brother was not well but caught 82' and
'I was knitting Karl a sweater in which I had to use 14 skeins
of wool, each 60 feet long although two were only 28 feet'.

The German censors who examined the letters in the first instance reported that the writer was obviously attempting to communicate with the man in plain language code and that he was
probably an allied agent. This he most emphatically denied, but
the circumstantial evidence was against him. He had no idea
who Anna was, he said. But he could not argue away the clear
indications that he was in regular communication with her. How
else could she be familiar with the details of his private life? Nor
could he give any satisfactory and convincing explanation of the

frequent references to numerals. It only remains to add that the Germans were not at all favourably impressed by his unsupported protestations of innocence—even in the torture chamber. They executed him, and in so doing lost a useful collaborator.

Station M worked on the principle that its output must be good enough to defy the most microscopic examination and chemical tests. Thus it produced no document which was not an exact imitation down to the smallest detail of what it purported to be. The necessary technical processes were handled by a panel of experts, whose services were for the most part given free. Among them were Canada's leading authorities on the manufacture of special inks and paper.

In the field of political warfare Station M devised a letter-writing campaign which was designed to cause alarm and despondency in enemy circles. The letters were genuine; the writers were recruited individually among enemy or neutral nationals opposed to the Axis and they did not know that they were contributing to a general scheme. They were asked to correspond regularly with friends and business acquaintances in occupied Europe, and to include in their letters subversive material (prepared by Station M), which revealed lack of faith in the Axis cause but was not so obviously defeatist in tone as to seem like deliberate propaganda. Risk of endangering addresses was kept to a minimum. Letters were often purposely sent to persons who were known to have died and to businesses which had closed down. So long as the subversive material was seen and noted by the enemy censors and other authorities it served its purpose.

On the assumption that the Nazis were undertaking letter-writing propaganda of their own, a campaign was planned to discredit information coming from Germany. It would have been easy to apprise friendly newspapermen in the United States of the available evidence. But Stephenson considered that this would be inadequate and he decided that something more substantial should be fabricated. The operation was entrusted to Station M. For example, the well-known columnist Walter Winchell received a letter which had been mailed in Lisbon by an American merchant seaman, who wrote that during a voyage from Hamburg to Brazil he had been told by a Jewish refugee that all approved correspondents in Germany with abroad were sent a monthly bulletin of news by Dr.

Goebbels's Information Ministry to be included in their letters to foreign destinations. To substantiate this story the sailor enclosed a printed slip which he told Winchell had been inserted by the German censorship in another letter which had been returned to the sender because it had not included the stock sentences, and also a copy of the current bulletin in which these sentences were supposedly issued in Hamburg.

It was a fine story for Winchell and his twenty-five million readers. Neither he nor they had ever heard of Station M.

Then there was the game called Vik which had been invented by an exiled Polish professor, who was a sabotage and 'resistance' expert during the First War. Described as 'a fascinating new pastime for all lovers of democracy', its purpose was to subject Fascists and Fascist sympathizers in neutral countries to continuous petty persecution with the object of wasting their time, confusing their affairs, fraying their nerves and getting them into trouble with the local population. Vik was launched by means of cheaply and anonymously printed booklets in English, French, Spanish and Portuguese, which were the product of Station M and were distributed with the greatest secrecy by Stephenson's agents throughout South America. Allied sympathizers were urged to organize themselves into teams and to compete with one another by scoring points for every annoyance or embarrassment caused to the Nazis and their confederates. 'From this it will be seen that a skilfully played game of Vik can be not only a source of great amusement to the players but also a real and valuable contribution to the Democratic Cause', to quote from the accompanying instructions. 'Remember that our Axis friends are highly susceptible to ridicule!'

Here are some of the petty persecutions which Station M recommended. A Nazi could be telephoned at all hours of the night and when awakened could be apologetically assured that it was the wrong number; the air could be made to disappear mysteriously from his motor tyres; shops could be telephoned on his behalf and asked to deliver large quantities of useless and cumbersome goods—payment on delivery; masses of futile correspondence could reach him without stamps so that he was constantly having to pay out small sums of money; his girl friend could receive anonymous letters saying that he was suffering from an unpleasant disease or that he was keeping a woman and six children in Detroit; he could be cabled apparently genuine instructions to make long, difficult and expensive journeys; a rat might die in his water-tank; his favourite dog might get lost; and street musicians might be hired to play *God Save the King* outside his house all night. With a little thought, Station M advised, it should be possible to invent at least five hundred ways of persecuting a victim without the persecutor compromising himself. 'Remember always', the instructions concluded, 'that in playing Vik you are in your own small way acting as a fighting member of the forces of Democracy. Therefore be silent, secret and discreet.'

This campaign of ridicule was supplemented by the publication and surreptitious distribution of abusive pamphlets attacking certain named Nazis. A typical example was the one concerning Werner Von Levetzow, head of chancery in the German Embassy in Rio, who had previously been 'tipped' as the next German Ambassador to Argentina. He was a tall half-German, half-Danish 'superman' type, who had married a Krupp heiress shortly after the outbreak of war. This lady had left him not long after their arrival in Brazil, alleging that he was impotent. Naturally he was the butt of many jests in Rio society on his supposed lack of virility, and Station M exploited them to considerable advantage. 'Gentlemen', the pamphlet warned male Brazilians. 'This man, this Levetzow, is capable of robbing you of your money, your businesses and your country, but NEVER of your wives . . . HE CANNOT.'

After the majority of Latin American republics had either entered the war on the allied side or else had severed diplomatic relations with the Axis powers, following the Rio Conference in January, 1942, Station M's scope as a subversive agency was necessarily reduced. Besides the activities already mentioned, it had one major achievement to its credit in the production of documents which resulted in the closing down of the Italian L.A.T.I. airline in Brazil, thus stopping the biggest gap in the economic blockade.

5

In early May, 1941, Stephenson received a message from Edgar Hoover which called for immediate action in a field in which the F.B.I. was precluded from operating by the terms of its presidential directive. The message was to the effect that Major Elias Belmonte, the violently pro-Nazi Bolivian Military Attaché in Berlin, was in touch with Nazi elements in Bolivia and understood to be planning a *coup* with the object of over-throwing the existing pro-British Bolivian Government of President Peñaranda and establishing a pro-Axis military dictatorship. Hoover added that President Roosevelt was most anxious that evidence confirming this report should be obtained and put into his hands as quickly as possible. The President's anxiety may have been due to the fact that Bolivia was the main source of supply for the United States of wolfram, the ore from which the ferro-alloy tungsten was derived for use in steel and arms manufacture, and he may have feared that such a *coup* might stop the flow of this essential commodity to American factories.

Stephenson immediately sent off one of his agents to Bolivia to investigate and plan a counter-offensive. This agent happened to be the present writer, so that he can speak with first-hand knowledge of subsequent events. As a matter of courtesy—and also as a precaution in case the agent should become em-barrassingly involved with the local authorities—the British missions in the various territories which Stephenson's emissary was to traverse were officially informed of his visit, though not of its precise purpose. For some reason, possibly due to bad flying weather, he had to spend twenty-four hours in Peru, where curiosity prompted the British Minister to invite him to lunch. On arrival at the Minister's house in a suburb of Lima, the agent discovered that he was by no means the only guest, and that the lunch party was a large mixed one, consisting mainly of prominent Peruvian gentlemen and their wives. Unfortunately, the Minister was neither so tactful nor so dis-creet as his colleague in La Paz. (After his retirement on pension, he joined a well-known firm of turf accountants in London, being the only former diplomat of the British foreign service ever to have done so.) No sooner was the assembled company seated at table than His Britannic Majesty's repre-sentative turned to the present writer and addressed him in tones which reverberated round the dining-room: 'So you've come down here to do a secret-service job, have you?'

The unfortunate individual to whom this question was directed did his best to laugh it off. But the uncomfortable impression remained that it would be news in the German Legation by tea-time, so that he was relieved when he got on his way next morning without mishap and was flying over the Andes to the remote Bolivian capital beyond Lake Titicaca.

The news he was able to gather in La Paz confirmed the original report. It appeared that Major Belmonte in Berlin had been corresponding with the Bolivian Chief of Staff and hinting at a possible *coup*; also that the Government had got wind of this and was seriously concerned that Belmonte and his Nazi friends might attempt to bring off the *coup* under the guise of a military revolt. He further learned that the plans for the revolution were expected to be despatched from Berlin in a German diplomatic bag consigned in charge of a courier to the German Legation in La Paz. Chance put him in touch with a Bolivian who claimed to have some knowledge of Belmonte's project, and having collected all the information he could from this source and made certain other arrangements he returned to New York and reported the results of his journey to Stephenson.

Meanwhile, as a precaution, Stephenson had cabled one of his agents in Brazil instructing him to watch out for any courier carrying a German diplomatic bag which was believed to contain 'incriminating documents of the highest importance', and arriving at Recife by the Italian airline L.A.T.I. and going on to La Paz. The agent was told to possess himself of the documents or, if the courier should succeed in evading his attentions, to report his movements so that appropriate action could be taken elsewhere. In due course, the agent reported that a German named Fritz Fenthol had arrived ostensibly representing the German Potash Syndicate and had left by air for Buenos Aires whence it was thought he planned to go on to Bolivia. Contact was established with his female secretary who for a monetary consideration supplied Stephenson's agent with particulars about Fenthol and his correspondence. According to her he was carrying a sealed letter addressed to the German Minister in La Paz. Shortly afterwards the local F.B.I. representative informed his headquarters that he understood that a British agent had managed to deprive Fenthol of a letter while he stood next to him in an overcrowded lift in the German Bank Building in Buenos Aires.

At the beginning of July, Stephenson informed London that the United States authorities were aware that some document had been intercepted and were 'expressing anxiety that no time should be lost in passing it on to them if of interest'. London replied asking for the full text of the document which was 'most urgently required here by the highest authorities'. This was followed up a few days later by another message to the effect that the Bolivian Government should be warned as soon as possible so that it might suppress the *coup* 'if and when it takes place' and suggesting that the matter should be discussed frankly with the Americans who should be left to take action if they so wished. ('In any case absolutely essential that warning should be conveyed with least possible delay.')

Stephenson thereupon handed the letter to Hoover, who was as gratified as he was surprised to receive it. Hoover at once passed it to Secretary of State Cordell Hull, and Hull lost no time in sending a photostat copy to the Bolivian Government, after he had shown it to President Roosevelt.

The letter, typewritten in Spanish and bearing what was apparently Belmonte's signature, was dated June 9, 1941, from the Bolivian Legation in Berlin, and addressed to Dr. Ernst Wendler, the German Minister to Bolivia. 'Friends in the Wilhelmstrasse tell me that from information received from you,' so ran the letter, 'the moment is approaching to strike in order to liberate my poor country from a weak government and from completely capitalist tendencies. I go much further and believe that the *coup* (*el golpe*) should take place in the middle of July since I consider the moment to be propitious.' Cochabamba and Santa Cruz were to be the focal points of the projected rising, since they were centres which were 'most friendly to us' and 'have prepared conditions and have organized our forces with skill and energy'. The writer went on to state that he knew from some of his friends that meetings were being held without being molested by the authorities and that 'nightly exercises' were taking place. ('Further, I see that large quantities of bicycles have been collected which will facilitate our movements by night since motor cars and trucks are too noisy.') The writer also discussed the plans for his arrival by air to take over with the help of the younger elements in the army. ('Actually I have always counted upon them and it will be they, without doubt, who will give me the greatest co-operation in the important work which we are carrying out in my country.') The keynote was rapidity of action. The letter continued:

> We must rescind the wolfram contract with the United States, and also substantially modify the tin contracts with England and the United States. The handing over of our airlines to the interests of Wall Street is treason to our country. . . . Since my short time in the government service I have been fighting this. Why hand over the country to the United States on the pretext of financial aid which will never come? This irritates me! The United States will follow their age-long policy: to obtain great advantages in exchange for small loans, and even these loans we are not allowed to administer. Bolivia does not need American loans. With the triumph of the Reich, Bolivia needs work and discipline. We must copy, though on a modest scale, the great example of Germany since National Socialism came into power. . . .
>
> I hope that the last word will be my flight from here to complete the work which will save Bolivia in the first place, and afterwards the whole South American continent, from North American influence. The other countries will quickly follow our example, and then with one sole ideal and one sole supreme leader, we will save the future of South America and will begin an era of purification, order and work.

The repercussions, when this remarkable communication reached La Paz, were spectacular. On July 19, the Government proclaimed a nation-wide state of siege and the police began to round up suspect Nazi sympathizers. At the same time Dr. Wendler, the German Minister, was declared *persona non grata* and ordered to leave the country. A number of prominent Germans and Bolivian civilians, including the local correspondent of the German Transocean news agency, and thirty officers headed by the chief of the Cochabamba military zone were arrested. Four anti-British and anti-American newspapers were suspended, while the others obediently reproduced the incriminating Belmonte letter. Belmonte himself was struck off the Bolivian Army List. The Chief of Staff identified the signature on the letter as genuinely belonging to the Military Attaché.

As a reprisal the Bolivian Chargé d'Affaires in Berlin was given seventy-two hours to leave Germany. Two days later, in Washington, Sumner Welles, Acting Secretary of State in Hull's absence, announced that the American Government had assured Bolivia of full assistance if her expulsions of the German Minister resulted in 'an international incident' and had informed the Government in La Paz that Dr. Wendler would not be permitted to enter the United States.[1]

That the Germans were engaged in subversive activities in Bolivia at this time there can be no doubt, although the precise extent to which Major Belmonte was involved in them must remain a matter of conjecture. Two-and-a-half years later the Germans got their own back in some measure when they helped to engineer the military revolution which overthrew President Peñaranda and his Government on December 20, 1943, and installed Major Gualberto Villarroel as President, in spite of the fact that the new Bolivian Government remained aligned with the Allies in consequence of United States pressure.[2]

However unorthodox the methods by which the Belmonte letter was obtained, the operation must be judged by its results. It probably averted a revolution, it certainly caused the expulsion of the German Minister and the arrest of a number of dangerous men and it prepared the climate for the Pan-American conference at Rio six months later when Bolivia and eighteen other Latin American states broke with the Axis powers and banded themselves together in a common scheme of hemisphere defence—'the decision that saved New World unity', as Sumner Welles called it.[3]

6

The next major operation carried out by Stephenson in South America resulted in the closing down of the L.A.T.I. airline.

During the earlier part of the war, Brazil was the terminus for one of the most important Axis channels of communication with the American continent. The Italian L.A.T.I. planes,

[1] *New York Times*, July 20, 21, 22, 24, 1941.
[2] Hull. II, 1388.
[3] Welles, 101.

which flew regularly between Europe and Brazil, carried German and Italian diplomatic bags, couriers, agents, diamonds, platinum, mica, chemicals and propaganda films and books. The Brazilian Government had no desire to obstruct the service. One of the Brazilian President's sons-in-law was the chief technical director of the line, and there were many other powerful Brazilians who had an interest in preserving its landing rights. In spite of the protests of the U.S. State Department, an American oil company supplied L.A.T.I. with fuel. L.A.T.I. constituted the biggest gap in the British economic blockade. Consequently the Special Operations Executive (S.O.E.) in London was anxious that something drastic should be done about it, and Stephenson was instructed accordingly.

The plan which he and his S.O. advisers devised in New York was to convey to the Brazilian Government a compromising letter which purported to have been written by someone in authority in the L.A.T.I. head office in Italy to an Italian executive of the company in Brazil and which would result in the cancellation of the company's concession to operate its transatlantic route. Stephenson's agents in Brazil immediately got to work and after some weeks they succeeded in obtaining a genuine letter which had been written by the L.A.T.I. president General Aurelio Liotta from the company's Rome headquarters. In forwarding it to New York, they suggested that the fabricated letter should be addressed to the airline's general manager in Brazil, Commandante Vicenzo Coppola.

The experts in Station M were able to simulate exactly the style of writing paper, the engraved letter-head and the form of type used by General Liotta. Fortunately Station M had been able to secure the small amount of straw pulp paper that was available in North America and was an essential requirement in the proposed operation. The embossing was copied with microscopic accuracy, and a typewriter was rebuilt to conform to the exact mechanical imperfections of the machine upon which the General's secretary had typed the original letter.

The deception letter was then composed in Italian, microphotographed and the microfilm sent to Stephenson's chief agent in Rio. It was dated October 30, 1941, from the Rome head office of L.A.T.I. 'There can be no doubt that the fat little man (*il grassocio*) is falling into the pocket of the Americans',

General Liotta was supposed to have written, 'and that only violent action on the part of our green friends can save the country. Our Berlin collaborators, following their recent conversation with the representative in Lisbon, have decided to intervene as soon as possible.' As this might result in a new concession being granted to the German airline Lufthansa, Commandante Coppola was urged to take immediate steps to make new friends among 'the green gentlemen' and do his best to see that all L.A.T.I.'s existing privileges were guaranteed under the new régime. ('Discover whom they would propose to nominate as Minister for Air and make the best dispositions possible.') The Commandante was enjoined to exercise the utmost discretion. 'The Brazilians may be, as you have said, a nation of monkeys (*una nazione di scimmie*)', the letter concluded, 'but they are monkeys who will dance for anyone who will pull the string.'

The 'fat little man' was of course easily recognizable as the Brazilian President Getulio Vargas, while the 'green gentlemen' were the Integralists, the political party opposed to Vargas, against whom they had already attempted a revolution with German help. As far as the President himself was concerned, the letter contained personal insult, abuse of his country, scorn of his foreign policy and suggested encouragement of his political enemies. Those who expected that this combination would cause the President to react vigorously were not disappointed.

Immediately after he had received the microfilm of the letter, Stephenson's man in Rio arranged for a burglary to take place in Commandante Coppola's house, at which a bedside clock and other articles were stolen. Coppola called in the police, and the affair received some publicity, which was what the British agent intended, as he wished it to become generally known that there had been such a burglary. Next, a sub-agent, who was a Brazilian, approached a reporter of the American news agency Associated Press and, after pledging him to the strictest secrecy, told him that he had taken part in the burglary of Coppola's house. He then went on to say that he had found something that looked interesting and proceeded to show the reporter a micro-photograph which he said he had found among the Commandante's belongings. When he saw that it was apparently a miniature reproduction of a letter from the

President of L.A.T.I. and had noted its contents, the A.P. man came to the conclusion that the original had been considered too dangerous to entrust to the ordinary air mail and that it had been smuggled into the country in this form to prevent possible interception. He immediately took it to the American Embassy and showed it to the Ambassador, who ordered some enlargements to be made. When he had examined these, he decided that the letter which had been micro-photographed was genuine, and he forthwith turned over the film and enlargements to President Vargas.

The infuriated President reacted exactly as Stephenson had hoped and surmised that he would. He immediately cancelled all L.A.T.I.'s landing rights in the country and ordered the arrest of the general manager of the line. The Commandante attempted to flee the country, having previously drawn one million dollars from the bank, but he was caught while attempting to cross the Argentinian frontier. He was later sentenced to seven years' imprisonment and his funds confiscated, while L.A.T.I. was fined $85,000 for infringing Brazilian law. Their aircraft and landing fields and all their maintenance equipment were likewise taken over by the Brazilian authorities and the crews and other Italian personnel were interned.

A few weeks later, when Brazil broke off relations with the Axis, the view was expressed in the U.S. Embassy in Rio that General Liotta's letter had been 'one of the main factors in persuading President Vargas to turn against the enemy'. The letter itself was not published, no doubt because of the insulting remarks it contained. But the Americans generously decided to share the secret with the British intelligence representative who worked in the British Embassy. A member of the American diplomatic staff accordingly produced a copy of the letter which he assured the Englishman had been 'pinched' by U.S. Intelligence. Stephenson's agent expressed fervent interest and admiration and warmly congratulated his colleague on his work.

Brazil's break with the Axis, which occurred during the Rio Conference, was of the greatest importance to the Allies, particularly the United States. Under a policy of strict neutrality Brazil could not have offered the use of her ports as she did to the U.S. South Atlantic Fleet as bases for patrolling the area. Another result was that the United States was permitted to build airfields in northern Brazil, which were essential for the transport of troops to Africa and the Mediterranean. Without these airfields the invasion of Algeria and Morocco could not have taken place in 1942.[1]

Of all the Latin American states the Germans were most strongly entrenched in Argentina, where it was estimated that there was upwards of a quarter of a million people of German descent besides 50,000 German nationals.[2] From this it might be supposed that Argentina presented extensive opportunities for 'special operations'. But this was not so, largely for political reasons. Pro-British feeling among the masses was combined with anti-Yankee sentiment, while the army was to a great extent pro-German as to some extent was the Government. Also, in spite of repeated prodding from Stephenson and other British official representatives as well as State Department, the Foreign Office in London kept delaying an announcement condemning Argentina's pro-Axis policies. Economics were also involved, since Britain's meagre civilian meat ration depended upon Argentine shipments of beef. Indeed the question of Argentina provided one of the biggest stumbling blocks in Anglo-American relations during the war. While Cordell Hull referred contemptuously to the 'petty commercial advantages of a long-term bargain with a fascist Government', a Foreign Office spokesman described the operation of dealing with the Secretary of State as like attempting to deal with Mr. Gladstone in his old age.[3] (Hull prided himself on being a Gladstonian Liberal.)

For these reasons the actions of Stephenson's agents in the Argentine were mainly confined to the combating of smuggling and the dissemination of propaganda. However, they did succeed in intercepting one remarkable piece of German intelligence which concerned Hitler's post-war plans for Latin America. This was a secret airlines map of the future showing how the sub-continent was to be divided and its territories redistributed between Argentina, Chile, Brazil, a new state called New Spain (consisting of Colombia, Ecuador, Venezuela

[1] Welles, 124.
[2] De Jong, 225.
[3] Woodward, 417.

and Panama, including the Canal Zone), and a colony comprising British, Dutch and French Guiana to be ruled by the France of Laval. The entire area was covered by a comprehensive airline network with a transatlantic terminal at Natal.

Nazi map of South America, purloined from a German courier

Handwritten notes in German referred to 'fuel reserves for transatlantic fuel' and the possibility of Mexican participation in the supply of fuel.

The map was purloined from a courier of the German

Embassy in Rio, when he met with an accident and his despatch case disappeared. As soon as he received it in New York, Stephenson gave it to General Donovan, who had by this date become Co-ordinator of Information, and Donovan passed it on to President Roosevelt. The President was greatly impressed and brought it into a speech which he made at a Navy Day dinner in Washington on October 27, 1941, and which was broadcast to the nation. 'Hitler has often protested that his plans for conquest do not extend beyond the Atlantic Ocean', the President declared. 'I have in my possession a secret map, made in Germany by Hitler's Government—by planners of the new world order. It is a map of South America and part of Central America as Hitler proposes to organize it. Today in this area there are fourteen separate countries. The geographical experts of Berlin, however, have ruthlessly obliterated all the existing boundary lines and have divided South America into five vassal States bringing the whole continent under their domination. And they have also so arranged it that the territory of one of these new puppet States includes the Republic of Panama and our great life-line, the Panama Canal. This map makes clear the Nazi design, not only against South America but against the United States itself.'[1]

A few weeks later, one of Stephenson's sources in touch with the German Embassy in Buenos Aires reported that after the President's speech Hitler had asked the Ambassador, Freiherr Edmund Von Thermann, for an explanation of the leakage. Apparently there were only two copies of the map. One was in the Fuehrer's safe; the other was with Von Thermann. A fierce inquisition took place inside the Embassy and eventually the blame was attributed to a former Civil Attaché and Nazi Party leader named Gottfried Sandstede. He was accused of having allowed the map to be copied.

The discovery of the map was convincing proof of Germany's intentions in Latin America and came as a considerable shock to all good citizens of the United States. Well might the President say, 'we have taken our battle stations'.

[1] *The Times*. October 29, 1941.

# CHAPTER VI

## C. O. I. AND O. S. S.

### I

UNTIL within a few months of Pearl Harbour, there was no domestic organization comparable with Stephenson's in the United States. The Army and Navy Departments had their own separate intelligence branches, while the F.B.I. was responsible for the collection of, and where necessary taking action upon, counter-espionage information. But until the middle of 1941 there was no body like B.S.C. which was engaged in co-ordinating and evaluating secret intelligence and planning propaganda and 'special operations' overseas which could be put into immediate execution should the United States become involved in the war. Stephenson frequently reverted to this theme during the early days of his association with Colonel Donovan; and, as already indicated, he made arrangements for Donovan to see everything he wished relating both to S.I. and S.O. activities during his visits to England. Indeed during his second visit on which Stephenson accompanied him as far as London at the end of 1940, Donovan had been shown the various S.O. stations in England by Air Commodore Sir Frank Nelson, an experienced business man and capable organizer, whom Dr. Dalton had appointed as the first chief of the Special Operations Executive (S.O.E.).[1] At this time, and indeed throughout the war, the propaganda division (S.O.1)—later to be known as the Political Warfare Executive (P.W.E.)—operated from Woburn Abbey, the Duke of Bedford's country house in Bedfordshire, while the physically offensive special operations staff (S.O.2) had their headquarters in an inconspicuous office in Baker Street,

---

[1] Sir Frank Nelson was succeeded as head of S.O.E. by Sir Charles Hambro, and later by Major-General Sir Colin Gubbins, who had previously been in charge of operations and training in S.O.E.

London, which was to become widely known, at least by name. (*'Qu'est-ce qu c'est, cette Baker Street?'*, one Frenchman was overheard asking another in a Paris café just after the liberation.)

When Donovan returned from his tour of the Middle East and the Balkans in April, 1941, and reported at the White House, President Roosevelt began to give serious consideration to the question, for by then Lend-Lease had begun to function and Congress was becoming accustomed to the idea of intervention on Britain's side on an increasing scale. At the beginning of May, 1941, Stephenson cabled London that he had been 'attempting to manoeuvre Donovan into accepting the job of co-ordinating all U.S. intelligence'. To this end he enlisted the help of various individuals whom he knew to have influence with the White House, notably the playwright Robert Sherwood, who wrote many of the President's speeches, and the sympathetic and pro-British John Winant, who had succeeded the defeatist Joseph Kennedy as United States Ambassador in London early in 1941. At the same time, he had to create a favourable climate of opinion in London where, although Donovan had made an excellent impression during his visits, there was some reluctance on the part of some of the older intelligence departments to his being provided with secret information of the kind with which Stephenson was already beginning to feed him, so that Donovan could pass it on to the President and further stress the need for establishing undercover services in the United States like Stephenson's own. 'At one point', Stephenson later admitted in characteristic language to Whitney Shepardson, one of Donovan's close associates, 'it became necessary to enlist the support of the great man at the top (Churchill) who fortunately for me, always saw eye-to-eye with me on all matters relating to British-American exchanges, and in his immediate entourage were some who kept an eagle eye on any suggestion of deviation from the great man's orders in relation to our friend Donovan by the departments concerned. General Ismay was one and Desmond Morton was another. Nonetheless, had it been comprehended in that building with which you are familiar (S.I.S. headquarters) to what extent I was supplying our friend with secret information to build up his candidacy for the position I wanted to see him achieve here, there would have been such a cold blast of horror sweep through it that on your first visit to it you would have had to find your way over one corpse after another!'

The idea that he himself should direct the new agency that Stephenson envisaged did not at first appeal to Donovan, nor was it by any means a foregone conclusion that he would be offered the appointment. Yet from Stephenson's point of view he was obviously the man for the job. In the first place, he had the confidence of the President, of the Secretary of State and of the heads of the Service departments. Secondly, he had made some study of, and had given considerable thought to, the conduct of secret activities. Thirdly, he had all the requisite vision, energy and drive to build swiftly an organization of sufficient size and importance ultimately to play an effective part in the war. Lastly, he had shown himself willing to co-operate fully with Stephenson and his B.S.C., and the value of his co-operation, as has already been seen, had been abundantly proved. But no decision was made for some time, despite what Stephenson called 'various pressures' being brought to bear in the White House.

Eventually, on June 18, 1941, Donovan was received by the President and after a long discussion agreed to accept the office of Co-ordinator of Information (C.O.I.), his duties to include the collection of all forms of intelligence and the planning of various covert offensive operations. He was to hold the rank of Major-General and to be responsible only to the President.

In telegraphing this news to London on the same day, Stephenson remarked that Donovan had accused him of having 'intrigued and driven' him into the job. 'You can imagine how relieved I am after three months of battle and jockeying for position in Washington', Stephenson added, 'that our man is in a position of such importance to our efforts.'

Donovan's appointment as head of C.O.I. was formally announced by Presidential executive order on July 11, 1941. His duties were defined as follows:

> To collect and analyse all information and data which may bear upon national security, to correlate such information and data, and make the same available to the President and to such departments and officials of the Government as the

President may determine, and to carry out when requested by the President such supplementary activities as may facilitate the securing of information important for national security not now available to the Government.

This directive was necessarily vague in its terminology, since the President obviously could not be specific about the functions of an agency which had been created to undertake work both secret and potentially offensive in character. But, in fact, Donovan had been entrusted with responsibility not only for collecting intelligence but for co-ordinating this product with preparations to conduct 'special operations' and subversive propaganda. 'Thus C.O.I. was in effect, if not in name, the American counterpart of B.S.C.', Stephenson later recalled, 'and that night I took five instead of four hours' sleep.'

Collaboration began at once. Together Donovan and Stephenson drew up the initial plans for his agency, both as regards establishment and methods of operation. On August 9, 1941, Stephenson informed London that Donovan's organization was rapidly taking shape, that central offices in Washington had been established with a nucleus of staff and were functioning, and that understanding with the Chiefs of Staff seemed satisfactory and that Donovan felt confident of their co-operation. ('He now has several competent assistants who seem to know their job and have a practical outlook.') His two mainstays among his small original staff were Colonel Edwin Buxton, a newspaperman from Providence, R. I., and a friend from First World War days—he had helped with Donovan to found the American Legion in 1919—and James Murphy, who had been his law clerk when Donovan was Assistant Attorney General. Ned Buxton became the chief executive officer of C.O.I., while Jimmy Murphy took charge of the counter-espionage side, although Murphy used to say with a cheerful grin that the real reason why Donovan had brought him into the new organization was 'to keep the knives out of his back'. The other prominent recruit to C.O.I. in the early days was Robert Sherwood, the playwright and friend of President Roosevelt, who was made responsible for propaganda to foreign countries, although (as will be seen) he did not remain throughout with Donovan. To secure the closest possible day-to-day liaison between B.S.C. and C.O.I., Stephenson set up a branch office in Washington to which he attached experienced officers in all branches of secret activity, and Donovan in turn established a branch office in New York. ('He now has working apparatus here and in Washington and should be able to safeguard secret documents.')

'The establishment of C.O.I. five months before Pearl Harbour represented more the promise than the fact of American participation in secret activities abroad', Stephenson has recalled. 'From my point of view C.O.I. was essentially a long-term investment and for some time it required more help than it could give in return. This was inevitably so for four main reasons. First, there was the obvious one that C.O.I. was a pioneer body lacking previous experience of its own on which to draw. Secondly, so long as the United States remained at peace his position was equivalent to Hoover's—that is to say, he had responsibility without power. For example, to conduct propaganda operations he needed, among other things, control of short-wave radio facilities; but broadcasting in the United States is a private industry and before Pearl Harbour the owners of short-wave stations could not be ousted or even coerced. In many instances they refused to follow C.O.I. directives or to use C.O.I. material. Again, the State Department was reluctant to risk identification with an agency whose covert functions clearly endangered United States neutrality and, despite initial promises to the contrary, largely withheld its co-operation which was needed to provide "cover" for his operations abroad.

'Thirdly, the older agencies, whose collaboration he required to carry out his task of correlating intelligence, were at the outset somewhat hostile, partly through scepticism regarding the worth of an organization which was of necessity staffed by amateurs, and partly through fear that C.O.I. would infringe on their own prerogatives. This was particularly true of the F.B.I., and to a lesser extent of the Service Intelligence Departments. Lastly, when war came, Donovan was expected by the Chiefs of Staff, as justification for the continuance of his organization, to produce immediate results despite the fact that he had insufficient time and authority to make adequate preparations.

'It is fair to say that it is likely that, if Donovan had not been able to rely upon B.S.C. assistance, his organization could not have survived. Indeed, it is a fact that, before he had his own operational machinery in working order, which was not until several months after Pearl Harbour, he was entirely dependent upon it.'

For example, before Pearl Harbour and for several months thereafter, the bulk of C.O.I.'s secret intelligence was supplied by Stephenson's organization from its various sources. Two short-wave radio services, which B.S.C. controlled—one for broadcasting to Europe and the other to the Far East—were made available to C.O.I. immediately after Pearl Harbour and, in Stephenson's words, 'they were the foundation of all American short-wave propaganda'. Experts in every branch of secret activities, intelligence, counter-espionage, subversive propaganda, communications, and 'special operations' of all kinds were put at Donovan's disposal. 'From the beginning the British gave him full co-operation', Stewart Alsop and Thomas Braden have written in their account of the Donovan organization. 'They told him how they trained their men, what weapons they had, and how they communicated with the resistance. Breaking the precedent of centuries, they even sent a man over to sit down with Donovan and explain the workings of British espionage.'[1] In fact, C.O.I. officers of all divisions, as well as C.O.I. agents, were in the beginning trained at the B.S.C. school in Canada, which was set up near Toronto in December, 1941. The school served as a model for Donovan's own training schools which were later established under the guidance of B.S.C. instructors.

'In short', said Stephenson afterwards, 'B.S.C. had a considerable part in the upbringing of the agency of which it was in a sense the parent. The effort thus expended would have been wasted only if C.O.I., to carry the metaphor a little further, had never grown to man's estate. In fact, from the story of O.S.S. which follows, it is evident that it proved extremely rewarding, for not only was Donovan's organization eventually equipped to discharge its responsibilities, but since it owed much to our efforts it was inevitably prepared to work in fullest accord with us.'

[1] Stewart Alsop and Thomas Braden. *Sub Rosa* (1948), pp. 16-17.

2

Mention has been made of the two short-wave radio services controlled by Stephenson's organization. Their broadcasts together covered Europe, Africa, the Middle East and the Far East, and were propaganda media of the utmost importance for the British war effort.

First, there was Station WRUL, which transmitted from Boston and was the only short-wave radio station in the United States which was not run for profit. It had been founded by a rich industrialist, Walter Lemmon of International Business Machines and was supported by several big charitable institutions. Its avowed purpose was to spread international goodwill. Its transmitting power—50,000 watts—was unsurpassed by any other station in either the Americas or Germany. It had a large international audience, linked together in an Association of Listeners in thirty different countries, and it received an average of a thousand letters every week. Its listening public in France alone was estimated at 400,000 strong at this period. Before Stephenson took a hand in its affairs, the greater part of its transmitting time was devoted to programmes in English, which were of course not in any way supervised by propaganda experts.

Through a series of trusted intermediaries Stephenson now began to supply Station WRUL with everything it needed to run a first-class international programme worthy of its transmitting power and declared policy. B.S.C. subsidized it financially. Stephenson's organization recruited foreign news editors, translators and announcers to serve on its staff. It furnished it with material for news bulletins, with specially prepared scripts for talks and commentaries, and with transcribed programmes. As a result, its foreign language broadcasts rapidly increased in number, variety and influence. By the middle of 1941, Station WRUL was virtually, though quite unconsciously, a subsidiary of the Stephenson organization, sending out covert British propaganda in twenty-two different languages and dialects, including Armenian, Iraqi, Senegalese and Serbo-Croat. It was controlled by a network of intermediaries drawn mainly from the various minority groups with which B.S.C. maintained contact. Material was prepared in Stephenson's offices and then passed to the different intermediaries, who gave it to the station, which regarded itself as completely independent, even if its independence was merely nominal.

In this way Stephenson was able to implement high policy directives from London. For instance, when the British Ambassador in Madrid, Sir Samuel Hoare, asked for an immediate propaganda campaign designed to convince General Franco and his advisers that Spain would be the loser if she entered the war on Germany's side, Stephenson was able to carry out the Ambassador's request. The broadcasts in Spanish were written by B.S.C. agents and the campaign successfully launched in June, 1941.

Thus it happened that an American radio station with an unsullied reputation for impartiality was, for many months during the most critical period of the war for the British, unknowingly harnessed to the task of broadcasting British propaganda on a scale almost comparable in quantity of output with the official B.B.C.'s Overseas Service. But to maintain control over it through intermediaries was no easy matter. None of the instructions, which B.S.C. issued covertly, had the backing of any legally constituted authority, and even Donovan, when he had officially entered the propaganda picture with the backing of the President's directive in July, 1941, had no power in practice to dictate the policy of what was after all a privately owned and administered American concern. Then the station management, docile enough at first, became more and more difficult to handle as WRUL's importance and influence increased. The directors sometimes rebelled against the tendentious tone of the broadcasts. And Lemmon himself, enjoying his new-found power, was often given to displays of self-assertiveness, which required tactful treatment. The enemy too was aware of the station's value as a propaganda channel and attempts were made to sabotage some of the transmissions, particularly of Free French material, by substituting other material on the ground that the broadcasts of the former were 'indistinct'. Close and constant watch had to be kept on personnel and every broadcast had to be carefully monitored by Stephenson's communications experts.

So long as the United States remained neutral, neither WRUL nor any other short-wave station could be taken over by any Government agency. Thus Donovan, who had been officially made responsible by the President for developing propaganda broadcasting for his country, lacked sufficient authority to discharge this responsibility on his own initiative. The most he could do was to supply the stations with material direct and hope that they would broadcast it. In fact, they usually refused to accept the C.O.I. directives, including ironically enough WRUL. Thus Donovan failed to commandeer the facilities of the short-wave stations for C.O.I., although he was able to use WRUL jointly with B.S.C. under cover. This was the situation within a fortnight of Pearl Harbour.

Incidentally, President Roosevelt always took a much greater personal interest in propaganda as an arm of warfare than did the British Prime Minister. For example, he was impressed by a series of broadcasts attacking Germany put out from London by Sir Robert Vansittart, the Chief Diplomatic Adviser to the Foreign Office and subsequently published under the title, *Black Record*. On November 7, 1941, while the United States was still neutral, he sent the texts of these broadcasts to Donovan with a memorandum saying he thought it could 'be used with great effect by some broadcaster in this country if it were edited to suit our needs'. Obviously, the more British or British Empire sentences or paragraphs could properly be deleted. 'Also,' the President went on, 'I am inclined to think that the efforts to prove that the Germans have always been barbarians for a thousand years as a nation go a bit too far. Those paragraphs should be stressed which place the blame on the German people for following utterly destructive leadership —and on the leaders themselves.' He hoped that Donovan would read 'this little record' because, as he had suggested, if it were revised for the American public, 'it might do a lot of good'.[1]

The significance of WRUL lay not so much in its value to Stephenson and his organization as an instrument for directing British propaganda abroad—although that was important—as in the fact that it represented a ready-made broadcasting

[1] Roosevelt. III, 399.

service for American propaganda, which was available to Donovan and, as we have already seen, was in fact turned over to him as soon as the United States entered the war. Had B.S.C. not undertaken this work, Donovan's political warfare activities after Pearl Harbour would have been considerably retarded, for while WRUL as such would have been at his disposal, he would have found in it little more than a powerful transmitter to serve his immediate needs. All the necessary preparations in the way of recruiting and training news editors, translators, commentators and announcers would still have been ahead of him. As it was, he had the nucleus of an excellent propaganda broadcasting service at his command.

Similar considerations applied to Station KGEI, owned and operated in San Francisco by the General Electric Company and the only station broadcasting to the Far East at this time. (Its service was later supplemented by KWID, a 100 kilowatt station erected as the result of Stephenson's endeavours.) Control of KGEI was obtained for Stephenson's organization through the general manager and chief engineer of the Malaya Broadcasting Corporation who happened to be on leave and represented themselves as interested in securing rebroad- casting rights for the Singapore radio station. In turn material put out by Stephenson and broadcast from KGEI and KWID was picked up and rediffused both by the Malaya Broadcasting Corporation from Singapore and the Australian Broadcasting Commission from Australia.

As in the case of WRUL, Donovan assumed control of the two services broadcasting to the Far East immediately after Pearl Harbour, while Stephenson and his agents, who had largely staffed both services, remained to give what advice and other help they could, as it were, from the side lines. It was a most harmonious and, from the point of view of the Anglo- American war effort, a most productive liaison in every field it covered, although, as will be seen, Donovan later had to hand over much of his responsibility for the conduct of political warfare to another agency. This was so for three basic reasons. First, C.O.I. had access through B.S.C. to essential material which Donovan's incipient organization could not obtain elsewhere. Secondly, C.O.I. regarded B.S.C.'s knowledge and experience, rightly or wrongly, as one of their most valuable assets. Thirdly, the individual officers concerned liked and trusted each other personally. They worked side by side, not as representatives of rival organizations inspired by mutual feelings of rivalry, but as friends in a common endeavour. They were devoted to a practical association, which had already accomplished much and might well accomplish more. In some ways it was a pity that in the all-important sphere of propaganda this co-operation was destined soon to be terminated.

One typical example may be given of how this co-operation worked in the short period between Pearl Harbour and the handing over by Donovan of his responsibilities for overt propaganda to the newly created U.S. Office of War Information six months later.

In May, 1942, when Japan had overrun much of south-east Asia, and Japanese pride and self-assurance were at their height, Rear-Admiral Toshio Matsunaga broadcast a talk in Japanese from Tokyo to Japanese-speaking audiences abroad, describing a tour of inspection which he had made through Japan's newly acquired empire. He described how captured American sailors were employed on forced labour, apparently in the Celebes. He said:

> They are engaged in the work of filling up the holes in the airfields. They are engaged in comparatively easy jobs. There are many who are suffering from hunger because they are not used to the Japanese type of food, and there are some who get very lazy because of the extreme heat. Those who do not do their part are beaten by the Japanese guards . . . Those who are hard to handle are severely beaten with a rope which is similar to the rope used by sailors. Because of the pain the lazy American prisoners continue the work with painful expressions on their faces.
>
> Indonesian natives who have lived on this island for a long time watch these prisoners, and they say: 'Previously these white people treated us like animals, and now the Japanese soldiers, who have faces similar to ours, are beating them' . . . The natives are very thankful for what the Japanese soldiers have done for them.

The broadcast was withheld from publication by the American authorities under the terms of the U.S. Army's official plan for psychological warfare against Japan, drawn up by Colonel Solbert and his assistants in the Psychological Warfare Branch and approved by the Chiefs of Staff, Secretary of War Stimson and Secretary of State Hull. The Army's reasons for opposing the publication of Japanese atrocity stories were that it might provoke reprisals against Japanese and Japanese-Americans in the United States and might encourage the Japanese to engage in further brutalities; also that the Army wished to fight the war 'according to the civilized rules'. There was a hint too that racial questions, which might induce negroes to side against the white peoples, were to be played down.

Stephenson's Japanese experts pointed out that this policy was based on a misconception of Japanese psychology. It failed to realize that Japanese atrocities were intended to destroy the prestige of the white races, as indeed Matsunaga had acknowledged in his reference to the Indonesian spectators, and as was shown by the fact that British prisoners-of-war were being worked as coolies in Malaya, where there was no shortage of native coolie labour. As Stephenson pointed out, by publicizing these facts, in conjunction with strong protests, the United States Government might help both to alleviate the conditions described and to undermine Japanese morale, since the Japanese are sensitive to 'loss of national honour'. These atrocities, he argued, could easily be interpreted as a proof that the Japanese Army was a gang of savage barbarians. Protests against them would, therefore, impel the liberal elements in Japan to curb the excesses of the militarists and ultimately to accept the allied propaganda theme that Japan was being betrayed by the military clique in power. It was recalled that, after the detailed reports of the looting of Nanking in 1937 were published in America, the officers responsible were punished, and that conditions in Hong Kong had noticeably improved after Mr. Eden's recent denunciation of Japanese methods in the House of Commons.

These arguments, vigorously repeated by Donovan in the official circles concerned, eventually had the desired effect, and the U.S. Office of Facts and Figures was directed to release this and similar stories. Whether they had much immediate effect in Japan is doubtful, although they unquestionably shocked the civilized world and provided substantial evidence which was subsequently used to good effect in the various Japanese war crimes trials.

### 3

At first sight it might be thought that the secret intelligence with which Stephenson was supplying the Donovan organization and so playing a vital part in its development was at the expense of Hoover and the F.B.I. Such was not the case. In 1941, the F.B.I. received from Stephenson's staff no less than one hundred thousand reports, memoranda and other documents on a wide range of subjects going considerably beyond security and counter-espionage matters. However, as has already been indicated, Hoover keenly resented Donovan's organization from the moment it was established, since he feared that its interests would clash with those of the F.B.I., particularly in Latin America, and his resentment was inevitably extended towards its British collaborators. At the same time Stephenson was faced with an acute problem in the shape of the introduction in Congress of a legislative instrument known as the McKellar Bill.

The publication of the Dies Committee's report on enemy subversive activities in the United States, as well as the discoveries which the F.B.I. was making on the same subject, had led to the promotion of a measure by Senator Kenneth McKellar, a Democrat from Tennessee, which transferred the registration of foreign agents in the United States from the State Department to the Department of Justice; it also amended most drastically the conditions under which these agents would in future be required to register. Under the impact of Pearl Harbour, the measure was quickly rushed through Congress, and at the beginning of 1942 it was sent to the White House. In its original form, the Bill made no distinction between agencies friendly to the United States and others, and generally it called for the production of all details of the work being carried on and how their funds were expended.

Immediately after the Rio Conference in January, 1942, which resulted in greatly increased opportunities for United States participation in secret activities in Latin America, a joint committee was set up for the purpose of co-ordinating all Anglo-American intelligence operations in the Western Hemisphere. At its first meeting, which was attended, among others, by Stephenson, Hoover, and Assistant Secretary of State Adolf Berle, the latter proposed that Stephenson's organization should maintain liaison with no United States Government agency other than the F.B.I. Stephenson naturally resisted this proposal and went on to refer to the McKellar Bill, pointing out that in its present form it would mean the end of British Security Co-ordination inasmuch as the Bill provided that 'all records, accounts and propaganda material used by foreign agents (whether allied or neutral, secret or open) would be liable to inspection by the U.S. Government authorities at any time'. Berle replied, with a knowing smile, that this was regrettable but that it was now too late to effect any modifications in its provisions since the Bill was already on the President's desk awaiting signature. The truth is that for some time past the State Department had been aware of some of the detail of B.S.C.'s secret activities, and there is no doubt that Berle, who had a hand in drafting the measure in its original form, hoped that the Stephenson organization would be unable to continue to function as hitherto.

Stephenson left the meeting before it was over and went immediately to the C.O.I. offices on Constitution Avenue, where he put the position bluntly to Donovan. If the Bill became law as it stood, then Donovan's organization might well fold up too. Donovan thereupon picked up the telephone and asked to be put through to the White House. He then requested an immediate appointment with the President which he was given. The result of this interview was that he was able to persuade Roosevelt not to sign the Bill unless and until it was modified to allow adequate safeguards for Stephenson's interests and those of B.S.C. A few days later the President vetoed the measure and sent it back to Congress. A month later the Bill was reintroduced in a form which relieved B.S.C. from the crippling provisions as to the compulsory disclosure of its records. It became law on May 1, 1942.

In its final legislative form the McKellar Act expressly exempted from registration, at the discretion of the Attorney-General, the agencies of foreign governments, 'the defence of which the President deems vital to the United States', provided that such agent engaged 'only in activities which are in defence of the policies, public interests or national defence, both of such government and of the defence of the United States and are not intended to conflict in any of the domestic or foreign policies of the Government of the United States'. As a result Stephenson merely had to file with the Department of Justice a statement of particulars of B.S.C.'s security functions and a list of its personnel. However, the fact remains that, if it had not been for Donovan's timely intervention with the President, no allied mission in the United States which did not enjoy diplomatic status could have carried on effectively, and not only B.S.C. but also C.O.I. would have ground to a halt.

Thus it was established that the F.B.I. no longer had the monopoly of collaboration with British Intelligence. The fact that it had lost this monopoly was inevitable not only on account of the emergence of Donovan's organization but because, with the end of neutrality, the U.S. Service Intelligence Departments G.2 and O.N.I., also insisted on maintaining direct liaison with B.S.C. But Hoover had shown himself more than once as the kind of man who does not bow easily to the inevitable—that was at once his strength and his weakness—and it took a long while to convince him that he could not succeed in his determination to exclude the British organization from contact with other U.S. intelligence agencies.

Berle, on the other hand, proved more immediately amenable. Stephenson had many discussions with him during 1942 in an effort to temper his hostility, and the Assistant Secretary of State was eventually persuaded that, to quote his own words, 'as a realist he owed it to his country to find the best method of co-operation with Great Britain'. Berle's changed attitude eventually provided the means of convincing Hoover that his efforts to control B.S.C.'s activities to his own exclusive ends were futile. In June, 1943, a memorandum from the Department of Justice to Stephenson, which bore unmistakable signs of having been composed at Hoover's instigation, directed B.S.C. to desist from direct contact with the U.S. armed services and maintain liaison only through 'approved military channels'. Since Stephenson knew that this directive was diametrically opposed to the wishes of U.S. services intelligence, he referred it to General George Strong, head of G.2, who stated unreservedly that 'he was not prepared to submit to an F.B.I. censorship'. At a subsequent meeting with Adolf Berle, which was attended by all the interested parties, Berle endorsed General Strong's view and ruled that B.S.C. should be allowed to decide for itself to which agencies and in what manner it would transmit its information. Hoover had no choice but to accept this ruling, and thereafter, it is only fair to add, he abided by it without apparent demur.

Fortunately the period of strained relations between B.S.C and the F.B.I. did not prove lasting. But while it endured, for about eighteen months, it was a difficult time for Stephenson, who was endeavouring to sustain Donovan and at the same time continue to supply Hoover with the security and counter-espionage intelligence which his organization still needed from British sources. For some months Hoover was convinced that Stephenson was deliberately withholding information from his agents in Latin America and passing it to Donovan instead. This was not true, but the impression remained and rankled. Sometimes, too, information on a particular subject in which he was interested had to be obtained from London, and the delays and consequent reminders sent before it was eventually forthcoming proved irksome to both parties. A good deal of correspondence, for example, took place by reason of Hoover's request for information on Communist activities in Britain before he was provided with the complete and exhaustive survey which he desired.

Incidentally this latter information was to come in useful when Hoover frustrated a plan of Donovan's to send a mission to Moscow in exchange for a mission from the Soviet Security Service (N.K.V.D.) to Washington. 'I think it a highly dangerous and most undesirable procedure to establish in the United States a unit of the Russian Secret Service which has admittedly for its purpose the penetration into the official secrets of various government agencies', Hoover wrote at the time to the President's close friend and adviser, Harry Hopkins. 'The history of the N.K.V.D. in Britain showed clearly that the fundamental purpose of its operations there was to surreptitiously obtain the official secrets of the British Government.'

The proposed exchange of intelligence missions was consequently blocked by the White House, although the author of *The F.B.I. Story* is perhaps not altogether correct when he states that it was 'quietly forgotten by everyone concerned'.[1]

Despite these difficulties, the former close and friendly relations between Stephenson and Hoover were eventually restored and no bitter feelings remained on either side. Even during the period of estrangement, the agents of their respective organizations often worked together in complete harmony, notably in Latin America, and some of the best results in joint counterespionage work during the whole of the war were obtained by their collaboration during this period, as is presently described. None realized the value of this collaboration in the interests of United States security more than Hoover himself and he was to express it in the most generous terms to Stephenson when the war was over. 'I have indeed regarded as fortunate the circumstance which brought about the establishment of your office in New York City and especially the designation of so capable and experienced a man as yourself to direct it', Hoover wrote to Stephenson on February 21, 1946. 'In retrospect I feel that the direct liaison between our organizations which resulted contributed immeasurably to our efforts in protecting the internal security of this country and to what I regard now as successful intelligence coverage achieved by your organization and ours on behalf of the whole Allied war cause.'

4

The period during which Donovan's growing organization largely depended upon Stephenson for material aid lasted, broadly speaking, until the summer of 1942 when C.O.I. was transformed into an essentially military body and was placed under the U.S. Chiefs of Staff, being henceforth known as the Office of Strategic Services (O.S.S.). This period was one of seemingly incessant and bustling activity in the Constitution Avenue offices and also at the General's house in Georgetown where, like Stephenson, he rarely slept for more than four hours a night, but unlike the quiet Canadian he did most of his entertaining at

[1] Whitehead, 199–200.

breakfast. This was the hour when he was particularly receptive to new ideas. 'Why don't you do it?', he would say to a breakfast-time visitor who had come up with some ingenious suggestion, or else 'Sure, let's give it a try'. The man would then go off and hire the necessary staff of assistants and soon they would all be working as a more or less self-contained unit under the Donovan umbrella. On other occasions, when he was particularly impressed, he would say, 'I'm going to handle this myself' or 'Leave it all to me'. Naturally he could not handle everything himself. Usually Buxton or Murphy would succeed in persuading him to hand over the execution of it to them, while letting him continue to keep a finger in the pie.[1]

If General Donovan did not shine as an administrator or personnel manager—it was said that he ran O.S.S. like a country editor, not like a business man—there can be no doubt about his creative energy and the magnetism of his personality which ultimately inspired the devotion of a war-time staff of 12,000 men and women. Nor were there any doubts about the reputation for personal courage he had won as a commander in the earlier world conflict. One dark night in Washington, he was involved in a nasty motor accident, when he was run down by an allegedly drunken driver and his legs were badly injured. (His friends said that the driver was an F.B.I. agent.) Next day he had a luncheon engagement in New York with Dr. Bruening, the former German Chancellor, and Mr. (now Sir) John Wheeler-Bennett, an expert on German political and military history. He was determined not to postpone the meeting, as many others would have done in the circumstances; it may be noted that Donovan was then nearly sixty years old. On the way to New York by train, he had his legs put into splints. He went on to the St. Regis Hotel, where he arrived punctually, spoke and listened well and was very courteous. He did not mention his accident and gave no sign that he was in pain, beyond (what was most unusual for him) drinking two stiff brandies-and-soda. He then returned to Washington.[2]

On June 13, 1942, a Presidential Executive Order abolished C.O.I. and established two new agencies in its place—the Office of War Information (O.W.I.) and the Office of Strategic

---

[1] Alsop and Braden, 20–22.
[2] Sir Robert Bruce Lockhart. *Friends, Foes and Foreigners* (1957), p. 10.

Services (O.S.S.). The former, under Elmer Davis, fifty-two-year-old author, ex-Rhodes Scholar at Oxford and news analyst for the Columbia Broadcasting System, was entrusted with responsibility among others for all overseas propaganda, except what was known as 'black', that is covert propaganda. The latter, headed by Donovan, was entrusted with C.O.I.'s remaining functions, in the words of the President's order, 'as an operating agency of the Government under the direction and supervision of the Joint Chiefs of Staff'. From these functions the Western Hemisphere was expressly excluded. In other words, in its designated field, O.S.S. was responsible for collecting secret intelligence, preparing intelligence appreciations for the Joint Chiefs of Staff (Research and Analysis), and the planning and execution of secret operations (including covert propaganda such as the operation of clandestine radio stations), and the training of personnel for 'strategic services'. In this context the term 'strategic services' was defined as 'all measures (except those pertaining to the Federal programme of radio, press, publication and related foreign propaganda activities involving the dissemination of information) taken to enforce our will upon the enemy by means other than military action, as may be applied in support of actual or planned military operations or in furtherance of the war effort'.

Incidentally, it was Robert Sherwood who was responsible for the amputation of the propaganda section from the body of C.O.I. He had organized this section, known as the Foreign Information Service (F.I.S.), in order to plan and carry on psychological warfare outside the Western Hemisphere, and having chosen to quarrel with Donovan on a point of principle —he wished his section to remain civilian in character, while Donovan would have it subject to military discipline like the rest of O.S.S.—Sherwood now transferred himself and his department to the Elmer Davis organization, where F.I.S. became the Overseas Branch of O.W.I.[1] As Stephenson put it, 'he and Donovan wasted no time on farewells'. Nor was the rupture ever healed. This was unfortunate, since both men were figures of outstanding ability and both were intimately concerned with the conduct of political warfare, so that smooth working and efficiency at military headquarters were not

[1] Sherwood. II, 935–6.

improved by the differences between the two bosses, especially as the differences were taken up much more violently by their respective subordinates. This developed into a major row when O.S.S. claimed the right to conduct all propaganda in the military field of operations. It could only be settled by General Eisenhower, as Supreme Commander of the Allied Expeditionary Force in Europe, creating an integrated Anglo-American Psychological Warfare Branch (P.W.B.) of his own, responsible for the execution of propaganda in the theatre of operations and taking its political guidance from P.W.E. and the Overseas Branch of O.W.I., the two civil agencies in London which were headed respectively by Sir Robert Bruce Lockhart and Robert Sherwood. Happily Sherwood and Lockhart worked together in the closest harmony.[1]

From the outset, before Sherwood moved to London, his relations with Stephenson were invariably most cordial. 'There goes a man of that rare treasure, complete integrity', Stephenson remarked to the present writer late one evening as we were walking along Fifth Avenue and espied Bob Sherwood in the distance. 'There are not many around, especially in the present rat race.'

Unfortunately for Stephenson his official relations with Sherwood were interrupted in the summer of 1942 soon after the creation of O.W.I. This was due to the arrival in Washington of a Political Warfare Mission from London in the charge of the Hon. (later Sir) David Bowes-Lyon, a brother of the English Queen and uncle of the present Queen. Bowes-Lyon proposed to take over all Stephenson's overt propaganda work, of which the most important was broadcasting to the Far East. This proposal was at first resisted by Stephenson on the ground that its implementation must impair, not only the continued operation of liaison arrangements which were working smoothly, but also the whole conception of co-ordinated activity which Stephenson's organization had successfully achieved in the United States. Sherwood was anxious that they should continue as heretofore and he sent a message to Ambassador Winant in London asking him to request the Foreign Secretary, Anthony Eden, in this sense. He was assured that they could be. But

[1] Bruce Lockhart, *op. cit.* p. 101. See also his *Comes The Reckoning* (1947), at p. 196.

inevitably they were not, since the decision had been taken to effect a separation of functions similar to that which had taken place between O.S.S. and O.W.I. In August, 1942, Stephenson accordingly handed over all the relevant files to Bowes-Lyon and gave him what help he could in the recruiting of expert staff, which Bowes-Lyon urgently needed. In an extraordinarily laudatory obituary notice which appeared in *The Times* on the occasion of Bowes-Lyons's death in 1961, it was stated that he was 'perfectly equipped' for the task of establishing relations with parallel American agencies on a basis of confidence. 'Both the work he did and the way he did it gained substantial praise from those on both sides of the Atlantic who had anything to do with those particular matters,' wrote *The Times*.[1] Be that as it may, Stephenson was certainly not included among these admirers, and the fact remains that relations between the Bowes-Lyon mission and O.W.I. were never so close or so productive as were the previous arrangements with B.S.C.

At the time the President issued his order establishing O.S.S., Donovan and Stephenson both happened to be in London, and it was therefore the occasion for discussions concerning the future collaboration between O.S.S. and its British equivalents. Out of these discussions there emerged agreements for pooling results of activities independently undertaken in the field of secret intelligence and for a working partnership in the field of special operations. Furthermore, O.S.S. decided to follow the example of British Intelligence by establishing a separate division to undertake counter-espionage overseas. So far as Europe was concerned, it was agreed that this work should be administered jointly by British Intelligence and O.S.S. from London.

Thenceforward Anglo-American collaboration in all forms of secret activity outside the Western Hemisphere steadily increased in scope and value, and while its emphasis inevitably shifted from the United States to the various operational theatres, notably after the launching of the 'Second Front' in Europe in 1944, Stephenson's organization had the responsibility throughout of maintaining and co-ordinating liaison with O.S.S. headquarters in Washington.

[1] September 14, 1961.

It is unnecessary to describe the detailed working of this relationship. But some examples of its product deserve mention. The material which B.S.C. purchased (for S.O.E. in London) from O.S.S., either by cash payment or under Lend-Lease, included much that could not otherwise have been obtained. For instance, in May, 1943, Stephenson informed Donovan that three ships with a minimum range of 3,000 miles, a maximum speed of at least 16 knots and four tons of cargo space were required by the British for 'irregular operations' in the North Sea. Donovan persuaded the U.S. Navy to release three 100-foot submarine chasers in the belief that they were to be used in exclusively O.S.S. activities. They were fitted with anti-aircraft and other guns, depth charges and radar, and they were transferred to Britain with great secrecy four months later. Throughout the winter of 1943–44 they ran the German blockade to and from Sweden, carrying not only valuable material such as ball bearings but also a number of important passengers. Similarly a varied assortment of commodities was obtained from the U.S. War Department, including radio equipment, cameras, landing craft and kayaks. On the other hand, B.S.C. supplied Donovan's requirements during the period when these were not in production in the United States. It provided him, for example, with all the equipment he needed for action preparatory to Operation Torch, as the allied invasion of North Africa was known. This included some out-of-the-way items such as land mines disguised as camel dung.

The underground needed money, and many delicate stratagems for the purchase of foreign currency had to be devised and carried out in the greatest secrecy. Here Donovan's friendly collaboration proved invaluable in securing large quantities of this commodity, often at very short notice. For instance, after protracted negotiations with the U.S. Treasury and the Bankers' Trust Company, B.S.C. joined with O.S.S. to pay the dollar equivalent of nearly two million Portuguese escudos. This money was required by British secret agents in Europe, and it was made available to them through the Lisbon office of José Bensaude, the Portuguese shipowner.

On another occasion, over eighteen million dollars in denominations of $50 and $100 were secretly transferred from

New York to London for the use of British and allied underground organizations in Europe before and during the eventual
invasion. It involved a long series of manoeuvres beginning in
1942 and ending two years later, which were known to no one
outside B.S.C. and S.O.E. in London except Donovan and two
of his officers. If the transaction had been direct between the
British Treasury and the U.S. Treasury, too many people
would have been involved with the result that both the despatch
and destination of the notes might easily have become known
to the enemy.

To get round this difficulty, it was arranged that one of
Donovan's men should draw the notes in large denominations
from the U.S. Treasury. The first three millions were accordingly
sent over in February, 1943, and were exchanged for one, two
and five dollar bills, collected in Britain. After being shipped
back to the U.S.A., these were paid into the U.S. Treasury by
the same O.S.S. officer who had drawn the large-denomination
notes.

Everything went smoothly until it became apparent that,
while one million dollars in large notes could go into one bag,
thirty or forty bags were required for the same amount in small
notes. Consequently, because of the shortage of aircraft cargo
space and the fact that ships in convoy took anything up to four
weeks to make the Atlantic crossing, the flow from east to west
did not equal the flow eastward. After the first three millions
had been drawn from the U.S. Treasury, despatched to London
and distributed to the Poles, for whom nearly half the total
was earmarked, the U.S. Treasury turned off the tap and
refused to allow any more drawings until a down payment
was made. In the cold eyes of the Treasury there was a limit
to an overdraft, even when the client was a U.S. Government agency.

Meanwhile London was urgently asking for another two
millions. The deadline was mid-March, for that was the last
lunar period during which there would be sufficient darkness
to enable planes to make the trip from England to Poland and
back without undue risk of detection. Partly by persuasion,
partly by the ungrudging help of Donovan and his men, and
partly by the timely arrival in America of the first two million
in small notes, the difficulty was overcome. By March 13, 1943,

the final consignment of the initial $5,000,000 had arrived in London for onward transmission to Poland. It was immediately transhipped and landed on Polish territory in almost total darkness. The plane made the return journey in safety, and the Polish underground was enabled to carry on for many more months without financial worries.

Four or five months later, a further $5,250,000 was sent over to Britain, but on this occasion there were not sufficient dollar funds in Britain to make repayment in American currency. Somehow or other a cheque or series of cheques would have to pass from the British Treasury to the U.S. Government, and yet neither the American Treasury nor the Foreign Funds Control agency could be informed of the existence of the transaction or the reason for it. Donovan's financial assistant solved the problem. He drew the notes from the U.S. Treasury on behalf of O.S.S. and handed them to Stephenson's office for shipment to the United Kingdom. The British Treasury effected repayment by sending a cheque to the Ministry of Supply, which instructed the British Purchasing Commission in New York to draw equivalent cheques in favour of Donovan's financial assistant personally. The latter then passed the payment back to O.S.S. The advantage of this arrangement was that large payments for unspecified purposes by the Ministry of Supply in London or its purchasing mission in New York were common enough for such a transaction as has been described to pass unnoticed.

Finally, between May and September, 1944, a further $8,000,000 were transferred in exactly the same way. This time Donovan's financial assistant asked to be informed roughly where the money would be spent, by whom and under whose authority; he also asked whether it would be circulated or hoarded and whether any large sums were likely to reach enemy hands. He was given this information on the understanding that he kept it to himself.

The war produced many examples of good Anglo-American relations, even if there were also some bad ones. None can have been more varied and at the same time more intimate and confidential than those which subsisted between 'Little Bill' Stephenson and 'Big Bill' Donovan and their respective organizations.

5

This is not the place for a detailed narrative of the achievements of O.S.S. The publication of a full and definitive history of Donovan's organization has hitherto not proved feasible, largely owing to the reluctance of the American authorities concerned to declassify much of the documentary material essential to such a project. However, because O.S.S. was in a sense the foster-child of B.S.C., it may be well to consider briefly what it achieved, as seen through the experienced eyes of British Intelligence and Special Operations. It is all the more desirable to put the record straight, since, while the actual war was being waged and O.S.S. was consequently obliged to hide its light under a pretty large bushel, it suffered from the jibes of columnists and others who liked to describe its initial letters as standing for 'Oh So Social', 'Oh Shush Shush' and 'Oh So Secret'. In fact, by war's end no less than 831 O.S.S. men had been decorated for bravery, men who in Donovan's words took 'some of the gravest personal risks of the war . . . on the express understanding that their heroism would have to remain unsung'.[1]

From the quantitative point of view the O.S.S. output was comparable with the combined efforts of the British S.I.S. and S.O.E., a most commendable achievement when it is remembered how little time Donovan was afforded to build up his organization and how many serious obstacles he faced at the outset.

There is a story told that, when the war was over and O.S.S. was about to be closed down, Donovan summoned one of his secretaries and said he wanted to look at the files.

'Which files, sir?' the secretary asked.

'All of them,' said the General. 'Now that it's all over and I have a little time, I want to read everything.'

The secretary called the department where all the reports from the various O.S.S. officers and agents overseas had been deposited. After several hours of concentrated research and analysis, the man in charge of the registry called back. Working

---

[1] Alsop and Braden, 26. See also article by John Chamberlain on O.S.S. in *Life*, November, 1945.

at a steady eight hours a day on a six-day week, he said, the General could complete a cursory inspection of all O.S.S. reports in sixteen and a half years.[1]

When he first began to send agents abroad, Donovan had to overcome the prejudices of the heads of the American diplomatic missions. For instance, Admiral William Leahy, the U.S. Ambassador in Vichy, has described his sense of surprise when a young Chicago lawyer arrived on orders from Navy Secretary Knox to become Assistant Naval Attaché at the Embassy. The Admiral soon discovered that he did not know which end of a boat went first and he wondered what kind of officers the Navy was commissioning. Some time later Leahy learned that he was a secret O.S.S. agent 'planted' in the American Embassy. However, the Admiral had to admit that he was 'a very good spy—capable and discreet', and that when the Embassy staff was imprisoned by the Germans in November, 1942, the Nazis were unable to make out a case against him, although they definitely suspected espionage. On the other hand, Leahy objected to Donovan's agents in southern France sending messages through the U.S. Consulate in Marseilles on the ground that this would be 'a serious reflection on our foreign service if we should be caught sending unneutral messages under the cloak of diplomatic immunity', and he ordered that the practice should cease. Later Donovan accused Leahy of interfering in his work. 'I told him that the diplomatic service was *my* business,' Leahy remarked afterwards.[2]

Qualitatively, too, it was Stephenson's considered opinion that much of O.S.S.'s work was without doubt of first-class importance judged by any standard. One example on the intelligence side deserves especially honourable mention. The head of the O.S.S. office in Berne was Allen Dulles, who was later to head the post-war Central Intelligence Agency (C.I.A.). To his office one night in 1943 there came a man known as George Wood, who was an important employee of the German Foreign Office in Berlin; during the next eighteen months Wood brought with him nearly two thousand microfilm photographs of 'top secret' German diplomatic correspondence between the *Auswärtigesamt* and twenty different countries. It

[1] Alsop and Braden, 21.
[2] William D. Leahy. *I Was There* (1950), at pp. 22, 71.

included reports from the German Military and Air Attachés in Japan, data on the structure of the German secret service in Spain and information regarding German espionage in Britain and the Irish Republic. An interesting example of the latter, which Wood supplied, revealed the existence of a secret radio transmitter in the German Embassy in Dublin which was used to direct submarine raids on allied shipping.[1]

This information was passed on to the British, but for a long time the British intelligence chiefs in London refused to believe that it was anything other than a deliberate 'plant' by the enemy on the gullible Americans. Eventually Stephenson, who was convinced of its genuineness, 'raised a riot', as he put it, in London, where he enlisted the assistance of the head of the Government Code and Cipher School. In due course, the cryptographers were enabled to check it against their own findings, with the result that its reliability was established beyond question.

Shortly after his return to New York, Stephenson met Allen Dulles, who had come home to report, and he congratulated him warmly on his success. At the same time Stephenson wrote to Donovan as follows:

> New York,
> *15th November, 1944*
>
> The visit here of your very able representative in Switzerland reminds me of the fact that when I was in London recently, I had the opportunity of going into the history and product of the 'Wood' traffic. This is certainly one of the greatest secret intelligence achievements of this war.
>
> I mention this exceptional case, but I must also express my sincere admiration for the way your whole S.I. organisation has been developed in what is, compared to the development of the various established secret intelligence organizations elsewhere, a phenomenally short space of time. I say nothing at this moment about what I have seen of the operations of your other departments which are no less outstanding, but I cannot help recording my delight that your 'I' side—which is, after all, the most delicate operation in foreign fields—has been so amazingly successful. All those with any real experience, who know something of its operations and achievements, are astonished at the progress which has been made.

---

[1] Alsop and Braden, 227. See also Andrew Tully. *C.I.A.: The Inside Story* (1962), at p. 42.

The receipt of this letter from his closest British friend and collaborator encouraged General Donovan to propose to President Roosevelt the eventual setting up of a permanent central secret intelligence organization in Washington. This he did in a memorandum, which was significantly dated three days after Stephenson's letter.[1]

Washington, D.C.
*18th November, 1944*

I have given consideration to the organisation of our intelligence service for the post-war period.

Once our enemies are defeated the demand will be equally pressing for information that will aid in solving the problems of peace.

This requires two things:

1. That intelligence control be returned to the supervision of the President.

2. The establishment of a central authority reporting directly to you.

Had Roosevelt lived to complete his fourth term in the White House, he would undoubtedly have taken what he called 'a direct interest in the proposed venture', and the considerable intelligence side of O.S.S. might not have been dissolved as it was by his successor. Also, C.I.A. might have escaped a lot of its initial teething troubles. But that is another story.

Besides the S.I. division, there were two other divisions in O.S.S. headquarters which produced useful intelligence and with which Stephenson's officers maintained regular contact. These were the Survey of Foreign Experts and the Research and Analysis Branch. Amongst other products, the former provided most important information concerning potential bombing objectives throughout Europe. The work of the latter in producing strategic surveys and topographical maps was generally regarded by the British as second to none. Between 1942 and the end of the war it turned out 8,000 map titles. 'It made its compilations available to me,' Stephenson has recalled, 'and I made certain that they reached those most directly concerned without a moment's delay.' Those whom the maps reached in this way included the British Prime Minister,

[1] Sanche de Gramont. *The Secret War* (1962), at p. 127.

and they were a conspicuous feature of his famous map room. Indeed, Churchill invariably took them with him on his official journeys. At the Quebec Conference in August, 1944, he called President Roosevelt into his room, pointed to the wall, and said, 'See, I've got them too!'

Mention has already been made of the counter-espionage division of O.S.S. In this connection Stephenson made available to Donovan the deciphered wireless communications between Germany and the various secret wireless stations in South America concerning the activities of Nazi agents. Most of this traffic was from Berlin to Buenos Aires and vice versa, the outward-bound traffic being relayed from a large German naval wireless station at Bordeaux in Occupied France. British cryptographers succeeded in breaking the relevant ciphers at an early stage, so that the messages were readable almost from the beginning. In fact, the only wireless intercepts that Stephenson was specifically barred from passing to Donovan were those of the most highly secret operational character concerning the movements and plans of the enemy's armed forces in the various war theatres, notably the Pacific and the Far East.

'On numerous occasions', Stephenson has recalled, 'when Donovan consulted me about reports and appreciations which were destined for the highest levels from various departments of O.S.S.—for example, Research and Analysis—I would suggest alterations based upon the real rather than the deduced situations, as evidenced by these particular deciphered enemy communications. He always followed my advice in this, and I assumed that he shrewdly guessed what actuated it. I endeavoured to the end to get the Combined Chiefs of Staff to authorize that Donovan should be made personally privy to this by far the most important source of secret intelligence, but it was never agreed. I always felt uncomfortable about it; but I think, because of his constant prior reference to me on important appreciations, I was able to remould somewhat some incipient mistaken deductions and conclusions.'

The final tribute to O.S.S. from the British side came in August, 1945, when, Germany having already been vanquished, victory was at last achieved over Japan. On that day, Major-General Sir Colin Gubbins, head of the Special Operations

Executive in London, wrote to General Donovan in Washington:

> . . . I send to you and all the Office of Strategic Services the congratulations of S.O.E. upon the splendid contribution you have made to the defeat of our common enemy, and grateful thanks for your co-operation with us all over the world.
>
> It has been a pleasure to work with you and all the men and women under your command. The close association of our two organizations is a forerunner of what can be achieved by the Anglo-American unity which we all feel is so important for the future peace and happiness of mankind.

# CHAPTER VII

## *PROPAGANDA AT WORK*

### I

THE multifarious activities of British Security Co-ordination which have been described in the preceding pages, involved a staff of considerable proportions. Indeed at the height of its operations the B.S.C. headquarters numbered close on a thousand men and women. In the knowledge that Canadians on the whole got on well with Americans, Stephenson turned in the first instance to his own country for recruits to his organization. Thus Canada supplied him with specialists in many fields, including an admiral, a general and an air-marshal. One of the most brilliant Canadians was a Toronto professor, who was in charge of communications and was able to adapt the Western Union Telekrypton ciphering machines to carry the immense amount of secret traffic (over one million groups) which passed daily between New York and the various organizations in London which Stephenson represented. In addition, the devoted and hardworking female secretarial and clerical staff was also largely Canadian.

On the other hand, many of the key executive jobs at headquarters were filled by British personnel, most of whom were specially sent out from England. Besides Sir Connop Guthrie, who has already been mentioned as head of the Security Division, and his assistant Walter Karri-Davies, the English business men and financiers, who at one time or another belonged to B.S.C., included Ingram Fraser, John Pepper, David Ogilvy, Herbert Sichel, Richard Coit, Ivor Bryce, Louis Frank, Barty Bouverie, Bickham Sweet-Escott and Walter ('Freckles') Wren. The English theatre and radio provided Benn Levy, Eric Maschwitz and Giles Playfair, while journalism produced Sydney ('Bill') Morrell and Christopher Wren, son of P. C. Wren of *Beau Geste* fame. The English Bar was represented by

Alexander Halpern, a naturalized British subject born a Russian who had been legal adviser to the Kerensky Government in Petrograd in 1917, as well as by the author of this book. Colonel C. H. ('Dick') Ellis, who spoke Russian as well as Alex Halpern did English, came from the Foreign Office in London, as also did Walter Bell. The War Office sent over Major-General Alexander Telfer-Smollett, who had been Lieutenant-Governor of Guernsey, and Colonel A. M. ('Bunny') Phillips. Finally there were four university dons, A. J. Ayer, G. A. Highet, K. J. Maidment and F. W. D. Deakin. 'Freddy' Ayer is now Professor of Philosophy at Oxford; Gilbert Highet, who married the novelist Helen MacInnes, occupies the Chair of Latin Language and Literature at Columbia and has become a United States citizen; Kenneth Maidment is Vice-Chancellor of Auckland University, New Zealand, and Bill Deakin, after being parachuted into Yugoslavia and winning the D.S.O. for his exploits with Tito's partisans, later became the first Warden of the newly created St. Anthony's College in Oxford.

With such a large organization as B.S.C., there was always the danger of leakages, particularly among the junior staff. Stephenson used to impress upon the secretarial personnel the need for care in this respect; he made a point of seeing that they got good living quarters in Manhattan; and they in turn were content to live comparatively limited social lives in view of their work. There were only two cases of anything approaching serious indiscretions, although fortunately these did not cause any substantial harm.

On the other hand, the precautions taken by the various London headquarters in sending out officers were sometimes wrapped in unnecessary mystery. Benn Levy, for example, was not given the address of the B.S.C. offices in Rockefeller Centre, though this was undoubtedly known to the Germans. Instead, he was told to memorize a certain telephone number, which he was to call as soon as he arrived in New York and say, 'This is Mortimer'. He remembered the number correctly, but he forgot his cover name. 'This is . . .' 'This is . . .' he kept saying after he had dialled the number. Finally he blurted out, 'This is Benn Levy'. 'That's quite all right', answered a voice at the other end of the line. 'We've been expecting you. Come right on up.' He was then directed to Room 3603, 630 Fifth Avenue.

Of course, it was sometimes difficult for the senior members of Stephenson's staff to conceal the true nature of their activities, particularly when they encountered friends from former civilian life. The present writer, for example, had been on terms of intimacy with the witty Irish poet and autobiographer, Dr. Oliver St. John Gogarty, in Dublin, and after Gogarty came to live in New York, which he did shortly before the outbreak of war, it was inevitable that sooner or later their paths should cross. Indeed this happened and their former close friendly relations were resumed. For a long time Gogarty never showed by the slightest hint that he was aware of what I was doing. Then one night I invited him to a small dinner party which I gave in my apartment. Besides Gogarty, the only other guests were from B.S.C.

In the course of the evening Gogarty asked for a sheet of writing paper. He scribbled away for a minute or two, and then handed me the result, saying to the assembled company, 'I think you will all like this'. It was a limerick, which read as follows:

> A lady of doubtful nativity
> Had a fanny of great sensitivity
> When she sat on the lap
> Of a Nazi or Jap
> She could detect Fifth Column activity.

Needless to say we were all highly amused, as also was Stephenson, to whom the original manuscript was subsequently presented. He in turn passed it on to the President's adviser, Ernest Cuneo, and no doubt it caused some hilarity when it was recited in the White House.

Stephenson also had many willing helpers outside B.S.C., who put their own resources and facilities at his disposal. Prominent among them was the Canadian Charles Vining, President of the Newsprint and Pulp and Paper Associations of Canada; also his old flying comrade from the First War, Tommy Drew-Brook, the Toronto stockbroker. Then there was the Hungarian-born British film producer Sir Alexander Korda, who had got his knighthood (so it was said) because Winston Churchill was so struck by the picture *Lady Hamilton*, based on Nelson's life story, which Korda made in six weeks in 1941. It is true that the Prime Minister saw this film eight times and was reported to have cried on each occasion;

doubtless he was also impressed, as was Stephenson, by its propaganda value, since Britain also stood alone for a time in the Napoleonic Wars and in Nelson's death and victory at Trafalgar had another 'finest hour'. Korda also played an active part in advising on the production of films for political warfare such as *The Lion Has Wings* and *Desert Victory*.

On one occasion, when eastbound transatlantic flights were heavily booked for many months ahead by top priority passengers, Stephenson managed to get Korda a passage in a Liberator bomber at short notice. At Dorval Airport in Montreal, a smart young R.C.A.F. officer fitted the film director with an inflatable life jacket.

In answer to his inquiry as to the purpose of this article of equipment, the officer said: 'It will keep you afloat for twenty hours, sir!'

It was mid-winter, intensely cold and blowing a gale. Korda was not impressed. 'But I do not want to be kept afloat for twenty hours,' he remarked somewhat plaintively in his characteristic Hungarian accent.

Korda did not enjoy the flight sitting on a parachute in an unheated bomb bay. He was unable to adjust his oxygen mask properly with the result that but for the prompt action of a fellow passenger who noticed his heavy breathing and change of colour he would undoubtedly have been asphyxiated. (As a reward for saving his life, Korda gave him a well-paid job with not too much to do in his film company's London office after the war.)

Stephenson himself often made the uncomfortable journey by bomber during the war. In December, 1943, he took his friend Ernest Cuneo to London in a Liberator. It was Cuneo's first war-time visit, and while the aircraft was *en route* across the Atlantic Stephenson asked him what he would most like to do or see during his tour of Britain. Cuneo replied that the greatest thrill he could possibly experience would be to meet 'the great man, Churchill'. Stephenson said he would arrange it.

On their first day in England, Stephenson arranged for Cuneo to visit an American Air Force Group which was stationed in Lincolnshire. As Cuneo departed by car for the air-force station, Stephenson set out on foot from Claridge's Hotel to keep an appointment at No. 10 Downing Street with the Prime Minister. It was a lengthy visit, as Churchill had many other callers, also friends of Stephenson, such as Lord Beaverbrook and Lord Leathers, and so the hours passed. Eventually Stephenson left about 3.30 a.m. and began to walk back to his hotel.

At the corner of Brook Street and Grosvenor Square, he recognized a familiar figure engaged in conversation with two young American Air Force officers. It was Cuneo.

'Come along, Ernie,' said Stephenson, after he had greeted his friend. 'We are going to call upon the Prime Minister at No. 10.'

'Good God, Bill,' the astonished Cuneo replied. 'Don't you realize it is four o'clock in the morning and we cannot possibly break in on the great man at this hour? Why, he may be asleep.'

'The whole of the forces of Britain are engaged in one way or another at this moment, and some of my own people are at this very moment dropping into enemy territory,' Stephenson remarked with apparent unconcern. 'Why then do you think that their leader should be sleeping at his post?'

By contrast, Cuneo was in a rather emotional state, having just returned from witnessing the departure on bombing missions of a number of United States Air Force personnel, with whom he had dined at their station in Lincolnshire, and having later watched the arrival back of the Squadron somewhat depleted as the result of action over their target. However, he agreed to come along.

When they reached Downing Street, they announced themselves and to Cuneo's surprise were immediately shown into a room where the Prime Minister was enjoying a well-earned drink with several of his colleagues. Churchill greeted the two newcomers warmly.

'Cuneo,' said the Prime Minister ruminatively, as the name struck a chord in his memory. 'Are you, by any chance, related to the Cuneo who served as navigator to Christopher Columbus?'

Cuneo's chest swelled with pride. Yes, indeed, he was a direct descendant of that famous Genoese sailor, he assured Churchill. Thereafter the visitor and the Prime Minister took to each other in the warmest possible fashion.

As they took their leave and with the first rays of the dawn retraced their steps to Claridge's, Stephenson asked the American what had impressed him most about Churchill.

Cuneo answered that it was his clothes. 'I was astonished to find this great Marshal of the Allied Forces dressed in such a simple garb as an overall.'

Actually the Prime Minister was wearing his 'siren suit' in case of enemy air raids, or his 'Zip' as he preferred to call it.

Next day Stephenson took his American friend to lunch with the Mountbattens in their penthouse overlooking Hyde Park. Lord Louis Mountbatten (as he then was) was the much-talked-of British Chief of Combined Operations and again Cuneo was suitably impressed particularly as he made a comment which greatly amused the company and was so often repeated afterwards that it became something of a classic.

The conversation turned on Mussolini and someone remarked that at least he had made the trains run on time. 'Yes,' Cuneo agreed, 'but perhaps the Italians would prefer that they didn't!'

Another diverting incident occurred at this lunch, which is worth recording. The other guests included the Foreign Secretary, Anthony Eden, who was seated beside Stephenson. During the meal the Minister made a whispered inquiry in his neighbour's ear as to the identity of his expansive American friend. Stephenson thereupon explained that Cuneo was a trusted adviser of President Roosevelt and a good friend of Britain, who was doing an excellent job in Washington as liaison between the White House, O.S.S. and British Security Intelligence in the United States. Eden expressed satisfaction.

As they were leaving, the Foreign Secretary took Mountbatten aside and asked in an undertone who Stephenson was. 'Why,' said Mountbatten in surprise, 'don't you know? He's your man in New York.'

As one of President Roosevelt's confidential advisers, Cuneo had an opportunity of observing something of Stephenson's role as an intermediary in certain high-level negotiations between the British Prime Minister and the U.S. President. In this connection his opinion of Stephenson is worth recalling. 'He always knew what neither of them could ever give,' Cuneo has said. 'Therefore the other never asked. He cut out the customary rigmarole whereby one statesman says to another: "If I asked you this in public, what would you say?" '

One of the more delicate subjects of a top-secret character which Stephenson had to clear personally with President

Roosevelt deserves a brief mention here. This was a project of strategic deception of the enemy in the shape of the body of a dead man which it was arranged should be released from a British submarine near the coast of Spain, where it would be washed ashore. The corpse was conveniently provided with faked plans of a 'second front' and had the desired effect upon the Germans, to whom the papers were passed by the Spanish authorities. Commander Ewen Montagu, the naval intelligence officer in charge of the operation, visited New York to discuss it with Stephenson and later gave a vivid account of its execution in his book, *The Man Who Never Was.*[1]

Another war-time acquaintance of Stephenson was Noël Coward. Stephenson, who had made Coward's acquaintance early in the war and was greatly impressed by his abilities, wished to employ him on propaganda and other secret work in the Western Hemisphere. Plans were made accordingly and Coward was preparing for his new job after spending the winter of 1940–41 entertaining the troops in Australia and New Zealand, when the news was broken to him by cable as he stopped at Bermuda on his homeward journey, that it was not to be. 'A greater power than we could contradict has thwarted our intents,' Stephenson informed him laconically.

Some of Coward's friends said it was because he had made a slighting remark about the Prime Minister's son Randolph at a dinner party and the news had got back to 'the old man'. However, it is extremely unlikely that Churchill would have concerned himself in a proposed personal appointment of this kind, although he probably would have felt (if his attention had been drawn to it) that Coward could be better employed devising and acting in theatrical and variety entertainment for the benefit of the British and Commonwealth armed forces. The truth is that Coward had many enemies among 'the Establishment', who for one reason or another objected to his official employment. At all events for Coward it was a bitter disappointment and as he subsequently was to admit, it cost him some black hours. But things probably worked out for the best, for if the job with Stephenson had materialized, he would never have written *Blithe Spirit* and *In Which We Serve.*

[1] The incident was also described in fictional form by A. Duff Cooper (Lord Norwich) in *Operation Heartbreak*.

Noël Coward did a wonderful war-time job on the entertainment side, which in the fairly lavish distribution of honours and awards afterwards did not seem to receive the recognition it deserved. But Stephenson always recognized his worth. He also treated him with characteristic kindness. Seeing him suffering from the after-effects of influenza while passing through New York at Christmas, 1943, after a particularly exhausting tour of the jungle camps in the Middle East and India, Stephenson packed him off to his property in Jamaica so that he could recuperate quickly in the tropical sunshine. It was Coward's first visit to Jamaica, and it led to his ultimately making a home there.[1]

Stephenson himself worked incredibly long hours at his wartime job, and his staff often wondered when he slept. At two o'clock one morning, during the New York 'dim-out', he was observed by the night shift leaving his office, and it was assumed that he was going to bed. But he did not stay there for long. At three-forty-five he telephoned from his apartment in Dorset House, which was not far away, to say that a chink of light was showing under one of the blinds. At five he was back at his desk, having bathed, shaved, and changed his clothes, ready for the next day's work.

On D-day in June, 1944, Stephenson, who was determined to be in on the launching of the 'second front', flew as a rear gunner over the invasion coast. Harking back to his days as a fighter pilot in the First World War, he was annoyed because he encountered no German aircraft to shoot at. But he could derive some satisfaction from the fact that the successful military operation which was just beginning, and which was eventually to throttle Hitler's forces, owed much to his own efforts and to the efforts of the brave people who had passed through his organization.

2

A country that is extremely heterogeneous in character offers a wide variety of choice in propaganda methods. While it is possibly true to say that most Americans are intensely suspicious of propaganda, it is certain that a great many of them are remarkably susceptible to it, even in its most patent and blatant

[1] Noël Coward. *Future Indefinite* (1954), pp. 194, 272.

form. It is unlikely that any propagandist would seriously attempt, with any prospects of success, to influence politically the people of Britain or France through the medium of astrological predictions. Yet in the United States this was done under Stephenson's auspices with effective if limited results.

In the summer of 1941, Louis de Wohl, a Hungarian who had been Hitler's personal astrologer, was sent over to the United States by Stephenson's London headquarters. But, while he was to be controlled by Stephenson, his instructions were that he must never mention Britain or show in any way that he was especially interested in Britain's welfare. His mission was to shake American public confidence in the invincibility of Adolf Hitler.

It was planned that the first prophecies which de Wohl would make on his arrival in the United States should coincide and harmonize with prearranged astrological and magical predictions of Hitler's fall to be made in other parts of the world. By this means it was hoped not only to convince the public but to alarm Hitler himself, who was intensely superstitious and a great believer in astrology. Accordingly, when de Wohl arrived in New York, Stephenson arranged a press conference for him at which the astrologer told newspapermen that Hitler's horoscope showed that his fall was now certain. The planet Neptune, he said, was in the house of death, making for a mysterious fate, and soon the progressed ascendant would be in a place where Neptune was at the moment of Hitler's birth. That very summer, de Wohl added, Uranus would bring the birth constellation into effect with grave consequences for Hitler.

A few days after these statements had appeared in the newspapers, other stories began to emanate from elsewhere. In fact, the arrangements which had been made were working smoothly. In Cairo a newspaper published in Arabic carried a statement by the eminent Egyptian astrologer, Sheikh Youssef Afifi, who was reported as saying:

> Four months hence a red planet will appear on the eastern horizon and will indicate that a dangerous evil-doer, who has drenched the world in blood, will pass away . . . This means that an uncrowned Emperor will be killed, and that man is Hitler.

At the same time steps were taken so that this story was duly picked up by American correspondents in Egypt.

Simultaneously correspondents in Nigeria filed a story which told of a report by a local District Officer in a remote district up country. It appeared that a priest called Ulokoigbe had seen a vision. In the priest's own words:

> In the light, I saw a group of five men on a rock. One was short, with long hair; the second was fat and shaped like the breadfruit; the third monkey-faced and crippled; the fourth had glass in his eyes like the District Officer; the fifth was leopard-faced. After a quarrel the fifth vanished. The cripple stabbed the breadfruit man in the back. The long-haired one cursed the glass-eyed one and pushed him from the rock. Then the cripple jumped from the rock leaving Long Hair alone. Long Hair seized the crown from the rock, but it did not fit his head and fell off. In a wild rage Long Hair slipped from the rock and fell shrieking like a madman. The crown was left in its proper place in the middle of the rock.

This easily recognizable description of Hitler and his principal lieutenants (Goering, Goebbels, Himmler and Hess) also appeared in the American press. People then began to sit up and take notice. Stephenson carried the matter further, and in order to enhance de Wohl's reputation, it was arranged that he would make a prophecy which would be actually fulfilled ten days later. After consulting the stars—and B.S.C.—the astrologer told the press that within the next ten days one of Hitler's allies would be found to be mad. Sure enough, inside the following week or so, a French naval officer who had escaped from Martinique was quoted as stating in Puerto Rico that the Vichy French Governor of the French West Indies, Admiral Robert, had become violently insane and could be heard shouting and screaming all night.

De Wohl's public was considerably impressed. He really seemed to know what he was talking about. Here was a prophet who made a prediction in New York which was immediately confirmed, first by an Egyptian astrologer in Cairo, and secondly by a Nigerian priest in the jungles of Africa. Furthermore, he had definitely said that within ten days one of Hitler's allies would become mad, and so it proved to be with Admiral

Robert. Certainly the astrologer's reputation shone as brightly as the stars of which he spoke.

After this auspicious beginning in New York, the astro-philosopher, as the newspapers called him, toured the country, and at public meetings, over the air, in widely syndicated articles for the press, he declared that Hitler's doom was sealed. Later, he delivered similar attacks upon the Vichy French Ambassador, Henry-Haye, and upon the isolationist Colonel Lindbergh. At the annual convention of the American Federation of Scientific Astrologers, which opened in Cleveland on August 5, 1941, de Wohl said of Lindbergh that he was part of the plague of technology which makes the weak-minded believe that a man who can handle machines well must be an authority on things of the spirit.

As for Hitler, he had shot his bolt. (Roosevelt, on the other hand, had a 'beautiful horoscope'.) 'Hitler's move on Russia was a great mistake', de Wohl told the convention, going on to point out that the date on which the German High Command decided to attack Russia was May 11, 1941, the same date on which Rudolf Hess landed in England. 'This is significant', he observed, 'because Dr. H. Spencer-Jones, the British astron-omer, scoffingly remarked in 1938 that if there was anything to astrology, its students should be able to predict important events for May 11, 1941.' He continued: 'Hitler is on the downgrade. The turning point came when Germany invaded Czechoslovakia in March, 1939. We can't predict a date for his defeat, but if the United States enters the war before next spring, he is doomed.'

Astrologer de Wohl returned to England after Pearl Harbour, having accomplished a fantastic but effective mission.

### 3

Besides the collection of secret intelligence directly concerned with the prosecution of the war, Stephenson succeeded in gleaning valuable information about internal American politics. It was based as a rule on statements of fact privately made, or views and intentions privately expressed, by the President himself, by his advisers and members of his Administration, and by the Chiefs of Staff and others in a position to determine or influence the shape of policy and strategy. This information was regularly cabled to London and repeated to the British Embassy in Washington.

Three examples may be given here. On the day after the Japanese attack on Pearl Harbour, Stephenson informed London of the losses and casualties which the President was to announce to Congress on the following day. 'At any rate', Roosevelt was reported as saying, 'this will be a salutary lesson to the Navy not to be too free with their criticism of the British.' The source of this information was Donovan, who had been received by the President at midnight on December 7/8, 1941, after one of the most hectic and exhausting days ever remembered at the White House. 'To think that all our planes were *caught on the ground*', the President continued in outraged indignation, as Donovan suggested a scheme for emergency defence of the Philippine beaches.[1]

Again, in November, 1943, Harold Ickes, the Secretary of the Interior, was reported as saying that 'no commitments on oil were made during the recent visit of Saudi Arabian potentates to Washington'.

Another example concerned Russian tactics in Washington. In April, 1944, Stephenson reported that the U.S. Navy and particularly the Commander-in-Chief Admiral King were strongly opposed to the active lobbying by the Russians for the extension of Lend-Lease for three years after the end of the war and 'assistance to establish a large navy'. The pertinent query came from King, 'Who are they going to use this goddamned fleet against?'

Through analysis of the intelligence available to him from his various sources, Stephenson was enabled to provide London with reliable forecasts of future events, such as the results of the Presidential elections held in 1940 and 1944, which were forecast with remarkable accuracy. In this context he reported at the beginning of February, 1944, that 'Roosevelt has undertaken to the Party that he will jettison Wallace as Vice-Presidential candidate', notwithstanding that Henry Wallace was himself unaware of this until within a few days of his rejection by the Democratic Convention five months later.

Roosevelt's Republican opponent in the 1944 election,

[1] John Gunther. *Roosevelt In Retrospect* (1950), at p. 352.

Thomas E. Dewey, was considerably influenced by the electoral analyses carried out in the country by the American Institute of Public Opinion, or the Gallup Poll, as it is commonly known. No doubt he was encouraged by the fact that Dr. George Gallup, who headed this organization, was himself an active Republican. Unfortunately for Dewey, the Gallup polls did not prove a reliable guide on this occasion, at least not in the earlier stages of the election, since they had Dewey in the lead almost until the last minute. It was later suggested that Gallup deliberately adjusted his figures in Dewey's favour in the hope of stampeding the electorate thereby. But this was quite untrue. The margin of error was a genuine miscalculation.

Meanwhile, in London, the British Prime Minister was naturally most interested in the result of this election, which came at the final critical stage in the war. Stephenson was accordingly asked to provide an independent forecast and he turned to Donovan for assistance in preparing 'a clinical analysis' of election trends. Donovan cleared the project with the President, who likewise expressed interest in the result. He then handed it over to David Seiferheld, a statistical expert with one of the most analytical minds in O.S.S. and asked him to re-evaluate the Gallup forecasts. The result was a finding that Gallup was 4 per cent. out in his calculations. In fact, Seiferheld correctly forecast the result in every single state except one.

This sensational information was passed to Stephenson by the President's adviser, Ernest Cuneo, who also acted as liaison between O.S.S. and Stephenson's organization.

'It's unbelievable', Cuneo told Stephenson, 'there are going to be some whitefaced boys in this country. . . . Dewey is calling up Gallup so often they have to have a clerk to answer him. Imagine a guy shaking so much!'

'And Gallup is trying to give Dewey service, I suppose?'

'Sure, he's one of Gallup's principal clients.'

A week before the election Stephenson sent the following telegram to London, laughingly telling Cuneo as he did so that he 'would be branded either an idiot or a genius'.

My estimates have consistently conflicted markedly with those of Gallup and other pollsters and political pundits . . .

and now show even greater divergence from largely accepted view than previously . . .

*My current analyses indicate victory for FDR in minimum repeat minimum of 32 states with 370 electoral votes and maximum of 40 with 487 electoral votes . . .*

Dewey minimum comprises North Dakota, South Dakota, Nebraska, Colorado, Kansas, Wyoming, Vermont and Iowa . . . Maximum includes foregoing plus Maine, Idaho, Wisconsin, Indiana, Michigan, Ohio, Minnesota and Illinois . . . Last four are Dewey's most doubtful ones and not improbable result anticipates his losing three or all four.

The results of the election were exactly as Stephenson had predicted. Dewey won all the eight states listed as his minimum, together with four of the remainder listed as possible gains. Roosevelt carried 36 states, with 432 electoral votes, although his popular vote was considerably reduced, the majority being only 3,000,000, the smallest in any presidential election since 1916.

Another prediction made by Stephenson concerned the important New York municipal office of Mayor. Early in 1944 he predicted that Fiorello La Guardia would not run again and that the next Mayor would be William O'Dwyer. At this time it was widely accepted that La Guardia would go forward again and almost taken for granted by the press. Eighteen months later O'Dwyer was elected by the largest majority in the city's history.

In regard to the Gallup polls, it is only fair to add that, despite occasional errors such as happened over the last Roosevelt election, Stephenson had a healthy respect for them and regarded their findings as more often than not extremely accurate. He was also aware that the Roosevelt Administration made covert use of them. For this purpose, Gallup's organization was employed to obtain answers to specific questions, and these were handed to the Presidential speech-writer, Judge Samuel Rosenman, who would pass them on to the President. There is no doubt that they exercised a considerable influence on the political strategy of the Administration. Much of the information gathered by the Gallup pollsters was made available to Stephenson through the co-operation of David Ogilvy, a brilliant young Scotsman, who had been one of

Gallup's associate directors and had made himself an expert on American public opinion.

Ogilvy was perhaps the most remarkable of the younger men to join Stephenson's B.S.C. This he did in 1942, shortly after his thirtieth birthday. It was a fortunate step for him; he later admitted that Stephenson had changed the course of his life. Not that his previous career had been unvaried, or for that matter easy. He had once worked as an assistant chef and washed dishes in the kitchens of a big Paris hotel, a job which he later exchanged for the equally hard one of selling cooking stoves from door to door in Scotland. Anyone who is familiar with the canny Scots housewife will appreciate that this was no sinecure. Yet Ogilvy turned out to be the company's top salesman and went on to write sales manuals before crossing the Atlantic to study American advertising techniques on behalf of his brother's advertising firm in London. Finding America what he called 'the most wonderful, delightful, marvellous country on earth', he promptly resigned his job with his brother's firm to become Dr. Gallup's right-hand man in Princeton. In conducting more than four hundred nation-wide surveys for Gallup, he gained a solid grounding in the methods of opinion research as well as a profound respect for it for purposes of advertising. (This experience was to stand him in good stead after the war when he started his own advertising agency in New York, which in an astonishingly short time became one of the most successful and spectacular concerns of its kind on Madison Avenue. 'The man in the Hathaway shirt', 'the diplomat who sent his son to Groton with money he saved buying Austins' and 'Commander Edward Whitehead, Schweppesman extraordinary' were all manifestations of Ogilvy's peculiar genius.)

Thus, when the time came, Ogilvy was able to arrange for a series of polls to be conducted at Stephenson's behest with the object of analysing the exact state of American public opinion towards Britain. These revealed, among other desiderata, that the defeats which Britain suffered in the earlier part of 1942 were having a most damaging effect on the American attitude to Britain and to the Roosevelt Administration. For example, it appeared in mid-February, 1942, that 63 per cent. of the American public believed that the British were doing all they

could to win the war. Three weeks later this figure had fallen to
49 per cent., the lowest point to which British prestige had sunk
since the beginning of the war. Furthermore, the reports showed
that there was a loss of confidence in the U.S. Government; one
American out of three now believed that the United States,
and therefore the Roosevelt Administration, was not doing its
utmost to gain decisive victory over the enemy.

Before Pearl Harbour, as has been seen, Stephenson's organization successfully spread covert propaganda, designed to
strengthen the interventionist groups throughout the country
and discredit the isolationists. As soon as the United States
formally entered the war, the first of these operations became
superfluous. But B.S.C. continued to analyse the publications
and broadcasts of former isolationists, and it found that, as the
bellicose spirit created by Pearl Harbour subsided and the Allies
continued to suffer crushing defeats, so the isolationist press
was encouraged to print anti-Roosevelt, anti-British, anti-
Russian and anti-Semitic propaganda of increasing vehemence
and in increasing quantity. There seemed to be a deliberately
concerted pattern in these attacks. An anti-British theme would
appear in one organ and be taken up by another until it had
spread throughout the country. The New York *Daily News*, for
example, was urging in February, 1942, that the bases in the
Western Hemisphere, which the British had leased to the U.S.
in 1940, should be 'confiscated', in case some day they should
play the same part as the Japanese mandated islands in the
Pacific had played in the Pearl Harbour attack. Thus the *Daily
News* at once appealed to American acquisitiveness, stigmatized
Britain as a potential enemy of the U.S. and opened up a vista
of future wars.

Evidence of deliberate isolationist activity was confirmed by
the records of an interventionist society called 'The Friends of
Democracy', to which B.S.C. had access and which together
with the results of the secret Gallup polls were embodied under
Stephenson's direction in a series of memoranda entitled *Fifth
Column Propaganda of the Axis in the United States*. They analysed
all the tricks which the isolationists were using and showed that,
while much of their propaganda was devised by native Americans, much was dictated by Germans, either through propagandists like Viereck or through short-wave broadcasts. They

showed how the same themes were used throughout the country in a manner which implied a consistent policy guided by a single group.

The first volume of *Fifth Column Propaganda*, which covered the period from December 7, 1941, to January 24, 1942, was handed by Stephenson to Donovan. After he and the leading members of his staff, such as Robert Sherwood and Archibald MacLeish, had digested it, the document was then passed to President Roosevelt, on whom it made a considerable impression. Indeed the President had not realized how widespread and how purposeful this propaganda was, for hitherto no official U.S. agency had been engaged in studying it. On February 23, 1942, the President delivered a speech to the nation, in which for the first time he denounced the 'rumour-mongers and poison-peddlers in our midst'. Prompted by Sherwood and MacLeish, he made use of a number of ideas which the report contained, and one long paragraph in his speech was directly inspired by it.

Thereafter the President's advisers, particularly those attached to the Donovan organization, requested Stephenson to pass them a copy of each memorandum as it was completed. On the President's instructions, a vigorous counter-attack was launched. Edmond Taylor of C.O.I. used the reports consistently through the campaign, while Joseph Barnes, Sherwood's chief assistant, handed numerous extracts from them to the *New York Herald-Tribune*, which embodied them in a series of articles. Every night for a week, C.B.S., drawing its information almost exclusively from the reports, devoted its principal news periods to talks on enemy propaganda and did the same with its coast-to-coast programme, 'Report to the Nation'. Dozens of articles, editorials and cartoons along similar lines followed. Finally, Archibald MacLeish's Office of Facts and Figures issued a booklet, which the author had obviously written with the reports on his desk, analysing Axis propaganda themes and showing the public how to detect them.

Having thus prepared public opinion for more direct action, the President was enabled to deliver a series of frontal attacks. A large number of the propaganda organs employed by isolationists and Axis sympathizers were banned from the mails, among them being Father Coughlin's *Social Justice* and William

Dudley Pelley's *The Galilean, X-Ray* and *Publicity*. Their publishers, with the exception of Coughlin whose indictment might have offended Catholic voters, were arrested and thirty-three of them were indicted at the largest treason trial in American history.

As the campaign against the fifth columnists continued, Stephenson was able to see how its progress was affecting American public opinion. The results, as polled by Gallup, were most gratifying. On March 11, 1942, only 49 per cent. of the American people thought that Britain was doing her utmost to win the war. Six weeks later, on April 23, this proportion had jumped to 65 per cent., although no important naval or military victory had occurred during this period to influence the public in Britain's favour.

His knowledge of Gallup's methods led David Ogilvy to the conclusion that a poll, if secretly organized in other countries, could assist in settling many political and ethnological problems without the confusion and possible corruption of a plebiscite. The results of such a poll, conducted in Spain at any time during the war, might have been used not only to guide British policy towards Franco, but also to determine what types of allied propaganda would be most effective. By the same means it would have been possible to assess the true strength of such political movements as the Integralist in Brazil or Sir Oswald Mosley's Fascist Black Shirts in Great Britain.

These ideas were set out in a report, entitled *A Plan for Predetermining the Results of Plebiscites, Predicting the Reactions of People to the Impact of Projected Events, and Applying the Gallup Technique to Other Fields of Secret Intelligence,* which was written by Ogilvy and forwarded by Stephenson to London in August, 1943.

Although it was received without enthusiasm at the time, both by the British Embassy in Washington and S.I.S. Headquarters in London, the fact remains that a year later the Psychological Warfare Board of General Eisenhower's Headquarters staff successfully carried out polls in Europe in the manner advocated by Ogilvy and endorsed by Stephenson. Since those days the U.S. Government has also made consistent use of Dr. Gallup's techniques, both overtly and secretly.

4

Throughout most of the war Stephenson was able to maintain effective relations with the American press, usually through intermediaries, and on occasion it was able to render him and the British cause most valuable service on the basis of material supplied by his organization, for example, by exposing the activities of the Vichy French. This liaison was desirable for two reasons, first, because there were occasional items which London wished to be placed in American newspapers, and secondly—and more important—newspapermen often possessed secret intelligence about American affairs which they could be persuaded to divulge provided they were kept supplied with exclusive information from Stephenson's sources.

Although Stephenson's office was in touch with all the principal journalists and feature writers in America, Stephenson himself was attracted by only two. These were Walter Lippmann, the shrewd commentator on foreign affairs, who wrote for the *New York Herald-Tribune* syndicate, and Leonard Lyons, whose gay and effervescent column on people and affairs ('In the Lyons Den') appealed to Stephenson's sense of humour. One evening, when the present author was in New York's celebrated Stork Club with Stephenson, he asked the quiet Canadian why he was so partial to Lyons. Stephenson replied, with a twinkle in his eyes: 'Len is always constructive and so kind and gentle that I feel I should be around to protect him from the big bad wolves!'

It is also pertinent to recount something of Stephenson's dealings with two other top-ranking columnists who were (and still are) very much part of the American scene—Walter Winchell and Drew Pearson. Both were in their early forties at this time, and so huge was their readership and audience which they commanded in their columns and broadcasts that they could make, as well as break, a man. Hence the deference with which they were treated by all alike, from the President downwards. They were generally feared because of their enormous power, and as a result they were exceptionally well informed of what was going on in America. They were, therefore, obvious though delicate sources for Stephenson to tap.

Winchell was a New Yorker, who had left school at the age

of thirteen for the stage, had graduated from vaudeville to theatrical journalism, and had become a dramatic critic, dramatic editor and eventually a columnist for the *New York Mirror*. His column, which was syndicated through more than 800 newspapers, was read by well over twenty-five millions daily, or one in every five or six of the entire population of the United States. There was no Senator or Representative whose constituents were not reached by his writings, and since Congressmen like votes, they were obliging to Winchell.

A Winchell column consisted of between twenty and fifty separate references to individuals or events. He wrote seven of these columns each week, intimate, important, airy or disconcerting notes about people and things. Thus a typical wartime column might contain as its principal feature a forthright, and possibly courageous, denunciation of some native-born fascist enterprise. But it would also include a score or so of minor items, ranging from a stroll of Marlene Dietrich along Fifth Avenue to a note that Mr. Fishbein, the gooseberry king, was about to be divorced from Mrs. Fishbein.

Among Winchell's friends was Edgar Hoover, who frolicked with him on occasion at the Stork Club, and was even indebted to him for the capture of the notorious gunman and Labour union racketeer, Louis (Lepke) Buchalter, whose gang had for years dominated New York's garment district and had forced the baking industry alone to pay them an estimated $1,000,000 for protection. Lepke surrendered through Winchell, because he knew that the G-men would not shoot him at sight, if he were in the company of so celebrated and influential a personage as the columnist. As the result of a radio appeal by Winchell, the gangster gave himself up to Hoover in person at a rendezvous previously arranged by Winchell at the corner of 28th Street and Fifth Avenue, New York City, on the understanding that his civil rights would be respected by the F.B.I. Sentenced to a fourteen-year term on a narcotics charge in 1941, Lepke was turned over to the New York State authorities two years later to stand trial, with two associates, for the murder of a Brooklyn storekeeper, for which crime he was duly convicted and sentenced to death. At the beginning of March, 1944, he was reprieved for the sixth time by the Governor of New York, Thomas E. Dewey, who was soon to become Republican candidate for President, and Stephenson sent the following telegram to London:

> Lepke reprieved forty-eight hours . . . Dewey is faced with complex situation for personal decision. He is progressing towards practically certain Republican nomination . . . Lepke's statement (which is being retained by Dewey in extreme secrecy) implicates important New Dealers . . . If worthwhile Dewey again reprieving Lepke for the purpose of deferring the final great exposé until just before election time, so that he may produce a knockout blow for the President at the crucial moment.

Presumably the maximum amount of information had been extracted from Lepke as this turned out to be his last reprieve. On March 2, 1944, he died in the electric chair at Sing Sing prison.

When President Roosevelt entertained Winchell at the White House, he opened the conversation, according to Winchell, by saying: 'Walter, here's an item for you.' Bundists, America-Firsters, Coughlinites and all the lunatic fringe of American isolationism probably concentrated more sheer hatred on Winchell's sleek grey head than upon that of any other one man. It is noteworthy that several of them went to jail or were indicted on charges of traitorous or treasonable conduct as a result of his disclosures. It is hardly necessary to add that his income was enormous—he himself boasted that he had 'salted away a couple of million'—or that he went in constant fear for his personal safety. The country estate to which he retired by day to sleep, bristled with sirens, electric eyes and other up-to-date forms of alarm.

Nevertheless Winchell was always a stout-hearted patriot, and he did his best to further the Anglo-American war effort by every possible means. To this end he asked a mutual friend to supply him with relevant factual information from time to time. The data which he requested was in fact obtained from Stephenson's office. Thus not only was Stephenson able to place items in Winchell's column, but on occasion he was able to supply him with 'copy' for a part or even the whole of the column itself. This happened, for example, in October, 1943, when the Argentine Government released on parole between thirty and forty of the crew of the German battleship *Graf Spee*, who had been interned, in breach of its agreement.

A column of over a thousand words was written, beginning:

> The following is an exclusive exposure of the attempt of the Argentine Government to send reinforcements to the Nazi submarine fleet . . . Every statement made can be proven . . . Of the facts I am sure. . . .
>
> This is an exclusive report to the people of the United Nations—of a pattern of treachery—of DELIBERATE INTERNATIONAL treachery—which has already stabbed one good neighbour in the back—and threatens the life-lines of every other nation battling the Axis . . . The Victim: Brazil . . . The Criminal: the gov't of Argentina . . .
>
> This is the second time that the Ramirez Government has broken its word of honour . . . We cannot shake the hands of men who are helping to send our flag to the bottom of the sea, while our fellow Americans are dying to keep it flying in the sky . . .

The article was handed to Winchell through the mutual friend and was subsequently published in its entirety. Furthermore, Winchell drew attention to it in his regular Sunday evening broadcast. After the Argentine Ambassador had been prompted by this to issue a public denial, the text of another column reached Winchell from the same source, and it likewise appeared in full. The following is an extract:

> '*Impossible and barbaric*' is the quote of the Argentine Embassy about my broadcast and column . . . The phrase is too valuable to drop—because 'impossible and barbaric' exactly describes the President of the Argentine. Here are the facts . . .

South American radio stations picked up the Winchell broadcast and relayed the story throughout the sub-continent. The result was that President Ramirez decreed that the crew of the *Graf Spee* were to be 'concentrated in small groups, which will be under the supervision of the Army and Navy'.

On another occasion, following a personal request from President Roosevelt to assist him in preparing public opinion for the drafting of army nurses, a complete column on the war effort of British women as an example to their American sisters was written in Stephenson's office. Here is how it began:

> *British Women—Orchids to Some Gallant Ladies*
> Britain is the ONLY country that has conscripted women for the fighting forces . . . Of about 16,000,000 women in Britain

between the ages of 14 and 59, over 7,000,000 are in the services or in paid employment . . . Of the single women between 18 and 40, 9 out of every 10 are in essential war work; the rest are either physically unfit or engaged in taking care of younger brothers and sisters or elderly parents . . . 467,000 are in the services; 56,000 are doing full time civil defence work; 6½ million are in industry.

The story was published by Winchell as it stood, and on the day it appeared Stephenson arranged through his contacts that Representative Emanuel Celler of New York should ask permission in the House to read it in full into the Congressional Record. The Speaker granted the Congressman's request. It was good publicity for the British contribution to the war, which was not infrequently under-estimated in the United States.

Again, in December, 1944, when public opinion in America was beginning to favour a lenient peace with Germany, Stephenson provided a useful piece entitled 'Humanity *v.* the German people'. It was a cogent argument against leniency, based on the facts of Hitler's bloodstained record. Once more, Winchell published it *in toto*, and what is more, he followed it up with three more articles on the same theme written by members of Stephenson's staff. Many Americans were profoundly influenced by these indictments, and little was heard thereafter about the desirability of 'soft' peace terms for Germany.

Finally, in January, 1945, the President asked for assistance in preparing public opinion for the passing of a National Service Act. Once again a suitable column was written for Winchell. It began:

> *Things I Never Knew*
> (About the National Service Act in Great Britain)
> That British people who cherish their personal freedom just as much as we do wasted no time in trusting their Government when the nation was in danger.

The article went on to explain how the act worked in England and how for the past four and a half years the Minister of Labour had been empowered to direct anyone to perform any service required, not just some persons, but all persons rich and poor alike.

Probably no man was closer to the President during the war years than Harry Hopkins, and it was fitting that he should pay Winchell a well-deserved tribute when the war was over, with which Stephenson incidentally warmly agreed. 'I don't know of anyone in semi-public life who stuck by Roosevelt as devotedly as did you', Hopkins wrote to him in July, 1945. 'You really fought against Hitler when it was none too popular and I think you deserve all the credit in the world for it. A more timid person would have backed away from that one.'[1]

## 5

To those who knew him during the war, Andrew Russell Pearson appeared a tall, tight-lipped individual, looking uncomfortably like a horse, a resemblance which was increased by his habit of snorting as he spoke. A Quaker from Illinois, he was occasionally heard addressing members of his family as 'Thou' and 'Thee'. He had received a more formal education than Winchell, having graduated from Swarthmore College (Phi Beta Kappa and other fraternities) and having travelled widely before settling down in the capital to write his celebrated 'Daily Washington Merry-Go-Round'—he had previously been a lecturer in geography and a successful foreign correspondent. His first wife was a Polish Countess. The garden pool of his Washington house in Dumbarton Avenue was stocked with goldfish bearing such names as Harry Hopkins and Harold Ickes. The cows on his Maryland farm were similarly christened—Cordell Hull, Henry Morgenthau, Ed. Stettinius and Eleanor Roosevelt. Cordell Hull was slaughtered in the spring of 1945 and eaten by Pearson and his family with relish.

Washington was Drew Pearson's beat. Cabinet Ministers, Senators and Congressmen were his servants. His methods of extracting information and rewarding his informants were similar to those employed by Winchell, although Pearson regarded himself as a much more serious reporter than his colleague, because he dabbled to a smaller extent in pregnancies, divorces and infidelities. Actually, he was less intelligent than Winchell, in spite of his superior education, and certainly

[1] Sherwood. II, 907.

far less trustworthy. He had a goatish indifference to the feelings of others, and was quite unperturbed if one of his disclosures cost a friend or acquaintance his job.

Pearson kept extensive records, both in his head and on his files, of the misdemeanours of important public men, mainly of politicians in Washington. He knew which Senators and Representatives had been financially 'taken care of' by big business lobbyists, and which had been unfaithful to their wives. Moreover, he was said to be adroit at hinting that he would not use the information, if they made a point of telling him now and again what was going on in their offices or departments. For example, he was said to have in his possession an affidavit signed by a railroad sleeping-car conductor vouching for the alleged homosexual activities of a well-known Washington political figure, Sumner Welles.

Before the war Pearson had a collaborator, Robert S. Allen. But after Allen joined the army, Pearson continued alone. The column was started in 1932, just after Pearson and Allen had published their book, *Washington Merry-Go-Round*. 90,000 copies of this work were sold, and Washington society was badly jarred by what the authors had to say of the private lives of its leading citizens. The book's success led Pearson and Allen to publish a daily column of similar character and with the same title. This column was even more popular and before long was appearing in more than six hundred newspapers with a readership of over twenty millions. Indeed it was second only to Winchell's in its influence on the public mind. During the war years, when it was written by Pearson alone, it lost none of its popularity, while in addition Pearson's Sunday evening broadcasts, which were made just two hours before Winchell's, had an estimated audience of 15,000,000.

Despite the changes which the President made from time to time in the Administration, Pearson contrived to remain in direct touch with at least three Cabinet Ministers at any given moment. For example, he was always able to telephone or visit Ickes, Morgenthau and Biddle. From these and other sources he obtained first-hand reports of all Cabinet meetings and on occasion he would quote in his column the actual words used by the President or a passage of dialogue which had occurred between Ministers during a session.

In Britain, of course, he would have been prosecuted at once for violating the Official Secrets Act. In the United States he was immune, provided that he did not publish information which might have caused the loss of American lives. Like Winchell, he was careful to foster the friendship of Edgar Hoover, and at suitable intervals went out of his way to praise him. His foresight paid him well. Once, Cordell Hull was so angry with Pearson that he swore to expose both him and his sources. Hoover was, accordingly, instructed by the White House to penetrate Pearson's intelligence system. 'Of course', Pearson casually admitted afterwards 'Hoover came along and told me about it. So I was able to take the necessary precautions.'

Although Pearson was a staunch New Dealer and an admirer of President Roosevelt, the President never liked his column. The trivialities which it contained apparently nettled him as much as the disconcerting anecdotes about members of his Administration. Once, when the President made a journey to Warm Springs, the column announced that a standing order for Danish pastry, of which the President was allegedly fond, had not been cancelled before his departure and that consequently Danish pastry was piling up high at the White House. Twenty-four hours later, three high officials paid separate visits to Pearson's house. 'For God's sake', they said, 'lay off the boss! Why are you always attacking him?' And they went on to explain that Danish pastry was not, in any case, the President's favourite confectionery. On another occasion, Pearson spread the story that Roosevelt enjoyed the tune 'Home on the Range'. For months afterwards, in consequence, the President could not escape 'Home on the Range' whenever he was within earshot of a band. Unfortunately, it was not Roosevelt, but his secretary, Marvin McIntyre, who liked it. Roosevelt detested it.

More serious was a charge of mendacity which the President brought against Pearson after a radio talk in which the latter declared that Hull wanted to see Russia 'bled white'. Both the President and the Secretary of State protested that Pearson was entirely wrong, and warned him that such statements might be construed as a dangerous affront to an ally. Pearson replied that the Russians had long been aware of Hull's 'consistently anti-Russian attitude,' and added: 'It didn't take me long to

tell them about it. However, if the President needed a scape-
goat, I am glad if anything I have said now assists the Administration to make it clear in words what certainly was not clear
before in deeds.' After the President's protest Pearson had large
placards printed displaying his own profile and under it the
words: 'The Man the President Called a Liar.' For Drew
Pearson it was good publicity.

But even Roosevelt acknowledged Pearson's value at election
time, and in 1944 he sent Harry Hopkins and the Chairman of
the Democratic National Committee, Robert E. Hannegan, to
speak to him. Each of them told Pearson how much the President admired him for his courage, adding that, although they
had had their differences in the past, the time was too critical
to allow small personal bickerings to hinder the cause. Pearson
was delighted and thereafter campaigned ardently for Roosevelt
and a fourth term.

Although a good deal of strategic information indirectly
reached Pearson from Stephenson's office in New York, this did
not produce results comparable with those in Winchell's case;
for not only did Pearson refuse to allow anyone else to write his
column for him but he frequently insisted in putting his own
interpretation upon the information he received. Nor was it
possible to prevent him from publishing at the same time a
considerable amount of anti-British material. This material,
some of it very violent, came to him from such sources as
Admiral Leahy, who had left Vichy to become President
Roosevelt's Chief of Staff, Assistant Secretary of War John J.
McCloy and others. Pearson did not publish it because *he* was
anti-British. He was not. He published it because it was 'hot'
news—for example, when McCloy told him that he (McCloy)
believed that Britain was deliberately delaying the launching of
the second front—and no one could stop Pearson from doing
so. On the other hand, he was dissuaded from publishing much
that would have been damaging to Britain. A great deal of it
was proved to be untrue or inaccurate and was discarded by
Pearson. Much of it also he was talked out of using, on the
ground that it would be harmful to Anglo-American relations
and therefore to the common war effort.

Although Pearson himself had no scruples in publishing
unauthorized information, he was nevertheless enraged when

Stephenson succeeded in penetrating his own intelligence
organization. But he never discovered how or by whom this
was done. Some of the background to this incident may safely
be revealed now.

It began on July 25, 1944, with the publication in Pearson's
column of the greater part of a confidential letter from William
Phillips, an experienced diplomat, who had been successively
U.S. Under-Secretary of State, Ambassador to Italy and the
President's special envoy in India. The letter, which had been
written from New Delhi in April, 1943, and was addressed to
the President, with a copy to Cordell Hull, summed up the
Envoy's impressions of India, and it did not make particularly
pleasant reading, least of all for the British.

According to Phillips, India was in a state of inertia, prostra-
tion, divided counsels and helplessness, with growing distrust
and dislike for the British, and disappointment and disillusion
with regard to Americans. The British had been completely
successful in their policy of 'keeping the lid on' and suppressing
any movement among the native Indians that might be
interpreted as being towards independence. British armies
dominated the picture; twenty thousand Congress Party
leaders remained in jail without trial. Phillips also remarked
that it was hard to discover, either in New Delhi or in other
parts of India, any pronounced war spirit against Japan, *even
on the part of the British*. Rather, the British seemed to feel that
their responsibility lay on the Indian side of the Burma-
Assam frontier. 'Unless the present atmosphere changed for the
better', he added, 'we Americans should have to bear the
burden of the coming campaign in that part of the world and
could not count on more than token assistance from the British
in British India.'[1]

The publication of these criticisms caused a considerable
stir, and was strongly resented in Britain. Sir Ronald Campbell,
the British Minister in Washington, immediately sought an

[1] Hull. II, 1493–4. According to Sherwood's account of the Teheran
Conference in November, 1943, which is based on the Hopkins Papers,
Roosevelt, at his first private meeting with Stalin, 'cautioned Stalin against
bringing up the problems of India with Churchill, and Stalin agreed that
this was undoubtedly a sore subject. Roosevelt said that reform in India
would have to begin from the bottom and Stalin said that reform from the
bottom would mean revolution.' Sherwood. II, 772. See also Churchill. V,
306.

interview with Cordell Hull, at which he lodged a strong
protest and requested the U.S. Government authorities to issue
a statement dissociating themselves from the views expressed in
the letter. Subsequently, on instructions from the Foreign
Office, Campbell called upon Eugene Meyer, the publisher of
the *Washington Post*, and made a formal complaint to him as
well. As it happened, this was of little or no avail, since the
*Post* was only one out of 616 newspapers in which the offending
column had appeared and in any event it exercised no control
over Pearson. However, the Minister reported his conversation
with Meyer in a secret telegram to the Foreign Office. To his
intense surprise, the substance of what he had cabled to London
was faithfully reproduced in Pearson's column a few days
later. Thus it looked as if Pearson had somehow or other
managed to obtain a copy of the original telegram from the
British Embassy.

It was an intolerable situation. Cordell Hull was determined
to find out who had given Pearson the text of Phillips's letter,
and the British Embassy began to search for chinks in its own
security. Meanwhile Stephenson set to work, and early in
August he discovered that Pearson had received a copy of the
letter from an Indian. Further investigation during the ensuing
three weeks revealed that the individual was an Indian
nationalist named Chamal Lal.

There still remained the matter of the Embassy telegram.
Towards the end of August, Stephenson was asked by London
to offer all possible assistance to the Embassy in its inquiries,
since other serious leakages had come to light. For instance,
Senator Albert B. Chandler of Kentucky had been able to
quote in a speech to the Senate the exact text of a cable from
Sir Olaf Caroe, the Secretary to the External Affairs Department in New Delhi, to the India Office in London describing
Phillips as *persona non grata* with the Government of India.

Within the next week Stephenson was able to send a full
report to the Embassy, showing that the leakages were occurring
through the Washington office of the Agent-General for India,
and naming those implicated. As a result, Major Altaf Qadir,
Third Secretary of the Agency and an ardent nationalist,
was obliged to leave the country. He had been borrowing
telegrams from the Agency's files and passing them to Pearson

and Senator Chandler as anti-British, Indian nationalist propaganda.

Pearson's publication of the Phillips letter probably caused more embarrassment to official Anglo-American relations than any other incident of its kind during the war. After Campbell's initial protests, Hull sent the President a memorandum to the effect that it was the State Department's feeling that 'it would be impossible to issue a statement satisfactory to the British, inasmuch as we share in general the views expressed in the Ambassador's letter'. The President agreed with Hull's suggestion that it would be preferable to make no public statement on the subject and that the British Embassy should be informed accordingly. But the British did not easily let the matter drop. On September 8, 1944, Lord Halifax called on Secretary Hull and, in Hull's words, 'very pressingly urged that the President at an early press conference refer to the Phillips letter without mentioning it and speak well of the Indian military forces, and then correct any impression that the British were not aiding in the war against Japan'.[1]

Although the President did not do this, he did join with the British Prime Minister a week later in making a joint statement at the Quebec Conference that all nations concerned with the war in the Far East and South-East Asia were 'ardent' to engage against the Japanese the massive forces they were marshalling. 'Far from shirking this task,' as Churchill later put it, 'the British Empire was eager to play the greatest possible part in it. We had every reason for doing so. Japan was as much the bitter enemy of the British Empire as of the United States. British territory had been captured in battle and grievous losses had been suffered.' Churchill thereupon offered that the British main fleet should take part in the major operations against Japan under United States Supreme Command, an offer which was immediately accepted by Roosevelt as Commander in Chief.[2]

[1] Hull. II, 1495.
[2] Churchill. VI, 134–5.

# CHAPTER VIII

## *FINALE*

### I

BESIDES the Vichy French and the Italian missions, Stephenson's agents succeeded in penetrating Japanese and Spanish diplomacy in the Western Hemisphere by covert means. At the same time others maintained contact with various foreign exiles and helped them to organize 'free' groups in order to strengthen the resistance movements in the enemy occupied countries. In particular, B.S.C. worked closely with the Poles, Czechs, Hungarians, French, Austrians, Norwegians, Italians, Germans, Danes, Jugoslavs and Dutch; also with the Spanish Republicans and Basques.

Notwithstanding language and other difficulties, Stephenson had reliable contacts inside the Japanese Embassy in Washington and the Japanese Consulates in New York and San Francisco, and from their reports, corroborated by other outside sources, it was evident some months before Pearl Harbour that the militarists in Tokyo were bent upon war. An incident in the middle of 1941 showed that the Japanese, in the event of hostilities with the United States, were preparing to transfer their espionage headquarters in the Western Hemisphere, which operated under diplomatic cover, from the United States to Argentina. From a source inside the Argentine Foreign Ministry Stephenson learned that two minor Japanese diplomats were being moved from Washington to Buenos Aires, and their real job Stephenson had reason to believe was espionage. In fact, they and their party had already sailed, and one of them, Hirasawa by name, was known to have been implicated in the forced resignation of Kichisaburo Nomura as Foreign Minister in 1939 and the supremacy of pro-Axis elements in the Japanese Foreign Office.

As a result of Stephenson's prompt action, Mr. Hirasawa and his friends were removed from their ship when it called at

Barbados, and from there they were flown to Trinidad, where Stephenson's representative had made suitable arrangements for their reception. On arrival in Port of Spain they were interrogated, photographed and searched, while their fingerprints were also taken. They were found to be carrying a number of British and American technical publications of value for intelligence work, maps upon which the locations of British and U.S. naval bases in the Western Hemisphere were marked, lists of Hirasawa's contacts and about $40,000 in U.S. notes, of which $15,000 were concealed in the lining of Mrs. Hirasawa's handbag.

Not unnaturally they claimed diplomatic privilege. But their diplomatic status was questioned, since it had been ascertained in the meantime that the Argentine Government had refused to accredit them, ostensibly because the personnel of all diplomatic missions in Buenos Aires was limited in numbers. However, Japan proceeded to evade this restriction by promptly raising its mission to the rank of an Embassy, and eventually the Argentines agreed to accept them. But by this time the British, as well as the Americans whom Stephenson had informed, had no intention of letting them go. After much discussion, they were taken under heavy guard by sea to Halifax. Here they were further interrogated by the R.C.M.P., assisted by the F.B.I., and following protests from the Japanese Government, they were finally repatriated to Japan accompanied by forty-seven pieces of baggage—but minus their $40,000, their maps and their technical publications.

In the middle of November, 1941, the treacherous Japanese special envoy Saburo Kusuru arrived in Washington. As Japanese Ambassador in Berlin he had signed the Tripartite Pact with Germany and Italy. His present mission was to try to push the United States into accepting Japan's overlordship in the Orient, and if and when that failed then to lull the Americans into a false sense of security with peace talk until his military masters were ready to strike. In this he was supported by the weak-kneed Ambassador Nomura, formerly Japanese Foreign Minister.

Stephenson had some success in penetrating the Kusuru mission with one of his agents who was a British subject and had spent fifty years in Japan and spoke the language fluently. This agent made contact with the envoy's secretary, whose

Ernest Cuneo

'. . . most engaging personality.'

David Ogilvy

'. . . admitted that Stephenson had changed the course of his life.'

General Donovan presenting Sir William Stephenson with the U.S. Medal for Merit, November 1946. Looking on are (*left to right*) Colonel Edwin Buxton, Assistant Director of O.S.S., Robert Sherwood and Lady Stephenson

' . . . timely and invaluable aid to the American war effort . . .'

name was Yuki, and had a series of meetings with him in a Washington apartment which had previously been wired for recording conversations. He spoke to Yuki of his love for the Japanese and told him that he felt he could use his influence to persuade Lord Halifax and the British Government to prevail upon the United States to appease the Japanese war lords.

The information obtained from the recordings was translated and transcribed and copies were sent by Stephenson each day to President Roosevelt. For the President it provided additional confirmation of Japan's attitude and of her future intentions which were becoming more and more alarming as each day passed, and it supplemented the Japanese diplomatic telegrams between Tokyo and Washington, which had been known to the American authorities for some time through the skill of the American cryptographers in breaking the Japanese codes and ciphers.

On November 27, the President sent his son James Roosevelt to Stephenson with a special message, the purport of which was not as yet known either to the British Foreign Office or to the British Embassy in Washington. The same day Stephenson telegraphed it to London. His telegram read:

> Japanese negotiations off. Services expect action within two weeks.

This news produced a considerable stir in the Cabinet offices in London and confirmation was immediately sought for it. The Foreign Secretary sent an urgent personal cable to the Ambassador in Washington, asking whether he knew anything about a report of expected Japanese military action, which had just come in. Lord Halifax happened to be out hunting in Virginia when the cable arrived—it will be remembered that the Germans had dubbed him 'Tallyholifax' at the time of his visit to Hitler in 1938—and he was now obliged to get off his horse and hurry back to the Embassy to cable his reply that he knew nothing of such a report. Another urgent cable was sent from London, this time to Stephenson, informing him that the Prime Minister and the Cabinet would be most interested to know the source of his information. Stephenson answered briefly: 'The President of the U.S.A.'

Two days later Cordell Hull saw Halifax and gave him the

news officially. 'The diplomatic part in our relations with Japan is virtually over,' he told the British Ambassador. 'The matter will now go to the officials of the Army and Navy . . . Japan may move suddenly and with every element of surprise.'[1]

How the surprise came just over a week after this interview is a matter of history.

It was now presumed that the Japanese would be unable to conduct much espionage in the United States, since their intelligence system before Pearl Harbour had been based exclusively on their Embassy and Consulates, as has been seen, and there was no evidence that they had made arrangements in anticipation of the day when these would be closed beyond transferring its direction to the Argentine. Indeed it is a remarkable fact that, so far as is known, only one agent in the United States continued to convey intelligence to the Japanese after Pearl Harbour.

This woman was called Velvalee Dickinson, who kept a dolls' shop in New York and had acted as a Japanese agent before the outbreak of war. After her arrest, in 1944, she told the F.B.I. that her late husband had been paid $25,000 by the Japanese Naval Attaché, Ichiro Yokoyama, on November 26, 1941, to furnish information to the Japanese. But all the evidence pointed to Mrs. Dickinson and not her husband as the recipient of this money, particularly as she had previously had another $35,000 in respect of services rendered to the Japanese Naval Intelligence Service.

It was Stephenson who first put the F.B.I. on Velvalee's trail when he gave Hoover the text of one of her letters, which had been intercepted by the Bermuda censors. She used to transmit her intelligence in plain language code which, like her dolls, was of Japanese manufacture, and it was contained in letters addressed to intermediaries in the Argentine. For example, 'I just secured a lovely Siamese Temple Dancer, it had been damaged, that is tore on the middle', meant 'I have just secured information about a fine aircraft carrier, it had been damaged, that is torpedoed amidships'. (This was the U.S.S. *Saratoga*.) Similarly, the meaning of 'I could not get a mate for this Siam dancer, so I am redressing just a plain ordinary doll into a second Siam doll', was 'They could not get hold of a sister ship, so a plain ordinary warship is being converted into a second

[1] Hull. II, 1088.

aircraft carrier'. Unfortunately the letter intercepted at Bermuda gave no clue to the identity of the writer, since it was unsigned and the address on the back of the envelope was that of a woman who, when subsequently questioned by the F.B.I., swore she had not written it; nor for that matter did she know anyone in Buenos Aires. The same negative result was obtained in the case of several similar letters which fell into the hands of the F.B.I.

Then Mrs. Dickinson made a stupid mistake. Hitherto the return mailing addresses which she used had been selected at random from street directories and they belonged to persons she had never heard of. But in a moment of spite she used the name and address of a woman with whom she had had a quarrel. When asked by an F.B.I. agent if she had any idea of who might have used her name, the woman thought for a moment and replied: 'I'll bet it's that Velvalee Dickinson in New York. I bought some dolls from her and because I couldn't pay her right away she's been after me with some nasty letters.'

Comparison of letters written by Mrs. Dickinson with the Bermuda intercepts showed that they had been composed on the same typewriter, and she was arrested on espionage charges. Since these charges would have been difficult to establish by circumstantial evidence alone, the U.S. Attorney handling the case decided to drop them and instead to accept her plea of guilty to violating censorship regulations. As the judge told her in passing a comparatively mild sentence, she was lucky not to have been tried and convicted as a spy, for in that event she would certainly have been sentenced to death or at least life imprisonment.[1]

Mention has already been made of the various minority groups of foreign exiles with which Stephenson's organization was in touch. For instance, it was through the Spanish Republicans and the Basques that he was able to penetrate the Spanish Embassies in Washington and Caracas.

Penetration of the mission in the United States was effected by the good offices of General José Ansensio, who had been Spanish Military Attaché in Washington during the Spanish Civil War and headed a small group of Spanish Republicans in the U.S. His people first of all suborned the butler and the chief messenger at the Embassy, with the result that both of these

[1] Whitehead, 164.

individuals were able to produce useful material, which included copies of papers from the Ambassador's desk and specimens of the Embassy seals and rubber stamps. A little later one of the typists who worked in the cipher room of the Embassy agreed to co-operate. The Secretary who was in charge of the safe where the cipher books were kept in a specially locked box when not in use had a bad memory, and he was in the habit of shouting across the room to his assistant and asking him for the combination. All the typist had to do (which she did) was to make a note of the numbers and pass them on to her friends.

Meanwhile, Stephenson's man in Washington discovered that one of the janitors employed at the Embassy was a Basque. Most Basques had remained loyal to President Aguirre, who had been forced to flee from Spain after General Franco's victory, and this one was no exception. At this time Aguirre happened to be in the United States and was in touch with B.S.C. He readily undertook to approach the janitor, and in due course the latter as readily promised his assistance.

The janitor was given the key to the safe combination, and one night, early in 1942, he opened the safe and took the locked box containing the cipher books to the wash-room of a nearby hotel. Here Stephenson's man was waiting for him in one of the lavatories. However, the mechanism of the box proved so complicated that when the time came for it to be returned to the Embassy it was still unopened. The janitor brought it back to the hotel on the following night, and this time Stephenson's man had made special arrangements for dealing with it. He took it to Stephenson's local office, where a skilled technician was soon able to discover its secrets. The box was opened successfully, the contents photographed and replaced, and the box was then returned to the janitor. In this way His Majesty's Government was provided with the means of reading all secret diplomatic messages which passed between the Spanish Foreign Office in Madrid and the Spanish Embassy in Washington for the remainder of the war.

The Spanish Embassy in Venezuela was also penetrated with the help of ex-President Aguirre. Stephenson's representative in Caracas had recruited the Spanish Ambassador's chauffeur and houseman as an informant. In August, 1942, he managed to have this individual presented to Aguirre, who was then on a tour of Latin America, which incidentally had been arranged by General Donovan at Stephenson's request. Aguirre persuaded the chauffeur-houseman to co-operate fully with the British. The results were equally satisfactory to those obtained in Washington, and two months later the Caracas Embassy's cipher books had been similarly dealt with.

2

One particular type of agent was operated on occasion jointly by Stephenson's organization and his American opposite numbers, namely the double agent, as a means of deceiving the enemy. Some particulars may be given here of this peculiar manner of individual, who has to serve two masters on opposing sides.

While the use of double agents has been described as the ultimate purpose of counter-espionage, it is at the same time a risky and very intricate operation. A man or woman who is already regularly engaged in espionage on the enemy's behalf must be persuaded or coerced to retain his employment but to transfer his allegiance to the other side. The choice of the right moment to exert such persuasion or coercion is one of the most difficult decisions that an intelligence officer can be called upon to make. His attempt may fail; and even if it appears to succeed, he has to face the possibility that the double agent may return to his original master and thus involve the officer in the appalling complications of a 'double double-cross'.

If the operation is successfully accomplished, however, the results are usually profitable. The potential value of a double agent is inherent in his ability to do four things. First, he can give information about other agents employed by the enemy, about their training, assignments and methods. Secondly, from the questionnaire with which he is supplied by his original employers he can explain what they want to know—and that is often an indication of the enemy's strategic plans. Thirdly, if properly organized, he renders it unnecessary for the enemy to place new and possibly unknown agents in his operational area, and consequently makes an important contribution to the security of his new employers' country. Lastly, and most important of all, he can be used as a channel to convey strategic deceptive information to the enemy. It is to this latter end that double agents must be eventually manoeuvred, for thus they play a valuable part in the cover plans for military operations of great magnitude.

The difficulties in exploiting the double agent are many. Not the least lies in the personality and character of the man or woman concerned. Double agents, with the knowledge acquired from working with two opposing intelligence services, are fully aware of their own value. While some may change sides for genuine ideological reasons or may initially accept employment from one side for the sole purpose of assisting the other, only too often they are motivated by a desire for money. In neutral countries, where it is not always easy or indeed possible to apply coercive methods, their demands are frequently exorbitant. But even when they operate in a belligerent's own country, their wishes must be studied to some extent in order to gain their co-operation and confidence, which are essential if they are to prove worth while. One of Stephenson's most important double agents working from New York, for instance, could only give of his best from a luxurious pent-house apart-ment, the bedroom of which was furnished with the person of a famous and expensive French actress. Many of the F.B.I.'s troubles with double agents, whom they tried to run, arose from their lack of understanding of the European mind and outlook, and from their inability to place in charge of a double agent an officer with a background likely to win his sympathy and friendship.

Another difficulty is that double agents are in constant danger of being arrested by the local police who naturally know nothing of their real purpose. For example, Stephenson's representative in Buenos Aires carefully recruited and 'built up' a potentially valuable double agent inside the Spanish-German smuggling ring operating from Argentina. Unfor-tunately, just before he could begin to produce information of value, he was arrested by the Argentinians on a smuggling charge and disappeared. Moreover, as already indicated, double agents may set out to penetrate the organization to which they have ostensibly transferred their allegiance in order to report back to the enemy on its structure, methods and intent. Or they may give him such information unwittingly. The 'double double-cross' can arise, too, when the enemy discovers he has been betrayed and so in return deliberately feeds the double agent with misleading information which will be accepted as accurate. Finally, double agents cannot be used to deceive the enemy unless they are supplied from time to time with true and useful intelligence material which they are allowed to transmit to the enemy, for otherwise the enemy will soon realize that their information is of no value and will discard them. But the natural source of such information is the Armed Services, and they are often most reluctant to release it.

Conscious of these various pitfalls, the F.B.I. were chary of using double agents in the early years of the war. They did, it is true, have one notable success in the case of William Sebold, which has been mentioned in an earlier chapter.[1] But their use of Sebold as a double agent was very limited, and he was not employed as a channel for strategic deception. In those days, before Pearl Harbour, Hoover regarded a double agent very much as a decoy, whose usefulness was to uncover other enemy agents hitherto unknown. Hence, in Sebold's case, the need for obtaining the release of pertinent information from the Army and Navy did not arise, as he could be kept operating with comparatively low-grade material.

The question was not thoroughly examined before Pearl Harbour, because, although Stephenson and Hoover were both interested in it, the U.S. Services had not realized its importance and were not prepared to give away any information. Stephenson had the greatest difficulty at this period in obtaining permission for the release of letters containing information sent by enemy agents in America; yet it was imperative to do so in order to keep the channel of communication open and thus pave the way for the ultimate detection of the sender. In April, 1942, he suggested to Hoover that the Chiefs of Staff should be invited to set up a joint inter-services committee, which would be charged with responsibility for facilitating the production of intelligence to be sent to Germany by double agents and of authorizing its release. Stephenson followed up this suggestion with a staff paper on the care and handling of double agents, with particular emphasis on their 'feeding'; and this paper was submitted to

[1] See p. 84.

the Chiefs of Staff and accepted by them. Nevertheless, as had happened in other instances, it was not acted upon consistently for many months. For example, an excellent double agent sent over by London was almost abandoned by the Germans because the F.B.I. were unwilling or unable to produce useful information to pass on to him.

Another difficulty, also of a purely domestic character, arose from inter-departmental competition, not to mention jealousies. The F.B.I. employed double agents (usually in conjunction with B.S.C.). So occasionally did the Army's G.2. Donovan's O.S.S. employed more. Naturally each agency kept its operations secret from the other, with the result that the F.B.I. would sometimes suspect and investigate an agent who turned out to be under the control of O.S.S.

In general, the theory and practice of operating double agents was one of the most difficult fields in which Stephenson attempted to educate both the F.B.I. and O.S.S., and it is open to doubt if they ever mastered the subject completely, especially the F.B.I. Nevertheless, as the war proceeded, increasing numbers of double agents were put into operation in the Western Hemisphere, mostly on Stephenson's initiative, and several of them are worth some brief detailed consideration.

One of the most important was a well-to-do young Yugoslav of good family and education, whose code name was 'Bicycle'. He hated the Germans who had arrested him and thrown him into prison when he was a student in Germany before the war, because in the course of student discussions he had praised the advantages of political freedom and democratic rule in contrast with the Nazi régime. Consequently when he was approached by a representative of the *Abwehr* in Belgrade early in 1940, he agreed to work for the Germans, but at the same time he got into touch secretly with British Intelligence. As a result of careful handling he was 'built up' as a valuable source in the eyes of the Germans, and during 1940 and part of 1941, he operated successfully between London and Lisbon. He was undoubtedly clever and always showed himself absolutely loyal to his British employers. Admittedly his tastes in clothes, women and entertainment were expensive—but then the Germans were paying largely for them. The only reward he ever asked for from the British was that after the war he might be appointed an honorary British Vice-Consul in his native Yugoslavia.

In August, 1941, after performing valuable service in Europe, he was sent by the Germans to the United States. The F.B.I. were advised of his arrival, having already helped to get him a passage from Lisbon. However, they insisted on taking him over and running him themselves. It was they who set up his radio station, composed his messages, and did his coding. Stephenson's staff gave advice and supervision whenever possible, but was often deliberately bypassed by the F.B.I., who were proud of their recent success with William Sebold and appeared to resent the advice of their friendly British collaborators in this instance.

The experiment was hardly a success. 'Bicycle' disliked the comparatively unsophisticated G-men who controlled him, and he was worried by their inability to produce strategic information for him to pass on to the Germans. The F.B.I., on the other hand, disliked his liberal manner of living, and kept making the impossible request that he should square up his financial affairs and reduce his personal expenses. However, in spite of these difficulties, eight letters containing secret writing in invisible ink were despatched by him to Germany in the autumn of 1941. These were supposed to be passed through the Bermuda censorship, but one of them—possibly because Stephenson had been advised too late to warn the censors— was picked out and sent to the testing laboratory, where the secret writing was fully developed, which of course rendered the letter useless for onward transmission. No doubt for the same reason the others took much longer to arrive at their German destinations than might have been expected.

Towards the end of the year the Germans instructed 'Bicycle' to report to Rio de Janeiro. There he saw the Assistant Naval Attaché in the German Embassy, Commander Bohny, and also the German secret intelligence chief, Alfredo Engels, who expressed complete confidence in him and instructed him to return to New York and build a short-wave radio for communication with Lisbon, Hamburg and Rio.

Throughout the first three months of 1942, the F.B.I. passed out messages which purported to come from him over his radio, but they gave B.S.C. no copies of these and no details concerning their success or failure. 'Bicycle' was not even taken to see the radio station which had been built for him, with the result that he was in danger of being caught out by a snap question from a genuine German agent in America or by a request to send a message at short notice. Soon the Germans were complaining that his reports lacked 'meat', and they began to suspect—particularly after the arrest of Engels in Brazil—that 'Bicycle' was working under control. After a strong personal protest by Stephenson to Hoover, the latter appointed one of his more experienced officers to take charge of the double agent and undertook to obtain a more regular supply of suitable information from the armed services.

In spite of these assurances, Hoover's men were unable to shed their original gang-busting methods in handling 'Bicycle'. For instance, when the Germans sent over some money for him, instead of allowing it to reach him without interference the F.B.I. attempted to draw the courier into a trap, which would of course have notified the Germans that 'Bicycle' was at least under the gravest suspicion. However, by making considerable efforts with the Joint Services Committee, Stephenson elicited enough information to keep 'Bicycle' at work until August, 1942. Then the F.B.I. finally decided to have nothing further to do with him on the ground that he was a liar and was too expensive to justify his retention. In fact, it was a tacit admission of their incompetence in this particular instance, and incidentally an instructive illustration of how to spoil a good double agent.

Another double agent, with whom considerable difficulties were encountered, although these had nothing to do with the F.B.I., was known as 'Springbok'. A German of noble descent —his grandfather had held a high office at the court of the Emperor William I.—he knew South Africa well (hence his code name) where he had built up a successful business before the war. He was also a man of powerful attraction to women, judging by the fact that he successfully seduced the wife of the B.S.C. officer in whose charge he was for a time. He was sent by the Germans to Brazil, where he defected to the British side. He operated mostly from Canada and gave most valuable information on the structure and methods of the German intelligence organization. This led to the arrest, among others, of Alfredo Engels and Herbert Von Heyer, the leading German agents in Brazil, and also of the spy named Leibrandt in South Africa who had orders to assassinate General Smuts and was later caught and executed. The main difficulty with 'Springbok', however, was to get his information back to Germany; and, when his intermediary in Brazil was arrested and the Brazilians published his name in the course of their investigations, the Canadians had to stage his arrest, which they announced had been done at the request of the British.

Other double agents were 'Moonstone', 'Bromo', 'Aspirin' (so named for the many 'headaches' associated with him), 'Lodge', 'Minaret' and 'Pat J'. When the end of the war came in Europe, radio channels were still being operated by the last three under control and were in daily contact with the Germans. One of the most successful was 'Pat J'.

This particular double agent was a Dutchman, who had worked for German intelligence during the First World War, had finally settled down in his own country as a dealer in radio and electrical equipment. His work brought him into contact with the German Zeiss optical instrument manufacturers' subsidiaries in Holland, which led to his being recruited by the *Abwehr* in the Hague in 1940. His new masters decided that he should be sent to the United States after a period of training; and at the beginning of 1942 he arrived in Madrid on his way to America. But in Spain he underwent a change of heart and came to the conclusion that he could not work against the allies of his own country. He revealed his story to the Netherlands Consulate in Madrid, which he had been allowed to visit on a routine matter connected with his passport.

The Dutch informed London, who in due course informed Stephenson and asked him to arrange if possible with the F.B.I. to accept 'Pat J' as a double agent to work in the United States. Hoover agreed and 'Pat J' was assisted to get a passage. Unfortunately he went down with a bad attack of pneumonia immediately after his arrival, but on his recovery he was able to provide valuable information on the working of the *Abwehr* in Holland and France. However, it was not until 1943 that he was able to establish radio contact with the Germans. But from then on the quality of his messages developed well, and he undoubtedly played a useful part in the general scheme of enemy deception.

Like so many German agents, 'Pat J' experienced the usual
financial difficulties, since payment by funds in neutral countries
was by no means easy and there were frequent delays before
this could be effected. Although the double agent was usually
well 'taken care of' in this respect by the British or the
Americans, he frequently had to pretend poverty in order to
give credence to this supposed condition. On occasions this
difficulty would create the ironic situation in which the
Germans were making every effort to despatch funds urgently,
while the deception material was held up in order to maintain
the pretence on the other side that sub-agents could not be
paid and hence no information was forthcoming.

On one occasion, towards the end of 1943, the Germans
advised 'Pat J' that funds would reach him shortly in the form
of eight rare and valuable postage stamps. A German agent
was accordingly despatched from Spain to Buenos Aires with
funds to buy the stamps and send them to New York for 'Pat J'.
However, on reaching Buenos Aires, the agent, who was an
alcoholic, converted the funds to his own use in the local bars
and finally dropped dead through excess of liquor. A few
months later, a somewhat nervous New York Jew handed
over $3,000 to an unknown man in a hotel bedroom in
Manhattan. The Jew knew that the funds had reached him in
contravention of the U.S. Currency regulations, but he was
under the impression that he was merely assisting a fellow
refugee in distress. The final recipient of the money was 'Pat J',
and it had been despatched by a Frenchman in Spain who had
been working for the Germans for some years. Incidentally,
although this Frenchman was only a small pawn in the
espionage game, it is worth noting that during the war he had
fleeced the German Intelligence Service by various means of
eighty million francs. When last heard of he was about to have
the major part of his takings forcibly removed by the French
authorities of General de Gaulle.

Further funds were sent to 'Pat J' at the end of 1944 by
means of another German agent who flew from Lisbon carrying
a diamond tie-pin and ring valued at $6,000. Continued and
ingenious methods of payment of a similar kind were made
and were ample proof of 'Pat J's' success as a double agent,
since they meant that the Germans clearly rated him highly.

'Pat J' was still transmitting when Germany capitulated, and it was planned that he should continue to do so in the event of any possible revival of German clandestine activities.

There is no doubt that what was done by Stephenson and his organization to assist the Americans in establishing double agents was well worth while, in spite of difficulties, and that excellent deception was practised upon the Germans particularly in regard to United States war potential.

## 3

One of the duties which Stephenson undertook for the London headquarters of both S.I.S. and S.O.E. was to recruit, train and despatch agents into enemy territory. There were many unforeseen obstacles in the way of fulfilling it.

Although the United States was the largest potential source of recruits in the Western Hemisphere, it could unfortunately never be exploited fully by Stephenson's organization. So long as American neutrality lasted, the U.S. Government did not wish recruits to be drawn from foreign minorities, and it could make its wishes effective through the Immigration and Justice Departments and the State Department, without whose permission it was virtually impossible for a prospective agent to leave the country.

The case of a Bulgar named Alexander Stoyanoff provides an illustration of this difficulty. This man was sent out by London to get false papers in America and return to Europe. The Immigration authorities, through their own inquiries, soon found out that his story was false, and Stephenson had to resort to a personal appeal on the highest level before Stoyanoff was cleared. Such pressure could only be exercised in exceptional circumstances, and a few first-class agents were recruited in this way. But to flout the will of the U.S. Government as a matter of policy would obviously have been very unwise.

After the United States entered the war, Stephenson was obliged to give an undertaking to the F.B.I. not to recruit any agents directly in the United States on behalf of his organization. A few were indeed recruited on his behalf by O.S.S. and sent to England, but this was an arrangement of which advantage could be taken only sparingly and very discreetly, since O.S.S. had difficulty in securing a sufficient number of agents to fulfil its own needs. The manpower authorities were unwilling to allow any fit man of military age to leave the country, and a draft board release, without which an exit permit could not be granted, was extremely hard to obtain.

Most of Stephenson's recruiting had, therefore, to be done outside the United States—in Canada, and to a lesser extent in Latin America. Even then the choice was limited, since it was found that with a few notable exceptions, such as the Yugoslavs, the members of foreign minority groups in the Western Hemisphere did not possess enough interest in the land of their origin to be prepared to return to it on an arduous and dangerous mission at the sacrifice of their existing comforts. Furthermore, many of them had forgotten their native language or could speak it only with an accent. Even when suitable recruits had been found and trained, Stephenson's difficulties were by no means over. Transport was always very tight and for a time after Pearl Harbour was virtually unobtainable. Party after party was held up. Sometimes as much as three months would elapse before an agent reached the United States from Latin America. Constant delays in sailing, changes in routine, and the multiplication of formalities, to which attention had to be given, represented what was perhaps the most irksome part of the job of recruitment. For nothing is more likely to discourage an agent, to damp his ardour and damage his discretion than interruption in his plans for setting out upon his mission.

To make the recruiting procedure consistent with the training scheme, and also to take advantage of the improved security and discipline which were possible under military regulations, Stephenson made arrangements with the Canadian military authorities whereby recruits were enlisted into the Canadian Army. This procedure worked out very well. It meant that men were put into uniform as soon as they had been effectively recruited. On completion of their training they were sent overseas in Canadian troopships. On arrival at a British port they would be discharged by the Canadian Army and absorbed by the War Office. Furthermore they were entitled to the full benefits of Canadian war-service gratuities and army pensions, and in this as in facilitating the whole recruiting programme the Canadian authorities could not have been more co-operative.

Thus Canada was by far the most fruitful field of recruitment, and Yugoslav-Canadians the most successful recruits, although some of the Italians recruited in Mexico were to accomplish outstanding work as leaders of the underground in various large Italian cities.

The training school, known as Camp X, was established in an old farm at Oshawa near Toronto in December, 1941. Here the new recruit was taught the importance of accurate observation; and his own powers of observation were frequently put to practical test by moving or removing objects in his room. He was taught how to shadow a man and how to escape surveillance himself; how to creep up behind an armed sentry and kill him instantly without noise; and how to evade capture by blinding his assailant with a box of matches. In the course in unarmed combat he learned many 'holds' whose use would enable him to break an adversary's arm or leg, to knock him unconscious or to kill him outright. He was also given weapon training. He learned to handle a tommy-gun and to use several different types of revolvers and automatic pistols, firing them from a crouching position either in daylight or darkness. He was instructed in the dexterous use of a knife, which could kill swiftly and silently if driven upwards just below the ribs.

Much of his time was spent in mastering the arts of sabotage. He was taught the simplest method of putting a motor vehicle out of commission without leaving any trace of his interference. He learned how to attach explosives to a railway track or an oil tank in a manner likely to cause the maximum amount of damage; how to make simple types of grenades as well as other explosive and incendiary devices, using material that could be easily purchased. Before the course was finished, he could make and write with secret inks, use different kinds of codes and ciphers for communicating with other agents, and interrogate a prisoner to the best effect. He was trained in parachute jumping. He took part in night exercises, in which one group of trainees would set out to sabotage a specific target, while others would be given the task of stopping them; and in exercises arranged by the Canadian Air Force, in which a raiding party would be dropped by parachute and would later carry out a mock attack with air support. Practical tests were also conducted in the city of Toronto with the aid of the local police, who at the same time were undergoing training in counter-espionage and counter-sabotage methods. A selected group of police in the counter-espionage squad, for instance, unaware that they were dealing with trainees, would be set on the trail of men whom they supposed to be genuine enemy agents. To pass this test the embryo agent would have to evade the police successfully.

In spite of the difficulties in recruitment, the school trained more than five hundred carefully chosen students, and conducted fifty-two courses. The courses were also attended by selected Canadian and American military personnel as well as by representatives of the F.B.I., O.S.S. and O.W.I. In addition, as has already been indicated, the school provided O.S.S. with all its initial instructors, books and equipment, and when it was finally closed down in September, 1944, its entire stock was bequeathed to O.S.S., who received it gratefully. Besides this, Stephenson had to supply S.O.E. in London with a variety of 'toys', as the various implements of sabotage and destruction were colloquially known. One of the more curious items was a gourd of curare, a dark resinous substance which produces instant death when injected into the blood stream. It was obtained by one of Stephenson's agents from some up-country Venezuelan Indians and forwarded to London in the spring of 1942.

The first agent to be recruited was recruited by Stephenson personally on the ship in which he travelled to America in June, 1940. He was an Italian, who later rose to become a Lieutenant-Colonel in the British Army. He was second in command of the Special Operations mission which went into Sicily with the first wave of assault troops, and he was instrumental in himself recruiting Sicilians for work behind the enemy lines. He performed similar missions at Salerno and Anzio. In December, 1944, he was parachuted into the country near Milan with the object of making contact with and encouraging the members of the Committee of Liberation, who incidentally had the highest respect for him and took their orders from him without question. The capture of Milan, for which he deserves much of the credit, was a model operation.

He led the liberation forces into the city and personally took over the Milan radio station. He was later granted the freedom of the city, while the British decorated him with the D.S.O. and M.C.

The value of the work performed by agents in enemy territory can hardly be overestimated. Without the material, communications, training and leadership by the British S.O.E. and (after November, 1943) by the American O.S.S., 'resistance' in the enemy-occupied territories would have been valueless from the military point of view. To give but one example, sabotage on the French and Belgian railways reduced the stock of serviceable locomotives to a point where there was an actual deficiency in the number required by the Germans at the time of the allied landings in Normandy. Between September, 1943 and September, 1944, sabotage in France alone accounted for almost as many as the total number of locomotives disabled by air action during the same period.

In no previous war had the resistance forces, to quote General Eisenhower's words, been 'so closely harnessed to the main military effort', and none appreciated this more than the Supreme Commander upon whose shoulders lay the responsibility for the ultimate military success in Europe. In this context, Stephenson's contribution and that of the training school which he organized was both impressive and effective.

### 4

Late on the night of September 6, 1945, William Stephenson, who happened to be on a routine official visit to Ottawa, called on Mr. Norman Robertson, Under-Secretary of State in the Canadian Department of External Affairs, at his private residence. With him he found Mr. Thomas Archibald Stone, Counsellor in the Canadian Embassy in Washington. Earlier that day Stephenson had heard a story to the effect that an employee of the Soviet Embassy had been in touch with the Department of Justice through the R.C.M.P., offering to furnish information, and he wanted to know whether Robertson knew anything about it. As a matter of fact, Robertson did. He told Stephenson that the head of the Intelligence Branch of the R.C.M.P. had informed him that a man who had given his name as Gouzenko and said he was a cipher clerk in the Embassy had made such an offer, and the intelligence officer had asked for guidance as to what action to take. The Under-Secretary had in turn consulted the Prime Minister, Mr. Mackenzie King, with the result that the R.C.M.P. were instructed to do nothing for the time being for fear of the diplomatic repercussions which might arise from a false step. ('Too hot a potato', the Prime Minister remarked), although this was not to prevent the R.C.M.P. from keeping a watch on the Russian.

Stephenson immediately realized that this man might well provide a unique opportunity for obtaining important details of the operation of the Soviet intelligence system in the Western Hemisphere. He also realized that the Russian's life might be in serious danger, if he had indeed defected, since the Soviet secret police in the Embassy would undoubtedly attempt to 'liquidate' him and would almost certainly succeed unless some prompt action were taken to protect him. Stephenson therefore urged that this consideration far outweighed the risk of any political repercussions which might result from giving the R.C.M.P. a free hand to deal with the case as they saw fit. The Under-Secretary agreed on reflection and telephoned the R.C.M.P., informing them privately that the Department was prepared to modify its previous instruction in the sense suggested by the Director of B.S.C. and adding that Gouzenko should be fetched and allowed to say what he wished on the following morning.

The amazing story of Igor Gouzenko has been told by many people, including himself, but it is necessary to give a few details here so as to clarify Stephenson's part in it.[1] Briefly, Gouzenko was a young Russian, aged twenty-six, a graduate of the Moscow School of Engineering, who after careful screening and training in the Soviet military intelligence academy had been sent out to work in the cipher department of the Embassy in Ottawa in 1943. He had a wife and young son Andrei, who had been allowed to join him in Canada, and now another child was on the way. His official duties were conducted in a specially sealed-off wing of the Embassy, to which not even the Ambassador had access, and he soon

[1] See particularly, Igor Gouzenko, *This Was My Choice* (1948).

discovered that his immediate chief, Colonel Nicolai Zabotin, the Military Attaché, was in charge of a complex and far-reaching espionage network in Canada.

He and his wife were astonished by the living conditions in which they found themselves compared with those at home in Moscow which they had been told were the highest in the world. The sense of personal security, freedom to speak as they liked and to look at and where they liked, the surplus of food and goods in the shops and supermarkets, the workers driving around in their own cars—this was the lot of the ordinary Canadian, and the lesson was not lost upon Igor and Anna Gouzenko—particularly when one afternoon Colonel Zabotin summoned him to his office and told him that instructions had come from Moscow for the immediate recall of Gouzenko and his family. A few days later, in response to a request from Zabotin pointing out that the Embassy was short of staff, these instructions were changed and Gouzenko was ordered to remain at his post 'for the time being'. But he and his wife realized that this was only a reprieve, and so they made up their minds that they must somehow contrive to stay in Canada. In due course, Gouzenko's successor arrived from Moscow and Gouzenko was allowed a few more weeks to explain the work to the newcomer. Then came the order to hand over on September 6, 1945.

'This is your chance to do something big for this country and yourself, and most of all, for Andrei and the new baby', his wife insisted. 'Canada is to be our home. Let us not take everything and give nothing.'

What Igor Gouzenko determined to give was complete documentary proof of the Soviet spy system in Canada. With this aim in view, he went through all the secret files, turning down the edges of those telegrams and other documents which he considered of particular interest. Then, on the evening of September 5—the day before he was due to hand over—he surreptitiously abstracted all the documents which he had marked, tucked them under his shirt and quietly left the Embassy for the last time.

It says much for his belief in the democratic processes of the country that he went straight to the offices of a local newspaper, the *Ottawa Journal*, and spread his precious documents on the

City Editor's desk. Having explained what they were, he was politely told that he should take them to the R.C.M.P. There he was told to come back in the morning.

Next day was an exhausting one as he trudged from office to office with his wife and child, seemingly getting nowhere. Finally, dispirited and weary, he returned to his apartment in Somerset Street, fearful of what might happen since he realized that by this time his failure to turn up at the Embassy for work coupled with the disappearance of the secret documents must have been discovered. He therefore appealed for help to the neighbours who lived in the same staircase. One of them, a sergeant in the Canadian Air Force, called the local police, and another took the Gouzenkos in and gave them a bed for the night. The police agreed to keep an eye on the apartment building.

Shortly before midnight a party of four men from the Soviet Embassy arrived and forced their way into the Gouzenko apartment by the simple expedient of breaking the lock. The Embassy men were led by Vitali Pavlov, Second Secretary and chief N.K.V.D. (secret police) representative in the Embassy. The Gouzenkos' neighbours again called the police and reported that someone was trying to break into their apartment. A few minutes later the police arrived and found the Russians rifling the contents. 'He left some documents here and we have his permission to look for them,' Pavlov prevaricated in answer to the police query. After an angry scene with the police Pavlov and his men withdrew.

From the apartment opposite Gouzenko continued to keep watch, as he felt the N.K.V.D. men might return. For several hours nothing further happened. Then shortly before 4 a.m. there was another knock at the door, this time a low careful one. 'But whoever it was left before I could identify him,' Gouzenko wrote afterwards. In fact, it was Stephenson and Stone, who had come to reconnoitre the position. (They thereupon returned to Norman Robertson's house and woke him up with the news of what had happened in the Gouzenko apartment house.)

Next morning Gouzenko was brought to R.C.M.P. headquarters, as arranged, while his wife and child remained in the neighbours' apartment under police protection. Not unnaturally he showed signs of the strain of the day before and indeed he was in a state of extreme nervousness as he sat down with the head of the intelligence branch and his assistant, an expert of long experience in dealing with Communist matters.

Gouzenko's first statements seemed so fantastic—how Soviet agents through contacts in the highest places had been collecting data on the atomic bomb—that they were difficult to credit until Gouzenko produced the documents he had in his possession. These consisted of the dossiers of three important agents, reports in the handwriting of other agents, a number of notes and a selection of some thirty recent telegrams which he had decoded. A preliminary survey of this material made it clear that the Soviet Union was conducting espionage in Canada on a large scale, and that a network of agents, operating inside various Government Departments, including the Department of External Affairs itself, and the Office of the United Kingdom High Commissioner, was being run by Colonel Zabotin and the staff of the Military Attaché's office. For example, one telegram signed 'Grant', which was Zabotin's cover name, dated July 9, 1945, read in part:

> Alek handed over to us a platinum with 162 micrograms of Uranium 233 in the form of acid, contained in a thin lamina.

The identity of 'Alek' was soon discovered. He turned out to be Dr. Alan Nunn May, a British physicist working on research into nuclear fission in the Montreal laboratories of the Canadian National Research Council. He had been a secret Communist and a willing Soviet agent for some time.

Other agents mentioned in the documents were Fred Rose, the only Communist M.P. in the Canadian House of Commons; Schmidt Kogan, alias Sam Carr, secretary of the Canadian Communist Party; and Miss Kathleen Mary Willsher, who was employed in the Registry of the U.K. High Commission in Ottawa and had access to the secret and confidential files. Miss Willsher, a well-educated graduate of the London School of Economics—she spoke French, German and some Russian in addition to English—had belonged to the Canadian Communist Party for the past nine years and passed the information she obtained from the registry files to Fred Rose. Mr. Malcolm

MacDonald, the High Commissioner, at first refused to believe that she had violated the Official Secrets Act which she had sworn to observe, and it was not until Stephenson showed him the documentary proof of her treachery that he resigned himself to the loss of one of his most efficient employees.

After this preliminary interrogation, Gouzenko with his wife and young Andrei were driven off to a 'hideout' in the country, where they were to remain heavily guarded but safe from the machinations of Comrade Pavlov and the N.K.V.D. When the time came for Anna Gouzenko's child to be born, she was taken to a local hospital where she posed as the wife of a Polish farmer, while an R.C.M.P. officer disguised himself as the farmer, visiting the hospital and talking in carefully rehearsed broken English. At the request of the R.C.M.P., a complete layette for the baby, who turned out to be a girl weighing seven pounds and twelve ounces, was specially ordered and sent up from Stephenson's office in New York.

Gouzenko's interrogation proved a lengthy business, and several weeks passed before the whole story had been pieced together, supplemented by information from London and Washington, since the trail led to Nunn May, who had returned to England, and to the United States, where a similar network of spies was found to be operating. Meanwhile, Stephenson had sent the R.C.M.P. two of his most experienced staff to help with the inquiries, while he put his secure tele-krypton facilities at the disposal of the Canadians for the purpose of communicating with London and New York, since there was a danger that the Canadian ciphers had been compromised. Incidentally, when one of Stephenson's men suggested to Mr. Robertson, the Under-Secretary of State, that the case should be given a cover name in all conversations and reports concerning it, the Minister pointed at the label on a bottle of Corby's Canadian rye whisky which stood on his desk and had been sustaining the tired group of men in the room—henceforward it was to be known officially as 'the Corby case'. Further to put the Russians off the scent, both the R.C.M.P. in Ottawa and the F.B.I. in Washington pretended to accede to the Soviet request to apprehend Gouzenko and hand him over to them by ostensibly instituting a nation-wide search for him in both countries.

At first, it was intended that concerted action should be taken towards the end of November, 1945, but the discovery of further evidence of similar espionage in the United States caused the Canadians to postpone their contemplated action for nearly three months. Meanwhile Zabotin and two of his principal assistants, whose recall the Canadian Government proposed to demand, anticipated this move by quietly leaving the country and taking ship back to Russia. Shortly afterwards, Drew Pearson, the Washington columnist and candid commentator, who had got hold of the story through some leakage, the source of which was never discovered, referred to it in two broadcasts. This made action imperative, and at dawn on February 15, 1946, the R.C.M.P. carried out their arrests. At the same time the Canadian Prime Minister appointed a Royal Commission consisting of two judges of the Supreme Court of Canada to hold a public inquiry into all the facts as disclosed by Gouzenko. Shortly afterwards, on March 6, the thirty-five-year-old nuclear scientist Alan Nunn May was arrested in England, and after a trial at the Old Bailey, convicted and sentenced to ten years' imprisonment. Fred Rose and the other Canadian were likewise tried in Canada and received prison sentences.

Not only did Gouzenko give evidence at upwards of twenty trials, which took place in Canada as a result of his disclosures, but his testimony before the Royal Commission was invaluable in constructing the most remarkable picture of international espionage to be presented in this century. 'You have accomplished an historic act,' Prime Minister Mackenzie King told him on the day the Commission's Report was published. 'The people of Canada and the world are your debtors.'

In saying this the Prime Minister merely endorsed the findings of the Royal Commissioners, Mr. Justice Robert Taschereau and Mr. Justice R. C. Kellock, who had stated that in their opinion: 'Gouzenko by what he has done has rendered great public service to the people of this country, and thereby has placed Canada in his debt.' It is not so generally known that but for the intervention at a critical moment of another Canadian, who never sought the limelight, Igor Gouzenko might not have been alive to tell his dramatic story.

5

With the surrender of Japan in August, 1945, Stephenson considered that his official work was virtually over and that it only remained for him to wind up his organization before he would be free to return to civil life and resume his business interests. With the ending of hostilities in Europe, most of his staff had already returned to their pre-war jobs or took new ones—some, like David Ogilvy, John Pepper and Sydney Morrell, decided to stay in America and make their future careers there. However, Stephenson kept on a few key men to help in the Gouzenko case, to which he had to give much of his personal attention during the next six months. Consequently it was not until the middle of 1946 that British Security Co-ordination was formally dissolved.

What he had achieved did not go unrecognized, although, to quote Robert Sherwood, his exploits, like those of Edgar Hoover, 'could hardly be advertised at the time'. He had already received the honour of knighthood at the hands of King George VI., his name having appeared in the New Year Honours List issued from Buckingham Palace in 1945. Towards the end of the following year he received the Presidential Medal for Merit, America's highest honour for a civilian. The citation signed by President Truman has been quoted in reference to the 'timely and invaluable aid to the American war effort in making available to the United States the extensive experience and resources of the British Government in the fields of Intelligence and Special Operations'.

The citation had been written by General Donovan, who sent it to the President with a covering letter in which he described as 'absolutely true' everything that had been expressed in it. 'Just as we have been insistent on the right of our country to have an independent secret intelligence service,' he added, 'so I would like our British colleagues to see that we recognize and appreciate the help they can give us.'

The award was made on the President's behalf by General Donovan in a simple ceremony in Stephenson's apartment suite in the top of the Hotel Dorset on West 54th Street, New York. The General pinned the decoration on Stephenson's coat in the presence of his wife and Robert Sherwood, former

Assistant Director of O.W.I., while Colonel Ned Buxton, who had occupied a similar post in O.S.S., read out the citation. At the same time Donovan gave him a photograph of himself which he inscribed:

> To Bill Stephenson whose friendship, knowledge and continuing assistance contributed so richly to the establishment and the maintenance of an American intelligence Service in World War II.
>
> Bill Donovan.

He was to receive one other remarkable tribute which must be mentioned. This was from the British Labour leader Dr. Dalton, under whose Ministry the Special Operations Executive had been developed. In 1947 Stephenson and his wife paid a visit to London in the course of which they met Dalton, who was now Chancellor of the Exchequer in the first post-war Labour Government. On his return to New York, Stephenson received the following letter :

> Treasury Chambers,
> Great George Street,
> LONDON, S.W. I.
> *29th July, 1947.*

MY DEAR SIR WILLIAM,

It has been a personal pleasure to me to meet you again during the past few weeks, and to renew our war-time association.

When I was Minister of Economic Warfare in Mr. Churchill's Coalition Government, I deeply appreciated the most conspicuous services which you were then rendering in the United States to the common cause. The appreciation of our American friends was shown by the most outstanding decoration which they conferred upon you.

I should further like to place on record the fact that you did all this of your own goodwill, and received no remuneration of any kind. This was a very generous and patriotic gesture, for which, on behalf of His Majesty's Government, I warmly thank you.

With my kind personal regards,

> Yours very sincerely,
> HUGH DALTON

Sir William Stephenson, M.C., D.F.C.

At this time Sherwood was working on his study *Roosevelt and Hopkins* (published in England under the title *The White*

*House Papers of Harry L. Hopkins*), and the brief passing tribute which he paid Stephenson in this work, when he described him as 'a quiet Canadian', whose activities 'produced some remarkable results which were incalculably valuable', gave him far more pleasure than the more formal compliments which accompanied the award of his British and American honours.

Meanwhile, Stephenson had gone to live in Jamaica, where he had bought a property at Hillowton, overlooking Montego Bay—'the finest house in the island', he called it. (Incidentally, it was his wife's choice.) His example was followed by several of his friends, including Lord Beaverbrook, Sir William Wiseman, Noël Coward and Ian Fleming, all of whom acquired estates on Jamaica's beautiful north shore at this time. For a year or so he showed little interest in the outside world and was content to enjoy life on this island in the sun. Only gradually did he recover his interest in commerce and industry. With some of his war-time associates, such as financiers Sir Rex Benson and Sir Charles Hambro in London, General Donovan in Washington, and a number of Canadian and American industrialists like Edward Stettinius, former chairman of the U.S. Steel Corporation, he formed the British-American-Canadian Corporation, which rapidly developed into the World Commerce Corporation, originally designed to fill the void left by the break-up of the big German cartels which Stephenson himself had done much to destroy. Thus he and his colleagues on the board raised an initial $1,000,000 to help 'bridge over the breakdown in foreign exchange and provide the tools, machinery and "know how" to develop untapped resources in different parts of the world'.

The World Commerce Corporation also played a useful part in the development and rehabilitation of economically backward countries. As one American newspaper editorial put it at the time, 'if there were several World Commerce Corporations, there would be no need for a Marshall Plan'. Barter trade was facilitated on a massive scale. A typical transaction took place in the Balkans in 1951. Yugoslavia and Bulgaria were short of dollars and also short of medicinal drugs. But each country had about $300,000 worth of paprika on its farms. World Commerce accordingly exchanged a year's supply of penicillin and sulfa for the paprika, which they then sold on other markets.

While normally working on a commission basis, the Corporation would sometimes forgo its profit if it felt it could help an impoverished or economically backward country by giving it the facilities of its international connections.

In 1948, Stephenson was asked by the then Governor of Jamaica, Sir John Huggins, to help the island to utilize its rich local resources of limestone and gypsum and so make it unnecessary for the Jamaicans to import cement from England. Stephenson agreed in the interests of public service, and he accordingly constructed a cement factory at Rockfort, on the outskirts of Kingston. Today Stephenson takes justifiable pride in the fact that the Caribbean Cement Company Limited is probably the most successful undertaking of its kind to have been established since the end of the war. Its annual capacity of 200,000 tons is now (1962) in course of being doubled as a result of an additional £2.8 million investment.

Soon after Stephenson's factory had begun to produce the much-needed cement for Jamaica's housing and public-works programme, Mr. Theodore Sealy, the editor of the Jamaica *Daily Gleaner*, visited London and gave a talk on the Home Service of the B.B.C. on February 18, 1952. He said:

> Most British thinkers on the Caribbean usually emphasize the need for social services. But the British people know from their own history that they have been able to purchase these services only after they had developed an industrial and commercial economy. It is very wrong, therefore, I suggest, for the people of Britain to think that the way to help the West Indies is to dress the shop window with social services.
>
> I much prefer the vision of men like Lord Beaverbrook and Sir William Stephenson, the international industrialist, who consider that the way to help Britain to raise the standard of living in those areas is to put capital in money and goods into the development of those countries, to create employment, to give more purchasing power. Then definitely out of the fruits of these developments will come all the social services which our friends in England talk so much about.

In the spring of 1952, Stephenson undertook a similar task in Newfoundland, when he became the non-salaried Chairman of the Newfoundland and Labrador Development Corporation, whose object was to attract private investment capital for the development of mining and other local industries. Or, as Stephenson himself succinctly expressed it, 'the ultimate aim . . . is an extra bottle of milk for the kids of Newfoundland'.

During the next few months Stephenson succeeded in interesting eight of the leading mining, industrial and banking concerns from outside in Newfoundland's economic possibilities, thus making available the many millions of dollars which these firms possessed. Then, having worked himself out of a job, he resigned. In thanking him for having completed his programme so rapidly, the Prime Minister, Mr. Joseph Smallwood, wrote: 'You achieved a magnificent result in a very short space of time, and I and the Government and people of Newfoundland must ever be grateful to you.'

In 1953, Stephenson was approached by an old friend, John Archer Dunn, who was a mining engineer and a director of the Selection Trust Group of Companies, of which his brother-in-law, Sir Chester Beatty, was chairman. Dunn came on behalf of the members of the Diamond Syndicate, who were extremely worried about the consistent thefts of diamonds from the South African mines and the smuggling of these stones, particularly those of the industrial variety, into America. The Syndicate's emissary was authorized to offer Stephenson the sum of one million pounds sterling, together with an additional blank cheque to be filled in by Stephenson in any sum he wished if he could provide a satisfactory solution of the leak, which amounted to something like £100,000 in value from the diggings every month.

It was an unparalleled offer, and its size was an indication of the faith the Syndicate had in Stephenson's record of achievement in the intelligence field. But Stephenson had no hesitation in turning it down flatly.

'I have just emerged from underground activities into the light of business, and there I intend to remain, Jack,' he told his friend. 'I don't think you realize what an octopus the Syndicate is grappling with. This is not a local affair confined to Africa. It is operated by an international murder gang which has world-wide ramifications. I am not afraid of it, but I have had enough of that kind of job, and I want to have time now to sit in the sun.'

Thus did the former British chief of intelligence decline to accept an assignment with an honorarium unique in the annals of criminal investigation. It was eventually undertaken as a police operation by Sir Percy Sillitoe, the former Director-General of the Security Service (M.I.5), though not for the sum offered to Stephenson. The subject later formed the background to one of the best of Ian Fleming's James Bond thrillers, *Diamonds Are Forever*. (Fleming took his title from the Diamond Syndicate's slogan.)

In his new industrial and commercial interests Stephenson did not forget his native Canada and above all his native province. In 1959, he became Chairman of the Manitoba Economic Advisory Board. 'He is a great Canadian,' John Pepper—one of his closest war-time and business associates, who succeeded him as Chairman of World Commerce—has said, 'and has done more than any other man in the world's markets to bring Canada's enormous potential to the notice of international investors.'

Stephenson lost one great friend at this time, which was a grievous blow to him, when the 'animating, heart-warming flame', which had won Sir Winston Churchill's admiration, was extinguished. On February 8, 1959, General William Donovan died at the Walter Reed Military Hospital in Washington. Besides their intimate war-time association, 'Big Bill' and 'Little Bill' had worked together in the formation of the World Commerce Corporation and they had continued to keep in touch during the difficult post-war years, when Donovan undertook fresh assignments overseas. For instance, Donovan had headed the committee formed by newspapermen to investigate the slaying in Greece in 1948 of George Polk, a C.B.S. correspondent. In this case, which had distinct political undertones, a Greek Communist was sentenced to life imprisonment and two others were sentenced to death in their absence. After a full investigation, Donovan had declared himself satisfied with the result. 'We must have peace by compulsion,' he said, on returning to America after witnessing the Berlin air lift. 'We must counter the Soviet subversive war by being strong enough.'

Later, in 1953, President Eisenhower had appointed him U.S. Ambassador to Thailand, where he served for two years, and materially contributed to the strong policy which arrested the Communist advance in South-East Asia at that time. It was typical of him that he accepted this dangerous and difficult task at the age of seventy, although he had earlier declined an ambassadorial post of the first rank. He was also chairman of the American Committee on United Europe, and in November 1956 he organized a refugee relief campaign which raised $1,500,000 to aid the Hungarians who had risen in revolt against the Soviet domination of their country.

Donovan's greatest feat was O.S.S. 'You may well have satisfaction in the achievements of the office and take pride in your own contribution to them,' President Truman had written to Donovan on the day O.S.S. was abolished by Presidential Executive Order (September 20, 1945). 'Great additional reward for your efforts should be in knowledge that the peace-time intelligence services of the Government are being created on the foundation of the facilities and resources mobilized through the Office of Strategic Services during the war.' The outcome, of course, was the Central Intelligence Agency, and none watched the growth of C.I.A., particularly under the expert guiding hand of Allen Dulles, with closer attention and with a greater sense of pride, than Bill Donovan and Bill Stephenson.

It was natural that Stephenson should have an occasional nostalgia for his 'cloak-and-dagger' days. But this has merely sharpened his appreciation of the overwhelming importance of intelligence in the contemporary world.

'As a whole, Intelligence operations consist less of the blood-chilling adventures we read about than of hard work, endless patience, highly developed technical skills, and infinitely careful and competent organization,' he has recently said. 'War has become a thing of instantaneous combustion, en-gulfing civilian and soldier alike. Surely it is plain that against enemy attack today, the first defence must be information: to find out when and where an aggressor intends to strike. That is the role of Secret Intelligence, and without it all other means of defence could prove to be of sadly limited avail.'

Thus, with singular and unerring perception, Sherwood's quiet Canadian, Sir William Samuel Stephenson, epitomized his own secret service story and the reason why it deserves to be remembered.

# SOURCES

THE principal authority used in writing this book has been Sir William Stephenson's official and private papers, supplemented by my own correspondence and personal recollections.

The only account of the man and his work, which has hitherto appeared in print, is an article by McKenzie Porter ('The Biggest Private Eye of All') in *Maclean's Magazine* (Toronto), December 1, 1952.

The following printed works have also been consulted:

ALSOP, STEWART, and BRADEN, THOMAS. *Sub Rosa*. New York, 1948.

BUTLER, J. R. M. *Lord Lothian*. Macmillan, London, 1960.

CHURCHILL, SIR WINSTON S. *The Second World War*. 6 vols. Cassell & Co., London, 1948–54.

COLVIN, IAN. *Chief of Intelligence*. Gollancz, London, 1951.

COWARD, NOËL. *Future Indefinite*. Heinemann, London, 1954.

DALTON, HUGH. *The Fateful Years*. Muller, London, 1957.

DE GRAMONT, SANCHE. *The Secret War*. New York, 1962.

DE JONG, LOUIS. *The German Fifth Column in the Second World War*. Routledge, London, 1956.

DRIBERG, TOM. *Beaverbrook*. Weidenfeld & Nicolson, London, 1956.

GOUZENKO, IGOR. *This Was My Choice*. Toronto, 1948.

GUNTHER, JOHN. *Roosevelt in Retrospect*. Hamish Hamilton, London, 1950.

HALL, H. DUNCAN. *North American Supply*. H.M. Stationery Office, London, 1955.

HULL, CORDELL. *The Memoirs of Cordell Hull*. 2 vols. Hodder & Stoughton, London, 1948.

LEAHY, WILLIAM D. *I Was There*. New York, 1950.

LEASOR, JAMES. *War at the top*. Michael Joseph Ltd., London, 1950.

LEVERKUEHN, PAUL. *German Military Intelligence*. Weidenfeld & Nicolson, London, 1954.

243

LOCKHART, SIR R. BRUCE. *Comes The Reckoning*. Putnam, London, 1947.
— *Friends, Foes and Foreigners*. Putnam, London, 1957.

MASCHWITZ, ERIC. *No Chip on my Shoulder*. Herbert Jenkins, London, 1957.

MEDLICOTT, W. N. *The Economic Blockade*, 2 vols. H.M. Stationery Office, London, 1952–59.

MOOREHEAD, ALAN. *The Traitors*. Hamish Hamilton, London, 1952.

ROOSEVELT, ELLIOTT. *The Roosevelt Letters*. Vol. III (1928–1945). Harrap, London, 1952.

SHERWOOD, ROBERT. *The White House Papers of Harry L. Hopkins*. 2 vols. Eyre & Spottiswoode, London, 1948–49.

STIMSON, HENRY L., and BUNDY, McGEORGE. *On Active Service in Peace and War*. Hutchinson, London, 1949.

TULLY, ANDREW. *CIA. The Inside Story*. New York, 1962.

WELLES, SUMNER. *Seven Major Decisions*. Hamish Hamilton, London, 1951.

WHITEHEAD, DON. *The F.B.I. Story*. Muller, London, 1959.

WILLERT, SIR ARTHUR. *The Road to Safety*. Verschoyle, London, 1952.

WINANT, JOHN G. *A Letter from Grosvenor Square*. Hodder & Stoughton. London, 1947.

WOODWARD, SIR LLEWELLYN. *British Foreign Policy in the Second World War*. H.M. Stationery Office, London, 1962.

# INDEX